Claude Simon: A Retrospective

Claude Simon
A Retrospective

Edited by
JEAN H. DUFFY *and*
ALASTAIR DUNCAN

LIVERPOOL UNIVERSITY PRESS

To Claude and Réa Simon

First published 2002 by
Liverpool University Press
4 Cambridge Street
Liverpool, L69 7ZU

British Library Cataloguing-in-Publication Data
A British Library CIP Record is available.

ISBN 0-85323-857-X *cased*
0-85323-867-7 *limp*

Set in Stone Serif and Sans by
Koinonia, Manchester
Printed in the European Union by
Alden Press Ltd, Oxford

Contents

Acknowledgments

We should like to express our profound thanks to Claude Simon and to Madame Réa Simon for the encouragement and support which they gave this project at every stage. This collection of essays had its origins in a conference held in London in 1999. Claude Simon sent a very warm message of welcome to participants and has given us permission to reproduce his photographs, including *Autoportrait 1997* on the cover; Mme Simon attended the conference and participated in a most stimulating and enlightening question and answer session. We are deeply grateful for these personal contributions to the project. Their kindness, generosity and interest add another layer to our continuing pleasure in reading and re-reading the novels of Claude Simon.

Our very warm thanks also go to the authors of this volume. We are as grateful for the stimulation of their ideas as for their patient cooperation throughout the various stages of editing and production.

We also wish to thank the following who made the original conference possible: the British Academy and the Universities of Sheffield and Stirling, for financial support; the Institut Français du Royaume-Uni, for financial support and for putting its premises at our disposal; Professor Jo Labanyi and the staff of the Institute of Romance Studies of the University of London, for assistance with the organisation and publicising of the conference.

Robin Bloxsidge of Liverpool University Press has been ever helpful and we should like to thank him.

As always we should like to thank our spouses and families for support and understanding.

Edinburgh and Stirling   Jean H. Duffy and
January 2001   Alastair Duncan

Message from Claude Simon to the Participants at the Conference held in May 1999

Je ne peux dire avec quel regret j'ai dû me résigner à ne pas faire ce voyage à Londres, tout d'abord parce que cette défection forcée me prive de rencontrer d'authentiques amis et je dirais même parents – car tel ou tel d'entre ceux qui se trouvent ici réunis et qui m'ont lu avec autant d'intelligence que de sensibilité (en matière d'art, l'une n'étant rien sans l'autre), me sont plus proches que bien des connaissances, même intimes, tandis qu'il existe une véritable parenté entre ceux que certaines dispositions de l'esprit lient plus étroitement que des rapports familiaux, ou autres, parfois seulement faits d'habitudes communes.

Par ailleurs, qu'il soit permis au très vieil homme que je suis de dire que le seul nom de cette ville où vous êtes aujourd'hui réunis, London, incarne pour lui la somme d'incroyables héroïsmes et d'immuables volontés qui, opposées solitaires pendant de longs mois au mal absolu, ont permis au monde libre de subsister, et à vous tous de vous trouver aujourd'hui ici.

Vous dire ma gratitude et mon émotion serait peu. Ce que je ressens est bien au-delà, parce qu'en vous lisant, faisant mon profit de vos réflexions et de vos analyses de mes livres, s'est accru en moi une conscience plus claire de mon travail. J'ai souvent dit que celui-ci me faisait penser à celui de ces artisans qui produisent des objets (pendentifs, cache-pots, plaques décoratives ou autres) au cuivre que l'on appelle 'repoussé', martelant la plaque de métal de sorte que ce qui est un creux à leurs yeux soit au contraire saillie en ronde-bosse pour le spectateur, mais artisan malheureux, condamné à ne jamais voir de ce qu'il a fait que l'envers caché d'un relief inversé.

C'est bien sûr un truisme que de dire que sans le lecteur qui participe complémentairement en le déchiffrant à ce phénomène de codage qu'est l'écriture, tout livre serait sans existence, et il ne pourrait se trouver mieux pour le dire ici que celle (j'ai nommé ma femme, Réa, qui est avec vous aujourd'hui) qui, toujours et avant tout autre, est la première à faire vivre au grand jour ces combinaisons de mots que je fabrique ('fabriquer' est le terme employé par Proust) avec plus ou moins de bonheur.

Et puisque je viens d'employer ce mot, laissez-moi vous dire que c'en est un pour moi très grand, en même temps qu'un très grand honneur, de savoir que vous êtes ainsi réunis pour parler de mon travail, et ceci grâce à l'initiative et au dévouement de ces deux amis que sont pour moi Jean Duffy et Alastair Duncan que je remercie en premier, ce qui est, en fait, une façon de vous remercier tous d'avoir pris la peine de rédiger vos interventions, de faire ce voyage et, au départ de tout cela, de me lire.

A chacun, donc, mes sentiments les plus chaleureux.

Claude Simon

Introduction: The Critical Reception of Claude Simon since the 1960s

Jean H. Duffy and Alastair Duncan

By the turn of the century Claude Simon had written fourteen novels and published a variety of shorter works including two volumes of photographs. His production spanned nearly sixty years, from *Le Tricheur*, begun in 1941 and published in 1945, to *Le Jardin des Plantes* (1997).[1] Like *Les Géorgiques* and *L'Acacia*, which preceded it in 1981 and 1989, *Le Jardin des Plantes* is a work on a grand scale, at once a personal memoir and a sweeping historical fresco. Like them, it recapitulates many of the main themes of his *oeuvre*, reworks familiar incidents and motifs, and rewrites his literary and personal past. It also offers new insights into Simon's own conception of the relationship between autobiography and fiction, of that between his novels and the *nouveau roman*, and of his place in literary history. Thus *Le Jardin des Plantes* invites Simon's readers and critics to reflect anew on the whole turning constellation of his work in the light of this bright new star. In this spirit was the present collection of essays conceived: contributors were invited to look back over Simon's work and to open new avenues suggested by *Le Jardin des Plantes*. A number of the essays in this volume were given their first airing at a conference held in London in May 1999. It had been hoped that Claude Simon would attend the conference. In the event he was unable to do so; the trace of his intention is to be found in the encouraging and very generous message that precedes this introduction. The bearer of that message was Madame Simon, whose acute questioning sharpened the focus of various contributions and who in turn answered questions about just how in practice many of Claude Simon's later novels have been written, from manuscript, through successive typescripts – typed and discussed

---

1 In 2001, after this volume went to press, Minuit published Simon's latest work, *Le Tramway*.

with her – and on to the correction of proofs. The purpose of this introduction is to set the volume in the broader context of Simon criticism and to give an outline of its contents.

Consideration of how in practice Simon's novels are written has not always been a characteristic of criticism devoted to his work. Indeed this focus contrasts sharply with the critical orthodoxy of earlier years. Within France, Simon's novels were for long seen in the context of the *nouveau roman*. Some of the critical and theoretical views adumbrated in Robbe-Grillet's polemical essays of the late 1950s and early 1960s were refined and hammered into definitive shape by Jean Ricardou in the 1960s and 1970s. Ricardou had close personal links with the writers of the *nouveau roman*. In the early 1970s, Simon and other writers attended a series of conferences held at Cerisy-la-Salle in Normandy, chaired or co-chaired by Ricardou, the proceedings of which were subsequently published in paperback. This created the impression that the disparate writers of the *nouveau roman* were, under Ricardou's leadership, becoming a coherent group of 'scriptors' of *nouveaux nouveaux romans*, an impression lent further plausibility by the formal characteristics of some New Novels of the 1970s, including works by Simon. The systematic rigour of Ricardou's arguments, no less than the force of his personality, compelled assent. He imposed a way of looking at Simon's novels that was persuasive but limiting. Underlying his criticism was an element of social and political critique: like others of his generation who had been active in *Tel Quel*, he adopted much of Althusser's analysis and rejection of 'l'idéologie dominante'. But he was even more influenced by the Saussurian concept that language is a system in which meaning depends on relationships within it rather than on reference to extra-linguistic reality. Thus he tended to identify 'l'idéologie dominante' exclusively with coherent narrative fictions in the realist tradition; and all his critical attention was devoted to studying the techniques by which certain novels subverted the 'referential illusion' and the manner in which fictions were generated intratextually by play on words and above all on their signifiers.

Ricardou's first substantial piece on Simon, 'Un ordre dans la débâcle' (1960),[2] was a largely thematic analysis of the breakdown of layers of order in *La Route des Flandres*. It predates the linguistic turn that he

---

2 *Critique*, no. 163, décembre 1960, pp. 1011–24 (reprinted with amendments in *Problèmes du Nouveau Roman*, Paris, Seuil, 1967, pp. 44–55).

took in the course of the 1960s. His essay on *La Bataille de Pharsale*, 'La Bataille de la phrase' (1970)[3] was the most comprehensive and most detailed application of his theory of textual generation. Ricardou was not alone, however, in taking the linguistic turn in 1960s. By the 1970s both Ricardou and the broader influence of structuralist narratologists, including Gérard Genette, were strongly apparent in a number of studies published in French. In 1973 and 1974 Dominique Lancereaux offered close readings of *La Route des Flandres* and *Le Palace* which demonstrated how words and fiction were generated and how punctuation gave rhythm to Simon's prose.[4] Gérard Roubichou's *Lecture de 'L'Herbe' de Claude Simon* (1976)[5] showed similarly, but in much greater detail, how the creative momentum of words produced meaning and an eventually coherent structure in that earlier novel. Lucien Dällenbach came to the fore, both in his contribution to the 1974 Claude Simon conference at Cerisy,[6] and in his analysis, in *Le Récit spéculaire* (1977),[7] of the subtleties of *mises en abyme* in *L'Herbe* and *Triptyque*.

During that same decade of the 1970s, Anglo-American criticism of Simon – with the notable exception of Stephen Heath's book on the *nouveau roman* (1972)[8] – was more traditionally academic, less combative, much less affected by structuralism and post-structuralism. Alastair Duncan and Stuart Sykes offered comparative studies of Simon and Faulkner (1973 and 1979),[9] while comparison with non-French novelists and novels was also the guiding thread of John Fletcher's *Claude Simon and Fiction Now* (1975).[10] J. A. E. Loubère's *The Novels of Claude Simon* (1975)[11] was the first large-scale study of Simon in English. It set his work in the context of twentieth-century literature and traced his

---

3 *Critique*, no. 274, mars 1970, pp. 226–256 (reprinted in *Pour une théorie du nouveau roman*, Paris, Seuil, 1971, pp. 118–58).

4 'Modalités de la narration dans *La Route des Flandres* de Claude Simon', *Poétique*, vol. 14, 1973, pp. 235–49; 'Modalités de la narration dans *Le Palace* de Claude Simon', *Littérature*, no. 16, décembre 1974, pp. 3–8.

5 Lausanne, L'Age d'homme.

6 'Mise en abyme et redoublement spéculaire chez Claude Simon', in *Claude Simon: Colloque de Cerisy*, Paris, Union Générale d'Editions, 1975, pp. 151–90 (reprinted in *Lire Claude Simon*, Paris, Les Impressions Nouvelles, 1986, pp. 151–90).

7 *Le Récit spéculaire: essai sur la mise en abyme*, Paris, Seuil, 1977.

8 *The Nouveau Roman: A Study in the Practice of Writing*, London, Elek, 1972.

9 Duncan, 'Claude Simon and William Faulkner', *Forum for Modern Language Studies*, vol. 9, no. 3, 1973, pp. 235–52; Sykes, 'The Novel as Conjuration: *Absalom, Absalom!* and *La Route des Flandres*', *Revue de littérature comparée*, vol. 53, 1979, pp. 348–57.

10 London, Calder and Boyers.

11 Ithaca, NY, Cornell University Press.

developing exploration of the formal possibilities of the novel from *Le Tricheur* (1945) to *Triptyque* (1973). A similarly wide-ranging eclecticism was shown in the collection of essays edited by Randi Birn and Karen Gould in 1981; *Orion Blinded: Essays on Claude Simon*[12] benefited from a preface by Serge Doubrovsky and contained both articles relating Simon to literary tradition and others, notably by Loubère, Karin Holter and Claud Duverlie, that studied the texture of the novels in ways influenced by the critical debate in France.

By the end of the 1970s, that debate – in so far as it concerned Simon – was beginning to take a new turn. In 1979 Stuart Sykes's *Les Romans de Claude Simon*[13] became the first book-length study in French. While not neglecting the matter of Simon's novels – 'Histoire, et la déformation qu'elle subit dans la conscience de l'individu' (p. 12) – Sykes emphasised most Simon's continuing quest for spatial coherence and its achievement in spiral and ternary forms. Sykes's book runs counter to Ricardolian orthodoxy. Commissioned by the Editions de Minuit, it signalled Jérôme Lindon's desire to set Simon's novels in a different and more Simon-specific context. In the event it was Simon himself who most effectively established a new critical climate. In 1981, in *Les Géorgiques*, he returned to the themes of family, history and war in a magisterially orchestrated reworking and deepening of his previous fiction. This was a novel to which formalist analysis could clearly not do justice. At a conference in New York in 1982 Simon, Robbe-Grillet and others voiced their dissatisfaction with the theoretical framework within which Ricardou had sought to contain them.[14] By then the revolt was already well underway in France. In a special number of *Critique* in 1981,[15] various critics, including Lucien Dällenbach, Alastair Duncan, Martin van Buuren and Jean Rousset, commented on *Les Géorgiques* or on Simon's work as a whole, taking account of Ricardou but offering parallel or revised perspectives. Lucien Dällenbach was to become the most influential voice of the post-Ricardou era. His postface to the paperback edition of *La Route des Flandres* has continued to shape the perceptions of new readers of Simon since it was first published in 1982.[16] Without naming Ricardou,

---

12 Lewisburg, PA, Bucknell University Press.
13 Paris, Minuit.
14 See Lois Oppenheim (ed.), *Three Decades of the French New Novel*, Urbana, IL, University of Illinois Press, 1986.
15 *Critique*, no. 414, novembre 1981.
16 'Le Tissu de mémoire', in *La Route des Flandres*, Paris, Minuit (Double), 1982, pp. 299–316.

Dällenbach used that essay to reject criticism that treats texts as a 'somme de procédés'; he placed subjective response, memory and identity at the core of his study. His monograph, *Claude Simon*, of 1988 amplified this turn: its lavish documentation emphasised the biographical origins of Simon's texts and the real work of their genesis.[17]

Dällenbach's influence on the French scene was exercised from abroad, from Geneva. Until well into the 1990s Simon criticism prospered more abroad – in Britain, the United States, Canada, Australia, Germany, the Netherlands, Scandinavia, Switzerland and India[18] – than it did in France. A characteristic of much Anglo-American criticism of the 1980s and 1990s was that it had by now assimilated much critical theory. In *The Subject in Question: the Languages of Theory and the Strategies of Fiction* (1982),[19] David Carroll examined Simon's work and deconstructed previous criticism in the light of Barthes, Lacan and, above all, Derrida. In *Claude Simon: New Directions*, edited by Alastair Duncan in 1986, close textual study of Simon was similarly, though less committedly, informed by readings of Barthes, Lacan, Lévi-Strauss, Derrida and Mircea Eliade.[20] In that volume Anthony Cheal Pugh began in theoretical mode the reflections on historiography which were to lead in 1990 to his strongly anti-Ricardolian exploration of the metamorphosis of Simon's wartime experience into fiction.[21] A number

17 *Claude Simon*, Paris, Seuil, 1988.
18 This listing of countries does not do justice to the extensive critical literature on Simon produced over the years in languages other than French and English, which the editors of this volume have not followed in detail. In the German-speaking world, Simon's work received an appreciative welcome in the essays of Gerda Zeltner (in the pages of the *Neue Zürcher Zeitung* and in *Die Eigenmächtige Sprache*, 1965, and *Im Augenblick der Gegenwart*, 1974), Kurt Wilhelm (*Der Nouveau Roman*, 1969) and Winfried Wehle (*Französischer Roman der Gegenwart*, 1972). Increasingly, in the 1980s and 1990s Simon's work became, in whole or in part, the subject of studies that combined insight with erudition: Jochen Mecke studied *La Route des Flandres* in the context of the literary treatment of time (*Roman-Zeit. Zeitformung und Dekonstruktion des französischen Romans der Gegenwart*, 1990); Wolfram Nitsch used Leiris's analogy of the 'tauromachie' to illuminate the links between violence and language in the novels of the 1960s (*Sprache und Gewalt bei Claude Simon: Interpretationen zu seinem Romanwerk der sechziger Jahre*, 1992); Thomas Klinkert traced Simon's reworkings of Proust and Faulkner in *Les Géorgiques* (*Bewahren und Löschen. Zur Proust-Rezeption bei Samuel Beckett, Claude Simon und Thomas Bernhard*, 1996). We also wish to salute Simon's Swedish commentator and translator, C.-J. Bjurstrøm and the pioneering work of M.-C. Kirpalani in India (*Approches de 'La Route des Flandres', roman de Claude Simon*, New Dehli, 1981).
19 Chicago, Chicago University Press.
20 *Claude Simon: New Directions*, Edinburgh, Scottish Academic Press, 1985.
21 'Facing the matter of History: *Les Géorgiques*', pp. 113–30; 'Claude Simon et la route de la référence', *Revue des sciences humaines*, no. 220, *Claude Simon*, 1990–4, pp. 23–45.

of contributors to *New Directions* were preparing the ground for elaborated versions of their arguments. In 1987, the title of Michael Evans's
work, *Claude Simon and the Trangressions of Modern Art* (1987), announced equal billing for the novelist and for the theory of frames and
framing through which his novels were viewed.[22] In *Claude Simon:
Writing the Visible* (1987),[23] Celia Britton used Lacan to establish a core
relationship between vision and desire in Simon's novels. Alastair
Duncan's *Claude Simon: Adventures in Words* (1994) recapitulated the
critical debate in successive decades; the final chapters reflect on the
novels up to *L'Acacia* (1989) in the light of theories of autobiography,
psychobiography and historiography.[24] The changing climate of critical
thinking can also be traced in the work of Ralph Sarkonak, from the
Ricardolian *Les Carrefours du texte* (1986) to the much more eclectic *Les
Trajets de l'écriture* (1994), in which close textual study of Simon's
works of the 1980s is informed by the later Barthes's concern with
semiosis and mimesis.[25] Mária Minich Brewer, editor of a special
number of *Esprit Createur* in 1987, set her *Claude Simon: Narrativities
without Narrative* (1994)[26] firmly in the context of postmodernist debate.
She rejects both the formalism of Ricardou and the postmodernism of
Jameson because each in its way diminishes the social, political and
cultural legacies that are borne by narratives, however fragmentary.

Of the six special numbers of periodicals devoted to Simon in the
decade between 1980 and 1990 only three were published in France
and two of these – *Critique* in 1981 and *La Revue des sciences humaines*
in 1990[27] – were dominated by contributions from abroad. The 1980s,
however, also saw Simon's stock begin to rise in his native country.
The award of the Nobel Prize in 1985 gained him new public recognition. *L'Acacia* (1989) confirmed his status as a repository of French
cultural inheritance: that novel's relatively accessible re-examination
of the themes of memory, family and war chimed with contemporary
French concerns with commemoration and sites of memory. At last, in
the 1990s, Simon's novels became a more widespread subject for post-
graduate research at French universities, a trend much accelerated by

22 Basingstoke, Macmillan.
23 Cambridge, Cambridge University Press.
24 Manchester and New York, Manchester University Press, 1994.
25 *Claude Simon: les carrefours du texte*, Toronto, Paratexte, 1986; *Les Trajets de l'écriture:
    Claude Simon*, Toronto, Paratexte, 1994.
26 Lincoln, NE, and London, University of Nebraska Press.
27 *Critique*, 'La Terre et la guerre dans l'oeuvre de Claude Simon', vol. 37, no. 414,
    novembre 1981; *Claude Simon, Revue des sciences humaines*, no. 220, 1990–4.

the choice of *La Route des Flandres* (1960) as a set text for the *agrégation* in 1998. To prepare students for this examination, 1997 saw the appearance in France of an unprecedented number of books on Simon. A few were collections of previously published essays; some were very competent student guides to *La Route des Flandres*. There was also the begining, however, of a flow of original books and articles that shows no signs of drying up and that was given fresh impetus by publication of *Le Jardin des Plantes*.

One effect of Simon's own continuing return to the reconstruction of troubled experience in memory was to encourage critics in the 1990s to re-open critical seams unmined since the 1960s. Merleau-Ponty's 'Cinq Notes sur Claude Simon' (1960)[28] formed the background to Michel Deguy's 'Claude Simon et la représentation' (1962)[29] which, using *Le Palace*, was the first article to study the relationship between memory and perception in Simon's work from a phenomenological perspective. John Sturrock also chose to situate his study, *The French New Novel* (1969), within the phenomenological debate.[30] In the early 1990s Jean Duffy returned to Merleau-Ponty to explore more systematically both spatial articulation in Simon's novels and the manner in which the pre-reflexive perceptual overloading characteristic of some novels dissolves the self and challenges conventional anthropocentrism.[31] The theme was taken up by Celia Britton in the first of the new Claude Simon series of *La Revue des lettres modernes* edited by Ralph Sarkonak (1994).[32] Britton illustrated the return to the referent – or rather, as she argued, the signified – by analysing how Simon's conception of language in the novel differs from that of Robbe-Grillet or Ricardou; her analysis confirms Simon's 'faith in language' that David Ellison had argued for in his 1987 essay on *Les Géorqiques*.[33]

28 *Médiations*, no. 4, winter, 1961/62, pp. 5–10, reprinted in *Entretiens*, 31, 1972, pp. 41–46, and in English translation in C. Britton (ed.), *Claude Simon*, London, Longman, 1993, pp. 35–38.
29 'Claude Simon et la représentation', *Critique*, no. 187, décembre 1962, pp. 1009–32.
30 *The French New Novel: Claude Simon, Michel Butor, Alain Robbe-Grillet*, London, New York, Oxford University Press, 1969.
31 'Claude Simon, Merleau-Ponty and Perception', *French Studies*, vol. 46, no. 1, 1992, pp. 33–52; 'Claude Simon, Merleau-Ponty and Spatial Articulation', *Romance Studies*, no. 20, 1992, pp. 59–73.
32 '"ce paysage inépuisable". Sens et référence dans la conception simonienne de la langue', *Revue des lettres modernes, Série Claude Simon 1: A la recherche du référent perdu*, ed. Ralph Sarkonak, 1994, pp. 97–120 .
33 'Narrative levelling and performative pathos in Claude Simon's *Les Géorqiques*', *French Forum*, vol. 12, no. 3, September 1987, pp. 303–21.

Quoting Merleau-Ponty, Britton concludes: '"il s'agit de produire un système de signes qui restitue par son agencement interne le paysage d'une expérience"'(p. 117).

This quotation may be taken to herald a number of more general studies which have taken seriously the phenomenological affirmation that a way of writing is also a way of seeing the world. Thus, following Dällenbach, Patrick Longuet in *Lire Claude Simon: la polyphonie du monde* (1995)[34] puts the *tabula rasa* of war at the heart of Simon's vision. From that experience of chaos springs the suspicion of all ordered forms of writing, the invention of new forms from the exploded fragments of experience and myths, and the uncanny melancholy of memory searching for points of reference and rest in an unstable world. Christine Genin's less allusive, more systematic study, *L'Expérience du lecteur dans les romans de Claude Simon: lecture studieuse et lecture poignante* (1997),[35] owes as much to Georges Poulet's *La Conscience critique*[36] as to Merleau-Ponty. Genin starts from perception: the motifs of seeing, sight and what is seen, a world of suffering and cruelty; she then turns to memory and its relationship with autobiography, time, history and genealogy; and finally to how Simon's texts are structured through analogy, intertextuality and the rhythmic musicality of his prose.

Longuet and Genin are typical of a trend away from the analysis of the form of individual novels and the differences between them. Instead critics have studied patterns of motifs, *topoi* and images in Simon's novels. The titles of both volumes of essays edited by Mireille Calle-Gruber in the 1990s – *Les Sites de l'écriture* and *Les Chemins de la mémoire*[37] – are programmatic in this respect, reflecting her conviction that 'une *oeuvre* s'écrit dans le jeu des rapports, des relations, des croisés qui constitue son tissu'.[38] Similar attention to sites of memory – earth, dwelling and land – had already been paid impressionistically by Didier Alexandre in his *Claude Simon* in the series *Lieux de l'écrit* (1991).[39] Bachelard, Gilbert Durand and Jean-Pierre Richard have become guides to this new charting of Simon's world. Annie Clément-

---

34 Paris, Minuit.
35 Paris, Champion.
36 Paris, José Corti, 1972.
37 *Claude Simon: Chemins de la mémoire*, Sainte-Foy, Le Griffon d'argile, 1993; *Les Sites de l'écriture: Colloque Claude Simon*, Paris, Nizet, 1995.
38 'Les Sites de l'écriture', in *Les Sites de l'écriture: Colloque Claude Simon*, Paris, Nizet, 1995, p. 8.
39 Paris, Marval.

Perrier has studied hands, gardens and colours;[40] while in *La Bataille des odeurs: l'espace olfactif des romans de Claude Simon* (1998) Jean-Yves Laurichesse explored smells associated with the elements, with human beings and with specific motifs, among them places of worship and desire, revolution and war.[41] Pascal Mougin's work is less Bachardelien in approach. His *L'Effet d'image: essai sur Claude Simon* (1997)[42] is a stylistic and thematic study of images based on quantitative data made possible by computer scanning. Mougin shows how images that import external references gradually, through elaboration and repetition, become part of a mutually reinforcing network of endogenous images. In *La Route des Flandres*, *Histoire* and *Les Géorgiques* he finds contrasting sets of images, particularly of hard outer surfaces and liquidity, elaborating and contributing to the themes of these novels.

Study of recurrent images has drawn some critics into reflecting on Simon's personal myths. Laurichesse points out that many of the sites of memory in Simon are sites of initiation. Like Vareille and others, he draws on Roger Caillois's *L'Homme et le sacré* and on Mircea Eliade to argue that Simon's work is informed by a sense of the sacred, 'un sacré sans divinité'.[43] The quasi-autobiographical nature of Simon's work of the 1980s and 1990s, linking back to his novels of the 1960s and to *Le Tricheur* and *La Corde raide*, has encouraged critics to venture into the autobiographical and the psycho-critical. Dominique Viart sees an autobiographical enigma subtending *La Route des Flandres*,[44] while Brigitte Ferrato-Combe's interrogative title – '*La Route des Flandres*: une autofiction?'[45] – conceals a survey of the trend towards autobiographical criticism. Laurichesse, commenting on Simon's own ironic account of trauma in *Le Jardin des Plantes*, affirms that 'le traumatisme premier est sans doute la mort de sa mère'.[46] And indeed the troubled nexus of emotions and complexes in relation to mother figures has recently received at least as much attention as the figure of the absent

40 *Claude Simon: la fabrique du jardin*, Paris, Nathan, 1998; 'Le Jeu des couleurs dans *Le Jardin des Plantes*', *Littératures*, no. 40, 1999, pp. 31–46.
41 Paris, L'Harmattan.
42 Paris, L'Harmattan.
43 *La Bataille des odeurs*, p. 107; J.-C. Vareille, 'A propos de Claude Simon: langage du cosmos, cosmos du langage', in *Fragments d'un imaginaire contemporain (Pinget, Robbe-Grillet, Simon)*, Paris, José Corti, 1989, pp. 77–108.
44 *Une mémoire inquiète: 'La Route des Flandres' de Claude Simon*, Paris, Presses Universitaires de France, 1997.
45 *Littératures contemporaines*, no. 3, 1997, pp. 169–82.
46 *La Bataille des odeurs*, p. 174.

father and his substitutes. For Ralph Sarkonak the eroticism of *La Chevelure de Bérénice* is permeated with a sense of loss and grief;[47] in his study of *L'Acacia*, Pascal Mougin places the threatening mother figure on the side of History and sees her, by analogy, as 'à ce titre responsable de la mort du capitaine'.[48]

Simon's linked themes of history and war have also been treated in and for themselves. Peter Janssens reviews critically the literature on this topic: following Carroll and opposing Dällenbach, he argues that history in Simon is not the return of the same, but of difference.[49] He demonstrates the spatialisation of history in Simon by taking up the geological metaphor which Simon once used to illustrate the schema of *La Route des Flandres*. A new direction has been opened up by Jean Kaempfer. Using *La Bataille de Pharsale* as his prime example, he establishes a typology of modern accounts of war by comparing them with earlier accounts from Caesar to Napoleon.[50] Modern accounts are characterised by the choice of a limited, subjective point of view, a dehumanised universe, and by a strong intertextual critique of the older controlled and epic accounts.

Kaempfer's book stands out somewhat from the current run of Simon criticism in that the new French critics have been less concerned with setting Simon in context than with exploring in detail the vast continent of his *oeuvre*. Yet exploration of the rich territory of Simon's cultural legacies has continued. Again, the foundation for this work were laid in earlier years. In the early 1970s, Françoise van Rossum-Guyon was the first to apply Bakhtin's notion of intertextuality to Simon's work. Her essays on *La Bataille de Pharsale* were the first chapters in an as yet unfinished tale of Simon's relationship with Proust.[51] Anthony Cheal Pugh's essay 'Du *Tricheur* à *Triptyque* et inversement' (1976)[52] was among the first to reflect on the intratextual play of references in Simon's work and on the textual memory required of his readers. In 1987, Michel Bertrand's *Langue romanesque et parole*

---

47 *Les Trajets de l'écriture*, pp. 33–86.
48 *Lecture de 'L'Acacia' de Claude Simon: l'imaginaire biographique, Archives des lettres modernes*, no. 267, Paris, Minard, 1997, p. 38.
49 *Claude Simon: faire l'histoire*, Villeneuve d'Ascq, Presses Universitaires du Septentrion, 1998.
50 *Poétique du récit de guerre*, Paris, José Corti, 1998.
51 'De Claude Simon à Proust: un exemple d'intertextualité', *Marche Romane*, vol. 21, 1971, pp. 71–92; '*Ut pictura poesis*: une lecture de *La Bataille de Pharsale*', *Degrés*, vol. 1, no. 3, 1973, K1–K15.
52 *Etudes littéraires*, vol. 9, no. 1, 1976, pp. 137–60.

scripturale: essai sur Claude Simon used a Ricardolian framework to study how intertexts of various kinds are incorporated into Simon's novels,[53] while Mary Orr's *Claude Simon: the Intertextual Dimension* (1993) is a comprehensive survey of intertextual references and intertextual approaches to Simon's work.[54] In *Passé et présent dans 'Les Géorgiques' de Claude Simon* (1992), Cora Reitsma-La Brujeere systematically studied the intertexts of that novel to conclude that it is something new in Simon's fiction, a form of historical novel that acknowledges the hypothetical, subjective and mediatised nature of its representation of history.[55] Pierre Schoentjes, for his part, found Jouve in *Leçon de choses* and illuminated *Les Géorgiques*, especially its *mises en abyme*, revealing resonances with Virgil, Proust, Lautréamont and Buffon.[56]

Simon's own recent publications, however, have helped push criticism beyond the realm of purely linguistic intertextuality: *Album d'un amateur, Photographies, 1937–1970* and his *Correspondance, 1970–1984*, with Jean Dubuffet,[57] have brought renewed reflection on his delight in the visual and his affinities with the pictorial. Brigitte Ferrato-Combe comments on Simon's use of painting as an epistemological model for his conception of the novel, both in his non-fictional writings and in *La Bataille de Pharsale*: she uses Freud to illuminate the various *topoi* associated with painting: the museum, the artist's studio and the gallery of family portraits.[58] Jean Duffy's *Reading Between the Lines: Claude Simon and the Visual Arts* compares Simon's aesthetic and practice with those of the artists he admires and the works of art he refers to in his fiction.[59] She considers defamiliarisation, generation, *bricolage* and Simon's formal and thematic links with Baroque art.

As the bibliography at the end of this volume demonstrates, *Le Jardin des Plantes* has itself already attracted considerable attention, including three numbers of periodicals devoted to it in whole or in

---

53 Paris, Presses Universitaires de France.
54 Glasgow, University of Glasgow French and German Publications.
55 *Passé et présent dans 'Les Géorgiques' de Claude Simon: étude intertextuelle et narratologique d'une reconstruction de l'histoire*, Amsterdam, Rodopi, 1992.
56 *Claude Simon par correspondance: 'Les Géorgiques' et le regard des livres*, Geneva, Droz, 1995.
57 Jean Dubuffet and Claude Simon, *Correspondance, 1970–1984*, Paris, L'Echoppe, 1994.
58 *Ecrire en peintre: Claude Simon et la peinture*, Grenoble, ELLUG, 1998.
59 *Reading Between the Lines: Claude Simon and the Visual Arts*, Liverpool, Liverpool, University Press, 1998.

part.[60] Dominique Viart's article in *Scherzo* outlines the chief novelties of this work, including its use of visual simultaneity, its exploitation of youthful memories, and its satirical and comic edge. His subsequent article traces the way in which Simon uses the journalist to portray both the writer as public figure and the origins of his impulse to write.[61] This quasi-autobiographical theme, pushed to a psychobiographical extreme by Pascal Mougin,[62] has been complemented by studies which consider the biographies sketched in the novel and their intertextual echos: Jean Duffy and Brigitte Ferrato-Combe have demonstrated how patterns of difference and similarity link the experience and aesthetic of the writer with that of the visual artists whom he portrays with varying degrees of sympathy.[63] The novel's apparent intent to write history has been studied by Didier Alexandre; with the help of Blanchot, he concludes his study of the published notebooks of Rommel by arguing that Rommel is above all a figure symbolic of death, inducing writing.[64] More detailed studies have been devoted to colour and animal imagery, the distinctive rhythm of Simon's prose, *Le Jardin des Plantes* as a form of travel writing, and the implications of trauma in the switches between first- and third-person narratives.[65] The variety of these studies speaks for the riches of this

---

60 *Claude Simon*, Scherzo, no. 3, avril–juin 1998; *Littératures*, no. 40, 1999; '*Le Jardin des Plantes*' *de Claude Simon, Actes du Colloque de Perpignan, Cahiers de l'Université de Perpignan*, no. 30, 2000.
61 'Remembrances et remembrement: cultiver les friches de la mémoire. *Le Jardin des Plantes*', *Scherzo*, no. 3, 1998, pp. 23–28; 'Portrait de l'artiste en écrivain. *Le Jardin des Plantes* de Claude Simon', *Cahiers de l'Université de Perpignan*, no. 30, 2000, pp. 9–24.
62 'Du *Tricheur* au *Jardin des Plantes*. La figure de la mère défunte', *Cahiers de l'Université de Perpignan*, no. 30, 2000, pp. 87–100.
63 J. H. Duffy, '"Ce n'est pas une allégorie. C'est une feuille tout simplement": Text, Intertext and Biography in Claude Simon's *Jardin des Plantes*', *Romanic Review*, vol. 89, no. 4, 1998, pp. 583–609, and 'Artistic Biographies and Aesthetic Coherence in Claude Simon's *Jardin des Plantes*', *Forum for Modern Language Studies*, vol. 35, no. 2, 1999, pp. 175–92. B. Ferrato-Combe, 'Simon et Novelli: l'image de la lettre', *Cahiers de l'Université de Perpignan*, no. 30, 2000, pp. 101–16.
64 'Le Renard du jardin: remarques sur l'insertion du personnage historique dans le récit simonien', *Cahiers de l'Université de Perpignan*, no. 30, 2000, pp. 67–86.
65 A. Clément-Perrier, 'Le Jeu des couleurs dans *Le Jardin des Plantes*', *Littératures*, no. 40, 1999, pp. 31–46; A.-L. Blanc, 'Le Jardin zoologique du *Jardin des Plantes*', *Littératures*, no. 40, 1999, pp. 47–58; M. Calle-Gruber, 'Une harmonie contre tendue: des principes de l'arc et de la lyre appliqués à l'écriture du roman chez Claude Simon', *Cahiers de l'Université de Perpignan*, no. 30, 2000, pp. 39–56; J.-Y. Laurichesse, 'Aux quatre coins du monde: *Le Jardin des Plantes* comme *album d'un voyageur*', *Cahiers de l'Université de Perpignan*, no. 30, 2000, pp.117–34; S. Darnat, 'L'Epiphanie du blanc', *Littératures*, no. 40, 1999, pp. 19–30.

novel and its multiple resonances with and beyond Simon's previous works. The present volume seeks to contribute to this continuing process of reflection.

David Carroll's and Mária Brewer's essays both situate Simon's work within the context of postmodern debate on the 'site'. Drawing on the work of Pierre Nora, Antoine Compagnon and Jean-François Lyotard, Carroll argues that Simon's fiction might be construed as a post-Holocaust literary 'site of memory'. Considered in the context of an age which is characterised by both a massive increase in our capacity to store and retrieve the past and a generalised feeling that our capacity for 'natural', collective memory has been, by and large, lost, Simon's 'memory-fiction' not only offers a critique of history and of 'history-memory', but also, by repeatedly re-remembering and rewriting (as opposed simply to remembering and writing) the past, exemplifies the process by which the post-Auschwitz writer constantly stages and restages the past in and as fiction and, in doing so, narrates the impossibility of transcending the past. Viewed in this way, Simon's aesthetic is seen to deviate crucially from that which has been derived from the Proustian concept of involuntary memory. Contrary to the aestheticisation of memory that literary criticism most usually assumes to be Proust's cultural legacy, in Simon's fiction time is lost over and over again and this loss, far from being transcended through art, is attested repeatedly in narratives that acknowledge the 'un-reality' of the past reality that they purport to narrate and that point not simply to what remains unsaid but also to the 'always-already forgotten' dimensions of past experience.

Mária Brewer's examination of the various ways in which Simon's fiction explores the incommensurable also draws on Lyotard's theory – in this instance his contributions to debate on incommensurability and postmodernity and, in particular, his concepts of the *différend* and the childhood of the event. Simon is seen to share with contemporary literary and cultural theory a fascination for 'sites' and for the divisions which separate them. Brewer reads Simon's work as a manifestation of 'the aesthetics of childhood' that represents a particular type of artistic response to incommensurability and that defines writing as a means of resisting the effacement of singularities in time, space and language. This reading is supported by the analysis of some of the numerous encounters between incongruous, anachronistic and anamorphic phenomena that are to be found in all Simon's fiction after *L'Herbe* and that take the form of instances of cognitive gaps, sensations of disconnection, communicative failure, discordances and oppositions. However, Simon is not simply concerned with the fragmentation, severance and loss of shared sites; he is equally concerned with questions relating to 'contact zones' and 'travelling cultures', the many travellers and farflung sites of *Le Jardin des Plantes* drawing attention to the importance of links and 'passages' in his work. Simon's writing counters closure, resists uniformisation and stresses, through his characters' shock encounters with the material specificity of places, people and moments, not only the diversity of the world, but also the multiplicity and diversity of the potential links among the elements of that world.

Celia Britton's and J. A. E. Loubère's essays are both concerned with the question of the articulation of trauma, with the writer's/protagonists' efforts to describe his/their experience and with the associative links that Simon's texts establish between the traumatic memory and other more mundane experiences. Britton's essay proposes a psychoanalytical reading of the interview series of *Le Jardin des Plantes*, arguing that, in its treatment of the war-episode which has been a keystone of Simon's *oeuvre* since *La Route des Flandres*, the 1997 novel constitutes a significant break with his earlier work. The evocation, during the encounter with the journalist, of the moments preceding the shooting of Simon's commanding officer acts as a 'liquidation', in Freudian terms, of the traumatic event that has been compulsively replayed in Simon's fiction over the last forty years. Britton demonstrates how, notwithstanding the insensitivity of the journalist and the ineptness of his questions, the unique, closed moment of trauma is gradually 'opened out' in the course of the interview and reconnected to other memories from Simon's past. This process is effected partly through spatial and temporal recontextualisation – the interview takes place in the present, indoors, in an upstairs room – that permits the establishment of a clear opposition between the traumatic experience and the reassuring context of the 'quotidien' in which it is recalled. The patterns of repetition within the interview, the use of the tape recorder which makes the traumatic moment both durational and infinitely repeatable, the variation on the familiar Simonian motif of the older–younger man relationship all combine with the changes in rhythm according to which the text switches in and out of the interview scene to bring about a more successful integration of the traumatic instant into the protagonist's memories than had been possible in previous novels.

The reiterated war-episode also figures prominently in Loubère's wide-ranging study of the theme of conflict in Simon's fiction. This essay offers a survey of the various manifestations of conflict in the novels – war, revolution, family confrontations, sexual tensions, man's struggle with the limitations of his own body – and shows that there is a close correlation between its prominence in a given novel and the level of linguistic dislocation in that novel. The various conflicts and tensions that mark the lives of Simon's characters are mirrored in and conveyed by the disruptions in the linear flow of narrative and language and, more specifically, through syntactical breaks, incomplete sentences, deviations from typographical norms and abrupt changes in rhythm. Thus, in those texts where the theme of conflict is particularly evident, the forward movement of the narrative is thwarted by the incursions of memory and by deviations from the norms of French syntax. However, this centrifugal effect is counterbalanced by a contrary tendency, the conflict motif acting as a kind of magnet that exercises a constant pull on the narration. Loubère's study tracks the effects of this double tension in Simon's fiction from *La Route des Flandres* onwards, analysing in particular the variations in rhythm that it engenders and drawing attention to the status of conflict as an 'energiser' that stimulates the writing process through the suggestion of numerous associative lines of development and that challenges the writer to try again and again to find words adequate to describe his experience.

Although ostensibly concerned with more light-hearted matters, Alastair Duncan's essay also considers the ways in which Simon and his characters respond to conflict and react to experiences of trauma. Duncan tackles the issue of humour in Simon by combining a consideration of the presence in his fiction of certain genres (satire, burlesque and comedy) with the close analysis of a representative sample of examples drawn from the novels that he has published since and including *Le Vent*. Duncan's analysis of Simon's satirical practice, an analysis broadly informed by Bakhtinian theory, focuses on the distancing role of satire and on the strategies – pointed contrast, parodic stylisation of professional language, juxtaposition of the incongruous and the contradictory, caricature, linguistic play, hyperbole – that are used to challenge the dominant values and ideology of a given community. Drawing on John Jump's definitions of high and low burlesque, Duncan proceeds, in the second section of his essay, to analyse the way in which Simon deflates subjects and experiences that would normally be considered to be significant and, in many cases, emotionally traumatic or physically threatening, while at the same time elevating the conventionally trifling or banal. Iser is the principal theoretical point of reference in the final section, which is devoted to comedy. Here, Duncan shows how in Simon, as in Beckett, comedy serves to mediate and to transform into laughter the anxiety arising out of the discrepancy between imagination and reality, the violation of norms and the subversion of prevailing values.

The question of intertextuality figures prominently in the essays of both Mary Orr and David Ellison. Orr's examination of intertextuality in *Le Jardin des Plantes* begins with a comparative reading of Simon's novel and Borges's *Garden of Forking Paths* that highlights a number of coincidences on the level of narrative content, theme and attitude to representation. These coincidences include similarities between fictional situations, the prominence in both texts of the theme of terror, the presence of mysteries, codes and clues that testify to the novels' affiliations with detective and espionage fiction, and the inclusion of various control mechanisms (false trails, dead ends, authorial representatives) that thwart the reader's desire for access to a single unequivocal truth. In the second part of the essay, Orr turns to some of the explicitly signalled intertexts, arguing that the extracts from Proust and Flaubert and, in particular, the extracts from correspondence with their contemporaries are part of a deliberation on the process of authorial decision making and on the relationship between literary production and academic and aesthetic evaluation. Thus, the inclusion of material from the 1971 Colloque de Cerisy on the *nouveau roman* and the account of the encounter between S. and the journalist draw attention to the same issues as the extracts drawn from the literary authorities of the past: the relationship between the work and the prevailing critical values; the process by which the text is released into the public domain. Finally, Orr argues that the unorthodox physical layout of certain parts of *Le Jardin des Plantes* should be read as a reflexive strategy designed to replicate one of the stages in the production of the manuscript.

David Ellison's contribution argues that, despite the familiarity of its themes and techniques, *Le Jardin des Plantes* effects a defamiliarising reframing of pre-existing material that forces a reconsideration of one of the most prominent preoccupations of Simon's *oeuvre*: the relationship between nature and culture. Ellison conducts his analysis in two stages. In the first section, he demonstrates, through an analysis of the description of the Jardin des Plantes which figures on pages 61 to 63 of the novel, that the botanical gardens that give the novel its title do not, as we might initially assume, serve as an anchoring point of reference in reality or as an interpretative key to the text. Close examination of the layout, design and ornamentation of the Jardin des Plantes exposes layers of artifice including references to Rousseau and to Bernardin de Saint-Pierre that suggest that the apparent contrast between the formal (and therefore 'artificial') French and the informal (and therefore 'natural') English sectors is, in fact, a false opposition, while the correspondences which Simon sets up between the initial description of the gardens and the description of a reproduction of Mme Vigée-Lebrun's *Paul et Virginie fuyant l'orage* point to the status of the Jardin des Plantes as a utopian 'non-lieu' that serves as a 'point de départ' for the 'departure from the real' on which, Ellison argues, Simon's writing is based. The second section of the essay is devoted to the exposure of another false opposition: the apparent counterpoint between the Proustian intertexts and the passages relating to the Second World War. Once again, artifice – here, the aestheticisation of nature and the tactics of love in the Proustian passages, the tactics of warfare in the Second World War passages – is the common denominator linking the two contrapuntally distributed series. However, if the overlay of artifice in the Proustian conversation piece reveals that intertext to be another false key to the text and to Simon's aesthetic principles, the implicit parallels between the physical conflict of the Second World War and the psychological/ emotional skirmishes of Proustian social and sexual intercourse draw attention to the productive dynamics of the tension between the literal and the metaphorical (i.e. between nature and culture) that lies at the heart of Simon's work.

If Ellison's essay considers the more general tension between nature and culture, *physis* and *techné*, Wolfram Nitsch's contribution focuses on particular examples of the man-made. Nitsch examines the roles and status of various types of machinery and media in the novels published in the 1980s and 1990s – the tape recorder in *Le Jardin des Plantes*, the train in *L'Acacia* and the cinema in *Les Géorgiques* – and argues that, in Simon, technology is presented in three very different, but not mutually exclusive ways: as a somewhat sinister inorganic phenomenon that belongs to the external material world and that impinges rather menacingly on the character's awareness; as an essential quasi-organic extension of the character's body, as an aesthetic stimulus and model of literary production. Thus, the 'murmure' registered by the tape recorder in *Le Jardin des Plantes* draws attention to the way in which verbal communication is jeopardised and frequently compromised by the intrusion of contingent noise. In *L'Acacia* the train carrying the protagonist to the Front is a component in and an image of the machinery of modern warfare, while in *Les Géorgiques*, the aggressive advertising, the insistent ringing of the bell signalling the start of the show and the disconcertingly jerky projection of the films confront the spectator with a material world which is both threatening and inescapable. However, despite their deficiencies, intrusiveness and menace, these machines and media have other positive and productive dimensions, serving to make the characters aware of phenomena that would otherwise go unnoticed, prompting the elaboration of narrative and linguistic chains of association and acting as telling *mises en abyme* for the mechanisms of literary production.

Lastly, Mireille Calle-Gruber and Jean Duffy focus on the role of the visual arts in Simon's work: Calle-Gruber examines his photographic practice, while Duffy explores the thematic, metafictional and generative roles played by Poussin's *Plague at Ashdod* in *Le Jardin des Plantes*. Calle-Gruber's close reading of a selection of images from *Photographies 1937–1970* highlights the common ground between Simon's photographs and his fiction. *Photographies 1937–1970* is shown to be underpinned by a number of thematic and formal concerns that are already familiar from his novels: notably, the passage of time and the challenges that it poses to representation, the tentative nature of artistic composition, the place of the observer/photographer/narrator and the internal formal coherence of the work whether that work be a novel or a collection of photographs. In *Photographies 1937–1970*, these concerns are expressed through a number of techniques, many of which involve language (the attribution of captions that add meaning(s) to the image or that highlight its polyvalence, intertextual allusion) or have equivalents in linguistic expression (synecdoche, metaphor). Calle-Gruber also argues that, in spite of the absence of photographs of Simon in the volume, the presence of a number of other features – the recurrence of images of graffiti that point to the relationship between photography and writing, the frame changes in certain sequences that testify to the organising consciousness producing the montage, the inclusion of images that can be read as *mises en abyme* – turns *Photographies* into an indirect self-portrait.

In her essay, Duffy argues that the description of Poussin's *Plague at Ashdod* that figures in *Le Jardin des Plantes* serves three principal functions. As one of numerous references to religious representations that occur in a wide range of quite different contexts in the novel and that testify at one and the same time to the number and diversity of the gods that man has fabricated and to the strength of his need to subscribe to some kind of 'truth', *The Plague at Ashdod* can be read as a kind of résumé of the history of religion and as a pointer to the intrinsic obsolescence of all systems of belief. Viewed in the context of a different set of cross-textual patterns, the description of Poussin's painting assumes a reflexive role as a *mise en abyme* highlighting Simon's anti-interventionist view of the activity of writing and his desire to dissociate himself from certain types of discourse. Simon's own conception of *écriture* as a process founded on the exploration of the evocative and associative power of language and the importance that he attaches to the aesthetic coherence of the work are examined in the final section of Duffy's paper, which is devoted to an analysis of the various serial motifs and linguistic correspondences that connect the description of Poussin's painting formally and thematically to the rest of the text.

In addition to the various clusters or subsets identified above, the essays are linked by a number of other thematic strands that run through the collection. The recurrence of topics in different essays has created numerous points of intersection and generated alternative and complementary critical perspectives on a range of issues. Following the terms of the invitation to the 1999 conference from which this volume originated, many of the contributors chose to focus upon *Le Jardin des Plantes*. The interview series in that novel has provoked particularly intense critical interest, the different perspectives offered by Britton, Carroll, Loubère, Brewer, Nitsch, Duncan and Duffy reflecting its prominence within the novel and highlighting its problematic interpretative status. The Proustian intertexts and the relationship between Simonian and Proustian aesthetics have also generated substantial interest in the contributions of Ellison, Orr and Carroll, while some of the other more obviously problematic sections of the novel – the description of the Jardin des Plantes, the film scenario that closes the text, the extract from the proceedings of the Cerisy colloquium, the references to the life and work of Gastone Novelli – are examined in more or less detail in several of the essays: respectively, Ellison, Orr, Loubère and Duffy (the description of the gardens); Brewer, Duffy, Nitsch, Orr (the film scenario); Duffy, Duncan, Brewer, Orr (the Cerisy intertext); Brewer, Orr, Loubère (the Novelli references).

However, although most of the contributions engage to some degree with *Le Jardin des Plantes*, most are also concerned explicitly or implicitly with broader issues in Simon's writing, and the theme of 'retrospection' that informed the organisation of the conference manifests itself in the number of essays that consciously revisit familiar Simonian *topoi*, often using critical ideas and models developed during the 1980s and 1990s to shed new light on old themes, or offering a reconsideration of certain topics in the light of perspectives suggested by *Le Jardin des Plantes*. Thus, the essays of Britton, Brewer, Carroll, Ellison, Loubère, Nitsch and Calle-Gruber are underpinned by questions relating to history and memory, while the contributions of Britton, Brewer and Calle-Gruber are also linked by the fact that they all discuss the question of the singularity of the moment and examine issues relating to the process of naming and unnaming reality. The reflexive and formal aspects of Simon's fiction are examined by numerous contributors. The *mise en abyme* figures in several essays (Orr, Duffy, Loubère); the importance of rhythm in Simon's novels is examined by Britton, Loubère, Brewer and Calle-Gruber; Nitsch examines the role of machinery as motor and model of literary imagination. Finally, Simon's conception of the role of the writer and his attitude to various types of discourse come under scrutiny in the contributions of Duffy, Ellison and Duncan. Thus, Duffy's analysis of the metafictional dimension of *The Plague at Ashdod* intersects not only with Ellison's demonstration of the way in which Simon distances himself, through a strategic choice of intertextual extracts, from the discourse of the aesthetic, but also with Duncan's analysis of satirical techniques deployed by Simon in his evocation of the various clashes of values, culture and class that so frequently characterise his characters' relationship with the communities in which they find themselves.

That the collection is characterised by so many points of contact and divergence and that it offers numerous different perspectives on single scenes, themes or techniques is indicative of the thematic richness and formal sophistication of Simon's work. Over the years, it has become increasingly apparent that Simon's collected works constitute an *oeuvre* in which each new text takes up where the earlier ones left off, offering unfamiliar perspectives on familiar topics, introducing new thematic strands that interweave with the old, furthering Simon's exploration of narrative form and providing a new vantage point from which to consider the work that preceded it. This volume had its origins in a shared desire to pay tribute to that *oeuvre* and the ever-new challenges which it poses for its readers, for *Le Jardin des Plantes* has not only posed new questions but has stimulated a reappraisal of earlier texts and a return to some of the unresolved issues and partially explored paths of Simonian criticism.

1

Thinking History Otherwise: Fiction and the Sites of Memory in Claude Simon

David Carroll

Ce qui constitue [les lieux de mémoire] est un jeu de la mémoire et de l'histoire, une interaction des deux facteurs qui aboutit à leur surdétermination réciproque... Seuls d'entre les livres d'histoire sont lieux de mémoire ceux qui se fondent sur un remaniement même de la mémoire... Même chose des Mémoires, qui sont des lieux de mémoire... parce qu'ils compliquent le simple exercice de la mémoire d'un jeux d'interrogation sur la mémoire elle-même.

Pierre Nora

Nous avons fait de quelques livres... comme la *Recherche du temps perdu*, des lieux de mémoire essentiels, parce que ce sont eux, c'est la littérature, qui nous aide à penser la mémoire autrement que sur le modèle de l'histoire.

Antoine Compagnon

In his multi-volume collection, *Les Lieux de mémoire*, Pierre Nora describes the contemporary period as having at the same time both a deficiency and surplus of memory. Surplus of memory in the sense that never before has it apparently been so easy to inscribe, store and retrieve memories of all sorts, both private and official, individual and collective. And never before have there been so many different types of archives and so many different forms of memory being stored. Also, and more important, never has there been such a demand for memories, such a determined will to remember, or such a broad consensus concerning the need for memory, the need not just for the 'great men and women' of history but for all individuals, no matter how insignificant, to gather, record and store their memories and family histories for themselves, their families and posterity. As Nora puts it, 'produire de l'archive est l'impératif de l'époque'.[1]

---

1 Pierre Nora, 'Entre mémoire et histoire', *Les Lieux de mémoire*, vol. 1, *La République*, Paris, Gallimard, 5 vols, 1984–92, p. XXVIII.

Such a surplus of memory may not, however, be as positive a contribution to the diversification and expansion of history as it might at first appear, for even though the decentralisation and democratisation of archives might be considered a positive development, Nora fears that the storage of information has increased so prodigiously and without reason that we now suffer as much as benefit from what he calls 'le gonflement hypertrophique de la fonction de mémoire'.[2] We may indeed even be at risk, he suggests, of being crushed by the 'terrorism' of historicised memory, evident in the indiscriminate filling of archives and the seemingly unbounded and uncontrolled will to remember and store practically everything.[3] If those who forget the past are bound to repeat it, it could also be said that those who strive on the contrary to retain or store everything from the past and to forget nothing risk being smothered by the sheer weight of the documents of the past or what Nora characterises as the 'avalanche of memory'.[4]

At the same time, Nora also argues that never before has there been so much talk about so little, the abundance and even surplus of talk about memory being the direct result of the absence of authentic memory, or of what he refers to as collective, lived memory.[5] Never have people been as distanced or alienated from spontaneous, collective expressions of memory in their different natural *milieux*,[6] distanced

2 'Aucune époque n'a été aussi volontairement productrice d'archives que la nôtre, non seulement par le volume que sécrète spontanément la société moderne, non seulement par les moyens techniques de reproduction et de conservation dont elle dispose mais par la superstition et le respect de la trace. A mesure même que disparaît la mémoire traditionelle, nous nous sentons tenus d'accumuler religieusement vestiges, témoignages, documents, images, discours, signes visibles de ce qui fut, comme si ce dossier de plus en plus proliférant devait devenir on ne sait quelle preuve à l'on ne sait quel tribunal de l'histoire [...] Impossible de préjuger de ce dont il faudra se souvenir. D'où l'inhibition à détruire, la constitution de tout en archives, la dilatation indifférenciée du champ du mémorable, le gonflement hypertrophique de la fonction de mémoire, liée au sentiment même de sa perte, et le renforcement corrélatif de toutes les institutions de mémoire' (*Les Lieux de mémoire*, vol. 1, p. XXVII).
3 *Les Lieux de mémoire*, vol. 1, p. XXVIII.
4 'L'avalanche n'a pas fini de nous emporter' ('L'Ère de la commémoration', *Les Lieux de mémoire*, vol. 3, *Les France*, part 3, pp. 1011–12).
5 'On ne parle tant de mémoire que parce qu'il n'y en a plus' (*Les Lieux de mémoire*, vol. 1, p. XVII).
6 Nora distinguishes, not without a certain nostalgie, between '*milieux*' and '*lieux*' of memory in the following way: 'La conscience de la rupture avec le passé se confond avec le sentiment d'une mémoire déchirée; mais où le déchirement réveille encore assez de mémoire pour que puisse se poser le problème de son incarnation. Le sentiment de la continuité devient résiduel à des lieux. Il y a des lieux de mémoire parce qu'il n'y a plus de milieux de mémoire' (*Les Lieux de mémoire*, vol. 1, p. XVII).

even from their own family memories and heritage, without a clear sense of belonging naturally and unreflectively to a single, unified, unquestioned heritage or national, ethnic, religious or political tradition or group, all of which had previously generated, stored and defended their own memories and the identities rooted in them.

Never before has history seemed to move so rapidly, leaving in its wake fragments and traces of memories of all sorts which, as they are left behind, become increasingly irrelevant and more quickly and definitively forgotten as new information, experiences and memories – as well as new modes for generating, storing, circulating and retrieving information – take their place. This potential 'terrorism' of memory arising from its overproduction is thus also a cover for a lack of foundation in or for memory, a form of (over)compensation for the loss of so-called authentic, spontaneous memory.

In the absence or distancing of traditional forms of memory is thus born the need for more memory, a need that can never be completely met and that thus generates increasingly diversified forms and sites of memory and a repeated questioning of the nature and status of the past and of the different ways it is retained and reproduced in the present. No matter how much memory is produced and stored, no matter how much talk there is of memory, for Nora there is, thus, at the same time never enough memory: inevitably too much programmed, artificial memory and never enough natural, spontaneous, collective memory. A surplus of memory smothers the present, while at the same time the shortage, absence or destruction of traditional memory creates a profound lack in the present. Nora's own essays fluctuate between, on the one hand, a romantic nostalgia for tradition and a simpler, more naturally collectivised retention and recognition of the past, and, on the other hand, a postmodern affirmation of the critical benefits of the conflictual diversity of 'little memories' and their multiple sites.

The nostalgic side of the essays Nora himself wrote for *Les Lieux de mémoire* conveys his sense of regret at the destruction or loss of traditional modes of memory and the collectivities who allegedly spontaneously lived them. What could be called the 'postmodern' side of these same essays, on the contrary, points to and even encourages the development of more critical, self-reflexive histories of memory that would not be smothered by the surplus of memory and yet would at the same time be free of nostalgia. These would be histories that would investigate and question predetermined notions of individual or collective identity and thus the memory sites that serve as the privileged locations of such identities. Histories that would challenge the dialectical recuperation of loss, conflict and contradiction in both general, redemptive meta-narratives (*pace* Hegel and Marx) and narratives of individual lives, whether biographical or autobiographical. And finally, histories that might also question the assumptions of both aesthetic and philosophical theories that posit memory as the unifying force that gives meaning to fragmented existence and value to the contingent experiences and realities of daily life and 'lost time' by raising them to a higher philosophical, literary or aesthetic level (*pace* Hegel again and of course Proust).

Nora argues that not just his own essays but all the essays in his collection are critical histories of this type, that they demonstrate how memory is not a 'natural' phenomenon for contemporary historians and, thus, why it has to be analysed more in terms of what it does than what it is, more in terms of its 'art of staging' of the past and its effects on the present than what it represents as the past. He refers to this 'art' as the fundamental 'literary dimension' of memory and claims it is the focus of the different approaches to history represented in his collection,[7] which he asserts represent nothing less than a 'new kind of history':

> a history less interested in causes than in effects; less interested in actions remembered or even commemorated than in the traces left by those actions and in the interaction of those commemorations; less interested in events themselves than their signification; less interested in 'what actually happened' than in its perpetual reuse and misuse, its influence on successive presents; less interested in tradition than in the way in which traditions are constituted and passed on; [...] a history that is interested in memory not as remembrance but as the overall structure of the past within the present: history of the second degree.[8]

The recognition of the fundamental performative, literary dimension of memory not only further emphasises the radical break with the nostalgia for 'natural memory', its traditions and its *milieux*, but also points to the need for history to be aware of its own mechanisms of staging and presentation and to become critical of itself, a history 'of the second degree'.

7 'Présentation,' *Les Lieux de mémoire*, vol. 1, p. VIII.
8 'From *Lieux de mémoire* to *Realms of Memory*: Preface to the English-Language Edition', in *Realms of Memory*, trans. Arthur Goldhammer, New York, Columbia University Press, 1996, vol. 1, p. XXIV.

Literature thus holds a key place in Nora's own treatment of the complex and fluctuating relations between memory and history, even though literature's exact role in the process of critical reflexivity remains largely uninvestigated by him. Nora claims, for example, that literature, until recently, was, along with history, one of the two forms of legitimation of memory. And even though he announces the demise of the novel, he still continues to give 'literary functions' an important role in determining memory's legitimacy. The difference is that these functions have now allegedly been assumed by history, which uses imaginary, literary forms to keep the past alive in memory:

> La mémoire, en effet, n'a jamais connu que deux formes de légitimité: historique ou littéraire. Elles se sont d'ailleurs exercées parallèlement, mais jusqu'à nos jours, séparément. La frontière aujourd'hui s'estompe, et sur la mort quasi simultanée de l'histoire-mémoire et de la mémoire-fiction, naît un type d'histoire qui doit à son rapport nouveau avec le passé, un autre passé, son prestige et sa légitimité. L'histoire est notre imaginaire de remplacement. Renaissance du roman historique, vogue du document personnalisé, revitalisation littéraire du drame historique, succès du récit d'histoire orale, comment s'expliqueraient-ils sinon comme le relais de la fiction défaillante? L'intérêt pour les lieux où s'ancre, se condense et s'exprime le capital épuisé de notre mémoire collective relève de cette sensibilité-là. Histoire, profondeur d'une époqe arrachée à sa profondeur, roman vrai d'une époque sans vrai roman. Mémoire, promue au centre de l'histoire: c'est le deuil éclatant de la littérature.[9]

If it is true that the blurring of the boundary between history and fiction has produced a new, hybrid form of history, the question Nora does not address is what form the novel has taken after the alleged demise of 'true' novels and the (re)birth of a new history in the form of the novel. History-memory emerges from its death to be reborn in the historical novel, or rather as history in the form of a 'truthful' novel; memory-fiction and the novel in its 'true form' simply disappear.

Whether the novel has actually died or whether it is really possible to distinguish between allegedly true and false versions of the novel, it seems legitimate to ask what fiction might still have to do with memory and with memory's changing relation to history. In his contribution to *Les Lieux de mémoire*, Antoine Compagnon sets the stage for this kind of investigation by showing how a novel as untraditional (and scandalous) as Proust's *A la recherche du temps perdu* (which could certainly not be considered either a 'truthful' or 'true novel' in conventional

9 *Les Lieux de mémoire*, vol. 1, p. XLII.

terms) became one of what he calls the privileged or essential sites of cultural memory for the French (but not the French alone). This happened not only or even primarily, claims Compagnon, because Proust's novel (if it is a novel) is rich in memories or discusses at length how memory works, or even because it demonstrates the powerful aesthetic effects of involuntary, 'essential' memory. It is rather because, as Compagnon asserts, history lives in such literary sites, and Proust's novel, like a select number of other literary texts, 'nous aide à penser la mémoire autrement que sur le modèle de l'histoire'.[10]

Compagnon thus seems to agree with Nora that literature in general and the novel in particular have served an important critical function in offering alternatives to historicised memory, whose unrestrained expansion constitutes for Nora, as we have seen, a form of terrorism or 'tyranny'.[11] It would follow, then, that if the novel were really ever to die, if there were in fact no more 'true novels' to question historicised memory and its truths and to provide alternate, fictional models for memory, then history-memory would indeed triumph over fiction, with the result that memory would be totally determined by and limited to whatever the accepted protocols of historical legitimisation happened to be.

Such, of course, is not the case, and Nora's announcement of the death of the novel is most definitely premature, as proclamations of this type always are. Fiction-memory is still alive in novels to challenge, undermine, supplement and offer alternatives to history-memory, even if novels do not necessarily have the form of 'true novels' with clearly identified characters, coherent plots and well-defined beginnings, middles and ends. Whether they are true to the form of the novel or represent its death,[12] it would be difficult to deny that the novels of

10 'La Recherche du temps perdu, de Marcel Proust', in Les Lieux de mémoire, vol. 3, part 2, p. 965.
11 In the last words of the last chapter of the last volume of Les Lieux de mémoire Nora defines the contemporary moment in terms of 'la tyrannie de la mémoire', but he also predicts that such tyranny will some day end: 'Le lit de la mémoire n'est pas indéfiniment extensible [...] Quand une autre manière de l'être ensemble se sera mise en place, quand aura fini de se fixer la figure de ce que l'on n'appellera même plus l'identité, le besoin aura disparu d'exhumer les repères et d'explorer les lieux. L'ère de la commémoration sera définitivement close. La tyrannie de la mémoire n'aura duré qu'un temps – mais c'était le nôtre' ('L'Ère de la commémoration', vol. 3, Part 3, p. 1012).
12 In his acceptance speech on receiving the Nobel Prize for literature, Simon attacked an unnamed critic who had maliciously wondered if the Nobel Prize committee in honouring Simon in this way was simply trying to confirm the rumour that the

Claude Simon constitute a powerful and relentless critique of both history in general and history-memory in particular. With the awarding of the Nobel Prize to Simon, it might even be possible to claim, in spite of (or perhaps even because of) his alleged responsibility for the novel's demise, that his texts have now been officially recognised as one of the 'essential', contemporary literary sites of memory.

However, if Simon's novels could be considered a 'site of memory', it would in fact be in a very different way from Proust's monumental novel and the site it occupies in cultural memory. For Simon's novels do not just provide models for conceiving of memory in terms different from those of history. They also challenge the aestheticisation of memory related to or derived from the version of Proustian involuntary memory that has entered the popular imagination exclusively in the figure of the 'madeleine' and that has been invested with symbolic value as a (or the) model for literary or aesthetic memory in general.[13] Simon's novels repeatedly stage the loss of transcendence of memory and the effects of this loss on and as the experience of history, rather than the triumph of literary or aesthetic memory over history. Moreover, the loss of transcendence in his work is not simply a stage on the way to a higher aesthetic truth but on the contrary definitive.[14]

But even the case of Proust is more complicated (and less a monument to the essential) than it might at first seem. For if Proust should be considered one of the last novelists of essential, aestheticised memory and thus the creator of one, if not the last, of the privileged literary sites of memory, he is also a novelist who prepared the way for

---

novel was definitively dead: 'Il [the critic] ne semble pas s'être aperçu que, si par "roman" il entend le modèle littéraire qui s'est épanoui au cours du XIXe siècle, celui-ci est en effet bien mort' (*DS*, 15).

13 Compagnon cites the 4,000 yearly visitors to Proust's aunt's house in Illiers (the model for Combray) and the 500 madeleines sold each week in the local bakery as signs of the symbolic investment in and sacralisation of Proustian memory (p. 927).

14 Régis Debray, in his 'Lettre à Claude Simon sur le roman moderne', acknowledges that reading Simon was particularly useful to him at a specific moment of his life: 'Au risque de vous faire de la peine, cher Claude Simon, je dois vous avouer que vos romans m'ont été naguère très utiles: c'est en lisant et relisant, une, deux, dix fois *La Route des Flandres*, en prison, à Camiri, vers 1969, que j'ai découvert l'impossibilité où j'étais désormais de me croire marxiste, hégélien, ou proustien (c'est à peu près la même chose). Vous m'avez révélé à moi-même en me révélant le noyau rationnel d'une fin de siècle où j'étais entré à reculons, les yeux tournés vers ses débuts, en m'ouvrant à l'univers qu'on a appelé depuis "post-moderne"' (*Éloges*, Paris, Gallimard, 1986, p. 72).

the demise of essentialist, transcendent forms of aesthetic or aestheticised memory and for the production of a multiplicity of conflicting memory sites, even or especially within literature. In spite of the investment in the 'madeleine' on the part of both literary tourists and numerous experts in the field of Proustian studies, involuntary memory can be seen in fact as only one moment, and not necessarily the deciding moment, of the Proustian investigation and staging of memory. Simon, following in Proust's wake, could be considered one, if not the most important of the novelists of memory in a world lacking in essential historical or literary forms of memory and over-supplied with constructed, fictional forms of memory, which are themselves lacking in transcendent but not critical possibilities.

Along with their repeated critique of History (most frequently found in Simon's work with a capital 'H'), and more specifically of the coherent, continuous, progressive form of History found in history books, Simon's novels also reject essentialist, aesthetic recuperations of the loss of historical transcendence and meaning. In general, Simon refuses to situate his work as a novelist within a post-romantic literary tradition that proposes to supplement the deficiencies of historical knowledge and representation by means of the creative or aesthetic imagination. An indication of his distance from the post-romantic tradition can be found in his repeated acknowledgements of his own lack of imagination and creativity and his admissions that he is incapable of inventing stories or creating characters or images on his own.[15] This explains, he claims, why he has always had to rely on personal memories for the subjects of his novels and on family documents, souvenirs and paintings as props, supports or stimuli for his writing.

In *Le Jardin des Plantes*, for example, S. (a character more directly linked to Simon than characters from other novels) responds to the questions of an insistent journalist concerning why the theme of war is so prevalent in his novels. S. replies in the terms Simon himself has often used in various interviews:

> 'J'ai dit que Oui c'était vrai que ça revenait souvent mais... Il a dit Pourquoi? J'ai dit que Vous savez je n'ai pas beaucoup d'imagination alors à part mes tout premiers bouquins qui n'étaient pas très fameux les suivants ç'a toujours été plus ou moins à partir de choses que j'ai vécues, de mes expériences personnelles, ou encore de vieux papiers de famille, tout ça...' (*JP*, 76–77).

15 For example, in an interview after the publication of *La Route des Flandres*, Simon boldly said: 'Je suis incapable d'inventer quoi que ce soit' (Claude Sarraute, 'Avec *La Route des Flandres* Claude Simon affirme sa manière', *Le Monde*, 8 octobre 1960, p. 9).

When literary creativity and imagination are severely limited or even lacking, personal experiences and the random bits and pieces of family and cultural memory ('tout ça') constitute the material the writer has at his disposal to work with and to work on. In other words, Simon-novelist, according to his own novels, is no inspired 'genius'.

The novelist is thus for Simon more an artisan than a creator. As he has often stressed, this means that writing should be defined primarily as a working on language, as the search among the possibilities offered by language to find new ways of transforming, complicating and linking together different memories, fragments of narratives, descriptions of objects and places, historical and individual time sequences, and individual words and sounds. Simon even used his acceptance speech for the Nobel Prize to attack his critics for ignoring or devaluing what he called the work of the novelist and for continuing to assume that the form of the contemporary novel was, or at least should be, determined by what he called a form of causality exterior to literature:

> 'Il semble aujourd'hui légitime de revendiquer pour le roman (ou d'exiger de lui) [...] une crédibilité qui soit conférée au texte par la pertinence des rapports entre ses éléments, dont l'ordonnance, la succession et l'agencement ne relèveront plus d'une causalité extérieure au fait littéraire [...] mais d'une causalité intérieure, en ce sens que tel événement, décrit et non plus rapporté, suivra ou précédera tel autre en raison de leurs seules qualités propres' (DS, 21–22).

Linkage between narrative sequences, phrases and even words does not thus depend, argues Simon, on any exterior referent, general plan, intended meaning or historically predetermined temporal sequence or chronology. Rather it is produced only by the work of the writer on language, the 'mot à mot' that constitutes the process of writing. The art of the novelist is thus an art of collage (or 'bric-collage'), as Simon has often claimed, not a creative art.[16] It should be judged not in terms of predetermined notions of 'the truth' or 'the real' but rather in terms of criteria that are never fixed and remain always to be established.[17]

---

16 For example, Simon has described the work of the writer in the following terms: 'Et pour qualifier ce travail de l'écrivain (qui, dans son détail ou son ensemble, me fait toujours penser au titre de ce chapitre du cours de mathématiques intitulé: "Arrangements, permutations, combinaisons"), il existe un mot lui convenant admirablement [...] c'est celui de *bricolage*' (Claude Simon, 'La Fiction mot à mot', in *Nouveau roman: hier, aujourd'hui*, vol. 2, Paris, 10/18, 1972, p. 96).

17 In *Le Différend*, Paris, Gallimard, 1983, and other works from the same period, Jean-François Lyotard emphasises the arbitrary nature of linkage and uses Simon as a prime example of a writer who sees the task of writing to be the discovery of new

The devices or material used as props for both imagination and memory in Simon's work are well known, because Simon has frequently described them in his novels and often discussed them in interviews with journalists and scholars in search of keys for understanding his work and his life. They range from the portrait of the ancestor in *La Route des Flandres*, to the postcards and family photos in *Histoire* (and in later novels), to various paintings, historical and family documents, to well-known literary and political texts of different types.[18] Recent novels increasingly rewrite and recast the memories narrated in previous novels – memories of the Spanish Civil War, the debacle in Flanders at the beginning of the Second World War, etc. – and create different links among these memories and between them and fragments of narratives not found in previous novels. They do not just remember and write the past but also re-remember and rewrite it; they do not just retell what was experienced but also relate what has already been remembered and written down as what was experienced. Simonian 'memory' takes the form of memory-fiction of a degree beyond the second degree.

The hypothetical novel that could be formed from the combination of all of what could be called Simon's 'novels of memory' might perhaps even be characterised as his own 'recherche du temps perdu' (especially given the long quotations from Proust in *Le Jardin des Plantes*). But as I have already indicated, Simon, unlike Proust, does not postulate the experience of the return of lost time and the

---

ways to link phrases. In his Irvine Wellek Library Lectures, Lyotard argued that, for Simon, the task 'consists in trying to start a sentence, to continue it, and to finish it […] Here is the labor of speech entering language in the middle in order to disclose the idiom it wants. Intransitively, to write is to seek, through the destination of writing. Even if there is neither a need nor a demand for writing any sentence, if no god addresses the writer any prescription to write anything, the necessity to begin, continue, and finish sentences, or better, phrases, remains' (*Peregrinations: Law, Form, Event*, New York, Columbia University Press, 1988, p. 4).

18 Increasingly frequently in Simon's recent novels, passages and scenes from previous novels, segments of interviews with journalists and critics, varied responses to his work in newspapers and journals, and even polemical accounts of colloquia and international meetings also serve as material supports for his writing. His recent novels do not in all instances avoid the temptation to settle accounts with critics or to denounce the political positions of other writers, both his contemporaries and those writers from the past whose positions on politics and literature he has repeatedly attacked in interviews and essays (above all, Sartre and Malraux). With their constant repetition, such attacks appear increasingly polemical and dogmatic, even if their explicit purpose is to denounce different types of political and literary polemics and dogmatism.

aesthetic transcendence of this loss as the origin or end of writing. Rather, in his novels, lost time returns only to be lost again, and then again, which makes Simonian memory (or re-memory) not the conqueror of lost time and of what cannot be remembered (time lost to memory), but rather a testimony to what is always lost or forgotten in or as memory. What is staged is not the past itself but the staging and the restaging of the past in and as fiction; what is staged in this type of writing of a degree beyond the second degree is also that something is always lost in staging, both in and as history and in and as fiction.[19]

The following example is only one among many possible examples from Simon's novels of the limits or inadequacy of memory (and ultimately of experience and consciousness themselves). It is one of the numerous and by now familiar descriptions in Simon's novels of a cavalry soldier's experience of the debacle in Flanders at the beginning of the Second World War and thus of his own memory (and of his memories, real and fictional, of that memory) of this event:

> *Il ne voit pas* les infimes particules de diamant laissées par la rosée sur la partie du pré encore à l'ombre de la haie, *il ne sent pas* le parfum végétal et frais des brins d'herbe écrasés sous son poids, *il ne sent pas* non plus la puanteur qui s'exhale de son corps [...] *il n'entend ni* les chants d'oiseaux *ni* les légers bruissements des feuillages dans l'air transparent, *il ne voit ni* les fleurs qui parsèment le pré, *ni* les jeunes pousses de la haie se balancer faiblement dans la brise du matin, *il n'entend même pas* les battements déréglés de son coeur et les vagues successives du sang dans ses oreilles. (*A*, 91–92, my emphasis)

What matters more in such passages is what was *not* seen, heard or felt, and not what was actually seen, heard or felt; what matters more is what *could not* be remembered, what was *not and could not* be told in narrative (except negatively), not what was actually remembered. Memory in such passages is thus profoundly negative, repeatedly acknowledging the forgotten – what was never experienced and what was experienced but not retained – at the very heart of memory itself.

This particular description of what is not seen, not heard and not felt, and the repetition of the negative itself in this rewriting or (re)memory of the experience make the unexperienced, unperceived, unconscious, always-already forgotten (because never fully experienced or understood) aspects of experience fundamental components

---

19 Debray contrasts Simon with Proust in the following terms: 'De Proust à Claude Simon, il me semble que le temps retrouvé devient définitivement perdu, la planche du salut, noyade' (*Éloges*, p. 78).

of both experience and its (re-)recall in or as either history or fiction. Simonian memory tells of the bits and pieces of what it retains and knows, but it also points to what it does not and cannot know, both what is remembered negatively and what remains forgotten in memory – even in negative, ironic, cynical forms of memory that retell the past by attacking and mocking the nature and function of memory itself.

In all recall and rewriting of the past, whether of a collective or individual subject, and regardless of whether memory takes the form of a formal history, a personal memoir or a fiction, there will always necessarily be something lacking in memory and something added to memory to compensate for its inadequacies: an indication both of something not heard, seen, felt, remembered or narrated and of something that points to, fills in for and supplements what is lacking. Moreover, it is not always possible to name or describe this 'something', even in the negative mode, as is done in the passage cited above, for it is not a *thing*. In other words, there will always be something not heard, seen or felt, something forgotten, even in attempts to describe what has not been seen, heard or felt. The negative mode used throughout this passage does not then only describe the 'not-experienced' and/or the 'not-remembered' as such; it also indicates that 'something' remains forgotten even in the negative presentation and narration/description of what was experienced and/or forgotten.

It is certainly no secret to readers of Simon that moments such as the above, because of the frequency with which they recur, are fundamental components of his novels. First of all, they are moments when all general plans and specific strategies for action are revealed to be not just inadequate but grotesquely deficient, moments when all order, even in the most traditional, disciplined and hierarchical elements of society, culture and thought, collapse or are destroyed. This destruction inevitably reveals an underlying, unspoken and unspeakable, violent disorder or chaos – a disorder that underlies not just experience (which might in part respond to the journalist's question of why descriptions of wars recur so frequently in his novels), but also meaning in general, 'la cessation de toute cohésion, de toute discipline (chose presque inconcevable dans un corps aux traditions aussi sévères et rigides que celui de la cavalerie), toute notion de commandement et d'obéissance apparaissant aux uns et aux autres sans objet, privée de sens, nulle' (*Les G*, 95). Such a breakdown of order results in the dispersion of random elements whose sequence and relation are now left to chance. The resulting cynicism and disrespect for any hierarchy, law, form or tradition that would command how these moments are to be experienced, represented or retold constitutes what could be called the 'origin' of Simonian memory and narrative, the void (of both form and meaning) around which and in terms of which memory and the repeated retelling and restructuring of the past are formed and reformed.

Simon's novels, as they repeatedly retell the breakdown of order in war and the end of traditional social, intellectual and cultural orders of different types, are not themselves really as much against History or at war with History, as some critics have argued, as they are testimonies to the non-recuperable negativity of history and the destruction of progressive, humanist historical myths and illusions. The novels are sceptical of History's greatness, and they bear witness rather to the insignificant experiences and the 'little stories' such greatness necessarily excludes. Perhaps one of the best examples from Simon's recent novels of such scepticism is once again a version of a soldier's experience of the debacle in Flanders:

> maintenant il avait simplement par-dessus la tête de toute cette histoire dont il doutait (en quoi il se trompait encore) qu'elle méritât qu'on l'écrivît avec un H majuscule et qui ne l'intéressait décidément pas [...] il lui semblait de moins en moins probable qu'il participât à une action historique [...] à moins d'admettre [...] que l'Histoire se manifeste (s'accomplit) par l'accumulation de faits insignifiants, sinon dérisoires, tels que ceux qu'il récapitula plus tard. (*Les G*, 304)

Simon's form of literary re-memory relates the insignificant, discordant, if not absurd, elements of historical experience, those that are told as admittedly inadequate approximations or ironic, even cynical accounts of lived experiences and historical events. That is all the postmodern writer's limited imagination and memory can produce; that is the best the constant writing and rewriting of the loss and violence of historical experience can do without repressing or covering over the insignificance, loss and destruction which are themselves experienced as essential components, even as the foundations, of history.

Jean-François Lyotard has argued in terms of other notable writers 'of memory' that, 'after Auschwitz', such a negative retelling of the past has to suffice, given the enormity of the crimes and the loss of lives in the Nazi extermination camps. Lyotard then describes how certain forms of art and literature continue to bear witness, in a negative mode, not to the past as such but to what he calls 'the forgotten' in or of memory:

Ce que l'art peut faire, c'est se porter témoin [...] de cette aporie de l'art et de sa douleur. Il ne dit pas l'indicible, il dit qu'il ne peut pas le dire. 'Après Auschwitz', il faut, à l'intention d'Elie Wiesel, ajouter un verset encore à l'histoire de l'oubli du recueillement auprès du feu dans la forêt (Célébration, 173). Je ne peux pas allumer le feu, je ne connais pas la prière, je ne sais même plus raconter l'histoire. Tout ce que je sais faire, c'est de raconter que je ne sais plus raconter cette histoire. Et cela devrait suffire. Il faudra bien que cela suffise. Que Celan 'après' Kafka, Joyce 'après' Proust [...] Beckett 'après' Brecht [...] que les seconds en date, incapables des premiers (je cite presque au hasard), mais capables par leur incapacité même, que ceux-là suffisent et aient suffi à porter témoignage négatif que la 'prière' est impossible et aussi l'histoire de la prière, et que reste possible le témoignage de cette impossibilité. Dans le monde où 'tout est possible', où 'tout peut s'arranger', l'écriture aussi reste possible qui déclare l'impossible et s'y expose.[20]

It would not be inappropriate to add Simon to Lyotard's list of exemplary authors coming 'after Auschwitz' and after the last of the great modernists (and it is certainly not a matter of historical chronology alone), those authors who expose themselves to 'the impossible'.

These 'belated authors', when compared to their predecessors in strictly modernist terms, could indeed be considered to be 'incapable'. But they should nevertheless be judged capable in another sense, argues Lyotard ('capables par leur incapacité même'), capable of narrating the impossibility of transcendence and even of effective, coherent, definitive narration. And as we have seen, in Simon's novels it is not just 'the prayer' (the recognition of divine transcendence and spiritual significance) or 'the history of the prayer' that is impossible, but also History itself, History as a spiritual or material divinity, all History that takes the form of the recuperation and transcendence of negativity.

However, even if such negative, fictional retellings of the past have to suffice or should suffice, they in fact do not and cannot suffice. This is in part because it would be impossible to ignore demands that what 'actually happened' should be told, demands that memory maintain a relation to the truth or the real, or risk being dismissed as being either deceptive or false. Responding to such demands, however, does not mean meeting them on their own terms, the terms of historical

20 Jean-François Lyotard, *Heidegger et les 'juifs'*, Paris, Galilée, 1988, pp. 81–82. In an interview with Bernard-Henri Lévy, Simon speaks of the effects of 'Auschwitz' in the following way : 'Le "trou noir" d'Auschwitz (sans parler du Goulag) a rendu tout discours "humaniste" simplement indécent. D'où sans doute, ce recours archarné au concret' (Bernard-Henri Lévy, '"… peuvent et doivent s'arrêter parfois d'écrire…" [Conversation avec Claude Simon]', *Les Aventures de la liberté*, Paris, Grasset, 1991, p. 21).

neutrality or objectivity. For example, at the insistence of the journalist in *Le Jardin des Plantes*, S. seems for a moment to struggle to remember his war experiences and narrate them as directly and accurately as possible. For the journalist, this of course means to remember his experiences without reference to exterior sources or without the support of fiction in general or of previous fictional accounts in particular. But, struggle as he might to respond to the journalist on the journalist's terms, S. nevertheless can only remember and present the past, not as an interiorised, familiar element of his life, but as an exterior, alien, unreal component of his existence: 'De nouveau je me demandai ce que tout ce que je lui racontais là pouvait bien représenter pour lui. Puisque aucune montre ne peut revenir en arrière […] Je tâchai de me rappeler. Mais même pour moi c'était maintenant comme quelque chose d'étranger, sans réalité. Je savais que je perdais mon temps, que c'était comme si je lui parlais dans une langue inconnue' (*JP*, 83). The reality of a past is necessarily foreign, not just to the journalist who had no direct experience of the war, but also to S., who in fact experienced it. To remember 'how it was' is also to be confronted both with an uneasy sense of the foreign unreality of 'what was' but is no longer, and with the inevitable, unavoidable incomprehension of those who demand the truth of the past and who want nothing more and will settle for nothing less.

In misunderstanding and refusing to accept the language and the forms of narration used to narrate the past in its foreign unreality, in refusing to acknowledge the fictive dimensions of the past as it is narrated after-the-fact, the journalist paradoxically refuses its historical reality as well, which itself is rooted in the experience of unreality:

> et S. dit que Non c'était bien pire […] et S. dit qu'encore une fois si on n'a pas vécu soi-même une chose du même genre on ne peut pas s'en faire une idée Parce que, dit-il, tout semblait se dérouler dans une sorte de brouillard d'irréalité Non ce n'est pas, comme le journaliste pourrait le penser, l'effet du temps plus de cinquante ans maintenant le brouillage de la mémoire, qu'au contraire il (S.) garde de toute cette affaire un souvenir très précis et que ce qui est précis c'est justement cette irréalité dans laquelle tout semblait se dérouler (*JP*, 262)

The best, most exact, complete, faithful memory of the experience of war is precisely of its unreality and of the limitations and unreliability of memory. In this context it is not the faulty memory of an ageing witness and narrator – another reason that memory might be unfaithful to the real – but the unreality of the experience itself and of the various accounts of the experience given in this and other novels and that Simon's literary memory repeatedly pieces together in different combinations and sequences.

The journalist in the novel, representing the demand for historical truth and realism, assumes that a clear and rigid distinction can be drawn between testimony and fiction, between the exact recall and narration of what happened and the creative recreation and embellishment of experience in fiction. Because of S.'s recognised international success as a novelist, the journalist wants to know the truth of these experiences because he considers them the source of S.'s novels. As in a court of law, he demands the facts and nothing but the facts, with no distortions, embellishments or omissions:

> Que non, S. ne devait pas prendre ça pour une critique, le journaliste ne se le permettrait pas et que d'ailleurs c'était très réussi mais que c'était encore plus intéressant d'entendre raconter sans ces enjolivements (que S. ne prenne pas ce mot en mauvaise part) les faits bruts simplement dans leur matérialité parce que Mais S. dit que Rien n'est simple, le journaliste disant Bien sûr mais quand même... Je veux dire qu'entre une fiction et le récit, le compte rendu objectif, neutre, d'un événement...Mais S. l'interrompt de nouveau et dit qu'il est impossible à qui que ce soit de raconter ou de décrire quoi que ce soit d'une façon objective (*JP*, 272–73)

It is impossible, claims the (fictional) writer of (fictional) fictions, who has an insufficient memory and little imagination, to give the journalist what he wants – the truth of his experiences without staging or embellishment – and remember and narrate the past in a totally objective, 'non-literary' way. The most faithful and complete memory is never in fact objective or complete; at the same time, fictions of the past cannot be considered simply as negations or distortions of the truth. By narrating what remains unreal in reality and indicating what is unsaid in narrative, what remains forgotten in memory and history, the novel provides a supplementary form of memory in a world in which History and historical meta-narratives cannot on their own provide sufficient or credible models for memory and the re-presentation of the past.

The loss of credulity in meta-narratives and the forms of transcendence they provide thus blurs, but does not eliminate, the border between historical truth and fiction. The border now needs, therefore, to be approached differently, to be treated as open and mobile, located within both history and fiction as much as outside each and separating one from the other. And if the present moment is defined, as Nora claims, in terms of 'la tyrannie de la mémoire', a tyranny in part resulting from the alleged demise of the 'true novel' and the form of legitimacy it once conferred on memory, then it could be argued that one of the critical functions of the novel, if it is to continue to survive after its demise, is to combat and resist that tyranny. Whether they are 'true novels' or not, Simon's fictions can rightly be considered one of the most important, not of the 'essential sites', but rather of the alternate sites of memory where history is thought 'otherwise', a literary site of memory where memory itself takes the form of a resistance to memory and literature takes the form of a resistance to literature.

2

(In)Commensurabilities:
The Childhood of Events and the Shock of Encounter in Claude Simon

Mária Minich Brewer

We are not *in* a context, but the context is in our ability to link. That's quite different.

Jean François Lyotard, 'Links'[1]

Quand le monde visible se sépare en quelque sorte de vous perdant ce visage familier et rassurant qu'il a (parce qu'en réalité on ne le regarde pas), prenant soudain un aspect vaguement effrayant, les objets cessant de s'identifier avec les symboles verbaux par quoi nous les possédons, les faisons nous.

Claude Simon, *Histoire*

It may seem paradoxical to speak of the incommensurable in Claude Simon when readers appear to have found considerable common ground for discussing his *oeuvre*. Numerous studies have treated the continued emergence of the workings of memory, the new realms of family history, the places of history, and the relationship of all these to his writing's dynamics. While these aspects of his work solicit consensus, the broader question of a *sensus communis* and the critical issue of incommensurability remain unexamined, out of harmony with the themes of correspondence, proximity, continuity and unity in Simon criticism. I do not wish, however, to revive critical debates in which rigid oppositions prevailed between representation and textuality, referentiality and literarity, and history and writing, oppositions which, with superb irony, have in any case become the material of fiction in the quotations in *Le Jardin des Plantes* (pp. 355–58) from the Cerisy colloquium proceedings. Rather, I propose to focus on occurrences in a variety of contexts that may be read as emblematic of Simon's writing. These occurrences all involve incidents of collision, accident, encounter and shock. The word incident itself, from *incidere*

---

1 'Links, the Unconscious, and the Sublime: An Inter-Phrase with Jean-François Lyotard', *Ellipsis*, vol. 1, no. 1, Spring 1990, p. 111.

(Lat.), to come upon, happen and fall upon, evokes a range of associations having to do with encounter, the incidental and the event of the singular. These incidents may be examined not only in terms of narrative discontinuity and fragmentation, but also in relation to a broader crisis of commensurability haunting the twentieth century's end and promising to engage us well into the twenty-first. Many literary and cultural critics talk of 'sites',[2] implying that spaces, histories and symbolic systems are not unquestionably held in common, and that their very uncertainty requires that they be laid out, measured and charted. Sites are instituted as cultural spaces, despite or due to the absence of a common standard of measurement for mapping their edges and distance with respect to one another. But can shared sites be taken for granted, except as necessary fictions, remainders and reminders of a collective purpose and a common memory? These, I believe, are some of the questions that literary studies confront today, questions that Simon's writing addresses in innovative and insightful ways.

Traversing multiple landscapes, times, textures and languages, his writing invents and itself becomes a passage where there is no path, a crossing where there is no bridge. It creates a complex and densely woven 'material' world whose phenomenological and referential status continues to be much debated. In writing that is exceptionally rich, sensual, tangible and diverse, Simon's language inaugurates links, passages and echoes between and across different times, histories, landscapes and voices. Moreover, his art of associating sound and movement as well as the visual and the linguistic anchors them to the material and symbolic conditions for linking and resectioning. In the 'society of the spectacle' (Debord) and the 'total visibility' (Baudrillard) of mass-mediated culture, the instant availability and manipulation of images globally gives viewers the illusion that everything is universally accessible (though only within the limits of the medium itself).[3] Read in this context, Simon's writing, which patiently explores the complexities of encounters between events, people, places and

2 See Mireille Calle-Gruber (ed.), *Les Sites de l'écriture: Colloque Claude Simon*, Paris, Nizet, 1995. Calle-Gruber suggests that the word 'site' evokes geographical location, archeological or geological survey or industrial space; however, 'il importe surtout d'entendre que *site* se donne comme *lieu d'opérations et de configurations*. Pas quelque incommensurable paysage dans sa réalité immédiate brute, mais un lieu de lisibilité et (donc) de visibilité' (pp. 8–9).
3 See Fredric Jameson and Masao Miyoshi (eds), *The Cultures of Globalization*, Durham, NC, Duke University Press, 1998.

materials, intimates that it is urgent to grasp these complexities as precisely and honestly as possible because of their possible disappearance from visibility and their destruction by time and oblivion. As readers, we are enjoined to consider seriously a variety of virtual, actual and past correspondences between worlds. In times of change and instability, how can literature effectively make relationships visible and enable readers to negotiate boundaries and borders, identify passages and traverse distant spaces, discourses, realities and idioms? Thinking about literature in terms of the (in)commensurable involves considering what ties endure between past and future, the memorable and the forgettable, the indispensable and the dispensable. What, in short, will remain visible and knowable and what will not: which configurations of landscapes, which sounds, gestures, bodies, people and texts?

The return of the autobiographical in contemporary writing, along with the valorisation of life-stories, is certainly involved in these questions. Critics have commented on the shift from proscription of the autobiographical, along with the referential, to the enthusiastic embrace of new realisms of identity in which autobiography seemingly returns to guarantee referentiality and history. Speaking of the works of the *nouveau roman* and *nouvelle vague* film, Lynn Higgins writes: 'in the early years it was their referential dimension that was most consistently overlooked or discounted. Now it is their mediated, textual dimension that is most easily overlooked.'[4] Autobiography serves as a *mise en abyme* of historiography. For Jean-Pierre Vidal, the scale seems to have tipped too far 'vers l'autre extrême, le vécu triomphant', so much so that it is appropriate to 'insister sur "l'indécidable" de ce biographique désormais presque trop innocent'.[5]

In Nathalie Sarraute and Simon, the 'return to the personal' and to childhood memories allows for experimentation with the boundaries of history and fiction and with uncertainties of genre, destination and address. I would argue, moreover, that the realm of childhood is itself in a profound way symptomatic of the crisis of common ground and the advent of the incommensurable in modernity. But incommensurability ought not to be confused with instances of miscommunication or mistranslation within what nevertheless remains a reassuring

---

4 Lynn Higgins, *New Novel, New Wave, New Politics: Fiction and Representation in Postwar France*, Lincoln, NE, and London, University of Nebraska Press, 1996, pp. 148, 149.
5 Jean-Pierre Vidal, 'Le Passé sous silence et la prise à témoin', in Calle-Gruber (ed.), *Les Sites de l'écriture*, p. 64.

and homogeneous world. Instead it involves divisions within languages, sites and the psyche itself.

The sites of childhood are many in Simon's novels: Montès's gaze upon the world in *Le Vent* is described as childlike; *L'Herbe* evokes a child's double initiation into language and desire through reading; *La Route des Flandres* stages Georges's childhood genealogical fantasies. Although, significantly, childhood memories are more limited in the 'formal' works of the late 1960s and early 1970s, *La Bataille de Pharsale*, *Triptyque* and *Leçon de choses* do contain important episodes. In *Triptyque*, scenes of two boys examining strips of discarded film and spying on a couple's love-making in a barn stress the boys' isolation and their exploration of the world about them. The realms of childhood memory are most fully elaborated in *Histoire*, *L'Acacia* and *Le Jardin des Plantes*, novels in which they are integrated with questions of representation, knowledge and experience. Lying at the intersection of knowledge and desire, reading and seeing, and discovery and loss, the space of childhood is defined by the extraordinary intensity of the child's contact and encounter with things and people.[6] One could say that all childhood experience in Simon's writing is that of one child, grasped at various times and points of intensity. Simon's adult narrators also engage with the world receptively, their memories marked by collisions or dis-junctures of verbal, visual, tactile and auditory faculties. At the opening of *Histoire*, for instance, waves of memories of his grandmother and her friends, as well as words and images, invade the narrator's semi-consciousness between waking and dreaming. In sum, childhood in Simon is remembered as being an encounter or crossing, out of which arise questions of representation, knowing and the commensurability between worlds as well as between words and things.

While the modes of description and recurrence give Simon's writing a consistency recognisable as eminently 'Simonian', there exists a further dynamic, which can be grasped through an aesthetics of childhood. As a social and symbolic subject (or object), the child is customarily thought to be eminently malleable, transportable and substitutable.

6 Simon's photographs of children show them dancing, playing, concentrating, fighting, captured in arabesques of movement or in graffiti they leave behind. While his photographic gaze details the lines of their movements and the textures of their threadbare clothes, they return his gaze in expressions that define the event as an encounter between intersecting and incommensurable realities. See Claude Simon, *Photographies 1937–1970*, Paris, Maeght, 1992.

Full of metaphorical possibility, childhood is certainly the site of multiple interpellations, ideological investments, projections and techniques of symbolic reproduction. In Simon's work, the child is never defined according to pre-given categories of psychology, ideology, or even literary representation, but is, instead, an irreplaceable site of feeling, seeing, remembering, questioning and knowing. As Ralph Sarkonak and Celia Britton have shown, Simon's scripting of the child's vision, especially in *Histoire*, may be read in terms of Freudian and Lacanian psychoanalysis.[7] More pervasively, 'desymbolisation' in Simon inaugurates a 'newness' of perception by erasing or suspending the proper names or designations instituting events, objects and experiences, which become uncertain or unfamiliar. Jean Duffy reads desymbolisation in terms of formalist 'defamiliarisation' and Merleau-Ponty's phenomenological analysis of the suspension of the categories and hierarchies of perception in situations of crisis where the identity of the subject is thrown into question.[8] She correctly identifies in Simon moments of crisis such as danger, trauma, illness and erotic excitement, in which the 'intentional arc' is relaxed, leading to a gap between the perceptible and the intelligible. Phenomenology presumes a coherent world, grounded on a common measure that is subsequently threatened by crisis. An aesthetics of the incommensurable, however, uncovers the shifting possibilities of linkages in language, the perceptible and the intelligible. The child is not so much represented from the outside or categorised according to sociological and psychological definitions; rather, the child is an instance of vision, feeling and sensation between different, shifting and often incommensurable worlds. Simon takes the labels off the 'child' and 'childhood', restoring to them their incommensurability as sites of recollection and memory, which are remade from the materials at hand. We might recall Merleau-Ponty's understanding of the 'intermediary person' in Simon, lying between the reflexive first-person consciousness and the distancing third person.[9] Simon's adult narrators' recol-

---

7 Ralph Sarkonak, *Claude Simon: Les Carrefours du texte*, Toronto, Les Editions du Paratexte, 1986, p. 156. Celia Britton, *Claude Simon: Writing the Visible*, Cambridge, Cambridge University Press, 1987, pp. 119–24.
8 See Jean Duffy, 'Claude Simon, Merleau-Ponty and Perception', *French Studies*, vol. 46, no.1, January 1992, pp. 33–52 and her *Reading Between the Lines: Claude Simon and the Visual Arts*, Liverpool, Liverpool University Press, 1998. See also Pascal Mougin, *L'Effet d'image: essai sur Claude Simon*, Paris, L'Harmattan, 1997.
9 Maurice Merleau-Ponty, 'Five Notes on Claude Simon', in Celia Britton (ed.), *Claude Simon*, London and New York, Longman, 1993, p. 37.

lection of childhood experience takes place in this intermediary space constituted in the space of writing. For Merleau-Ponty, as opposed to 'la perception structurante de l'adulte où les ensembles sont articulés et les détails organisés', the child's perception is extremely sensitive to details.[10] The child's egocentrism is not solipsism but an 'objectivité sans mesure' (p. 33). An incommensurable objectivity appears, therefore, at the site of the child, 'tourné vers une source d'excitations, vers un motif à mouvements et attaché à en éprouver les diverses possibilités' (p. 33).

Critics have discussed the importance of the archaic in Simon, versions of which have been identified in the privileging of what is 'outside or prior to history' (Duncan), the 'organic' and the 'elementary' (Dällenbach), the 'obscurité de l'être, l'opacité des temps' (Neefs) and the mysterious force outside history (Britton).[11] Françoise van Rossum-Guyon, for instance, defines Simon's project to 'remonter aux racines mêmes de la coupure et de la séparation, pour, en levant les voiles, en reconstituant à partir des ruines [...] en mettant les choses en rapport, situer les bords, recoudre les déchirures, réparer les blessures'.[12] The work of 'reparation' of an originary 'breach' is certainly relevant here, though I would argue that archaic separations need to be thought of as taking place within the problematics of the incommensurable rather than outside of or prior to it.

Claude Simon's own comments about his writing process are insightful in this regard. In *Orion aveugle* he writes: 'Je ne connais pour ma part d'autres sentiers de la création que ceux ouverts pas à pas, c'est-à-dire mot après mot, par le cheminement de l'écriture'.[13] Although such statements on his part have given rise to a variety of interpretations, what is at issue is something other than a defence of self-referential writing in a formal sense. Although writing is not the thing in itself, 'les mots possèdent par contre ce prodigieux pouvoir de

10 Merleau-Ponty, *Le Primat de la perception et ses conséquences philosophiques*, Paris, Verdier, 1996, p. 31.
11 See Alastair Duncan, *Claude Simon: Adventures in Words*, Manchester, Manchester University Press, 1994, p. 138; Lucien Dällenbach, 'La Question primordiale', in Jean Starobinski et al. (eds), *Sur Claude Simon*, Paris, Minuit, 1987, pp. 63–93; Jacques Neefs, 'La Grandeur de l'histoire', in Mireille Calle-Gruber (ed.), *Claude Simon: chemins de la mémoire*, Sainte Foy (Québec), Le Griffon d'Aigle, 1993, pp. 103–18; Patrick Longuet, *Lire Claude Simon: la polyphonie du monde*, Paris, Minuit, 1995; Britton, *Claude Simon: Writing the Visible*.
12 Françoise van Rossum-Guyon, 'Un regard déchirant: à propos de *L'Acacia*', in Calle-Gruber (ed.), *Claude Simon: chemins de la mémoire*, p. 126.
13 Claude Simon, *Orion aveugle*, no. 8, Geneva, Skira, 1970, unpaginated.

rapprocher et de confronter ce qui, sans eux, resterait épars'. Language has the power to bring together and confront what is separate, that is, incommensurable: 'parce que ce qui est souvent sans rapports immédiats dans le temps des horloges ou l'espace mesurable peut se trouver rassemblé et ordonné au sein du langage dans une étroite contiguïté'. Although the word 'ordonné' suggests that language itself serves to combine incommensurables according to an ordering process, elsewhere, for example in an interview with Mireille Calle-Gruber, Simon stresses his acute sense of the 'non-maîtrise du "réel", du savoir, de la perception, de la mémoire elle-même'.[14] He reacts strongly to any suggestion that he fragments the real, that the intervals in his writing result from a 'projet de déstabilisation', a will to anarchy or destructuring. Using the semantics of conjuncture, combination and crystallisation to define his writing, Simon emphasises language's capacity for contiguity, which I read as referring not only to relationships within language, but also to writing from within a poetics of memory as well as a problematics of linking (with) the incommensurable.

Sites of childhood

The work of the philosopher Jean-François Lyotard is closely associated with the problematics of the incommensurable in postmodernity. In *Le Postmoderne expliqué aux enfants*,[15] he identifies links between the incommensurable in avant-garde aesthetics, postmodernity and the symbolic realm of childhood. Speaking of the multiplicity of naming universes and the diversity of cultures, Lyotard writes that entry into culture occurs by learning proper names and the 'unités de mesure, d'espace, de temps, de valeur d'échange' (p. 56). His notion of the incommensurable takes us directly into the heterogeneous forces of culture as they are actualised in regimes of phrases, whose incommensurability follows from the decline of master-narratives.[16] In *Le Postmoderne expliqué aux enfants*, Lyotard is especially concerned with what he calls the murder of the instant and of singularity occurring in the reduction of the possibilities inherent in a multiplicity of idioms.

14 *Claude Simon: chemins de la mémoire*, p. 6.
15 Jean-François Lyotard, *Le Postmoderne expliqué aux enfants: correspondance 1982–85*, Paris, Galilée, 1986, p. 55.
16 Mária Minich Brewer, *Claude Simon: Narrativities Without Narrative*, Lincoln, NE, and London, University of Nebraska Press, 1995.

For Lyotard, a new understanding of the aesthetics of childhood, which is an artistic response to incommensurability, is to be found in Walter Benjamin's writings ('One Way Street' and 'Berlin Childhood'), which 'ne décrivent pas des événements de l'enfance, elles saisissent l'enfance de l'événement, elles inscrivent son insaisissable. Ce qui fait un événement de la rencontre d'un mot, d'une odeur, d'un lieu, d'un livre, d'un visage, n'est pas sa nouveauté comparée à d'autres "événements." C'est qu'il a valeur d'initiation en lui-même. On ne le sait que plus tard. Il a ouvert une plaie dans la sensibilité' (pp. 141–42). Lyotard conceives of 'experience' and 'existence' as idioms, points of untranslatable singularity that constitute a manner of deciphering 'ce qui arrive', what happens, and 'the task of having to bear witness to the indeterminate'.[17] Writing is a line of resistance drawn against the effacing of singularities and specificities in time, space and language, he argues, the means of opening on to new forms of expression without turning away from the sciences: 'on cherche au contraire, avec eux et par eux, à témoigner de ce qui seul compte, l'enfance de la rencontre, l'accueil fait à la merveille qu'il arrive (quelque chose), le respect pour l'événement' (pp. 150–51). It is in terms of Lyotard's concepts of encounter and the childhood of the event that I suggest Simon's writing may be read.

Lyotard's abiding interest in Simon's writing is significant.[18] He quotes Simon's response when asked by a representative of the Union of Soviet Writers: 'How do you imagine the task of writing?' to which Simon answered, 'It consists of trying to start a sentence, to continue it, and to finish it'.[19] For Lyotard, this process, which 'constitutes thinking or writing in its "entirety"', means 'the labor of speech enter-

17 Lyotard, 'The Sublime and the Avant-Garde', in Andrew Benjamin (ed.), *The Lyotard Reader,* Oxford, Basil Blackwell, 1989, p. 207. I quote the second, edited English version of this essay because it includes alterations subsequently made to the French text.
18 David Carroll has studied Lyotard's comments in the context of Simon's 'return to history,' which, writes Carroll 'should thus not be considered as the return to any historical or meta-historical (or formalist, for that matter) pre-text, but rather as the critical and unending search for possible modes of linkage' (David Carroll, 'Narrative Poetics and the Crisis of Culture: Claude Simon's Return to "History"', *L'Esprit Créateur,* vol. 27, no. 4, winter 1987, p. 53). Lyotard, writes Carroll, finds in Simon's work 'the search for undetermined linkages among elements of phrases and among different families of phrases', exemplary of a 'general narrative condition in which not only the form of narrative but more important the "unphrased", the "unnarrated", or the "unpresentable" are the stakes of the search' (Carroll, pp. 52–53).
19 Jean-François Lyotard, *Peregrinations: Law, Form, Event,* New York, Columbia University Press, 1988, p. 4. I quote from the English text as it was originally presented and published.

ing language in the middle in order to disclose the idiom it wants' (p. 4). Thoughts, in movement and subject to infinite change, have immeasurable boundaries. In Lyotard's *poetics of thinking*, the notion of the *différend* is related to the idea that all linkage between phrases is open, occurring without recourse to any unequivocal criteria (p. 8). The *différend*, he writes, means that 'une règle universelle de jugement entre des genres hétérogènes fait défaut en général'.[20] It is an 'état instable du langage où quelque chose qui doit pouvoir être mis en phrases ne peut pas l'être encore' (p. 29). Phrases obeying the rules of different phrase regimes are, moreover, untranslatable into one another (p. 79). Grievously, a *différend* opposes the phrase regimes of Holocaust victims and those of the perpetrators who condemn them to die. 'Je dirais qu'il y a différend entre deux parties quand le "règlement" du conflit qui les oppose se fait dans l'idiome de l'une d'elles alors que le tort dont l'autre souffre ne se signifie pas dans cet idiome.'[21] The real danger, in his view, comes not from the *lack* of consensus, which for Jürgen Habermas poses the greatest threat to a common democratic public sphere, but from the uniformising tendency of capital and its pervasive investments in and penetration of language as such.[22] At stake in literature, philosophy and perhaps in politics, he argues, is the necessity of bearing witness to *différends* by finding idioms for them.

Incommensurabilities: bodies, trains, languages and their *différends*

In Simon's work from *L'Herbe* onwards, an aesthetic of the incommensurable and shock emerges in the encounter between incongruous, anachronistic and even anamorphic realities. Simon has written about experiences of intense affect, exhaustion, hunger and fear, where there occurs a sense of being enclosed (Louise's sensation of being in a diving-bell in *L'Herbe*) or radically separated from the outside. In *La Route des Flandres*, Georges's memories of wartime marches are filled with a sense of being encased in mud, ice and fatigue. Scenes along the Flanders road in *L'Acacia* and *Le Jardin des Plantes* describe instances of a cognitive gap, a profound sense of unreality, somnambulism and disconnection. Donning a uniform results in a loss of and dispossession

20 Jean-François Lyotard, *Le Différend*, Paris, Minuit, 1983, p. 9.
21 Jean-François Lyotard, *Tombeau d'un intellectuel et autres papiers*, Paris, Galilée, 1984, p. 29.
22 On the importance of 'culture-révolte' in a new normalising and falsifiable world order, see Julia Kristeva, *Sens et non-sens de la révolte: pouvoirs et limites de la psychanalyse I*, Paris, Fayard, 1996, p. 17.

from one's own body, inside and out, 'leur chair, leur sueur elle-même, ne leur appartiendraient plus' (*A*, 239). The narrator's own voice returns to him 'à travers des épaisseurs de verre, incongrue, lointaine' (*A*, 104).

In the severance from, but also openness and vulnerability to, the outside world, the murmur or *rumeur* of history is perceived as an encompassing space of sound without progression. Without a sense of displacement in space or time, the real paradoxically becomes a movement negating movement. Such a view of history as the incommensurable may account for the powerful evocations of the din of human history in *La Route des Flandres*. The rhythms of horses' hooves symbolise a time without measure: 'le martellement monotone et multiple des sabots sur la route se répercutant, se multipliant [...] au point [...] de s'effacer, se détruire lui-même, engendrant par sa continuité, son uniformité, comme une sorte de silence au deuxième degré [...] le cheminement même du temps, c'est-à-dire invisible immatériel sans commencement ni fin ni repère' (*RF*, 28). Time and space, the bound context in which the cavalrymen move, become annulled as rhythm produces a further dimension of silence as infinite and limitless time. That is to say, history as conflict is a closed system whose catastrophic movements tend towards increasingly greater disorder and entropy. In Britton's terms, history is ultimately the negativity that escapes consciousness, an instance of the Lacanian real as an encounter that the subject always misses.[23]

The fault-lines of incommensurable worlds lie not only outside the subject, for the radical severance from the human community, history and time dispossesses the soldier from his own body, language and psychic integrity. In *L'Acacia*, the narrator perceives the sounds of the cavalry and the refugees' carts on the gravel, remarking on the symbolic link and separation between army and refugees, 'ce double courant, cette double procession cheminant en sens inverse [...] ce qui constituait pour ainsi dire à la fois le négatif et la complémentarité d'eux-mêmes' (*A*, 244–45). While they may in fact be within sight, earshot and even touching distance of each other, the two lines in movement are severed in many dimensions. The divide between them

23 Britton, *Claude Simon: Writing the Visible*, p. 145, where she quotes Lacan: 'du réel comme rencontre – la rencontre en tant qu'elle peut être manquée, qu'essentiellement elle est la rencontre manquée' (*Quatre concepts de psychanalyse*, 1973, p. 54). In Britton's account of the glimpse and the mirage in Simon, the visible is characterised 'as lacking, as never fully present, or as lost: and that is why it arouses such intense desire – the moment at which the mirage disappears is the essential moment of its staging as lost object of desire' (p. 173).

affects language itself, creating a frontier impeding communication between the soldiers and the fleeing men, women and children. Language, produced in this double and contradictory movement, suffers a severe mutation involving not only translation from a strange idiom into a familiar one, but the corruption of a border language or a language split against itself: 'ce fut à peine si chacun des cavaliers put saisir quelques mots, ou plutôt quelques sons articulés qui ressemblaient eux aussi à quelque chose de boueux, primitif, lourd, c'est-à-dire comme une ébauche de langue, un patois, ou plutôt une corruption de langue, un des [*sic*] ces dialectes à travers lesquels se comprennent les populations à cheval sur deux frontières' (*A*, 246). Less an instance of a mythic and originary language, this corruption of language results from the lack of common ground in a border zone that, as Simon's language deftly remarks, consists of not *one* but *two* borders. Moreover, linguistic corruption is not restricted to the *différend* between soldiers and refugees, for even the ritualised language between commanding officers and soldiers becomes fraught with unreality. The captain's address to the soldiers announcing the beginning of the war dissolves into a lack of signification: 'sa voix s'élevant alors avec netteté dans le silence, poussant devant elle, à chaque articulation de voyelles, de diphtongues ou de consonnes les petits nuages de vapeur aussitôt dissous' (*A*, 252). The breakdown in communication is founded upon prior breaks and ruptures in the social bond, ruptures themselves constituting *différends* between different idioms and regimes of phrases.

Paradigmatic encounters between contrary and incommensurable movements occur in scenes of impact that momentarily bring different worlds into collision. In *Les Géorgiques*, the recruits' train is stationed at a distance from the regular travellers' trains. A traumatising 'incident' or encounter with the civilian train occurs nevertheless, opening an anamorphic dimension of space and time. Simon's writing enacts the movement, noise, shaking of the ground and swirling of snow accompanying the hallucinatory vision of the passing train: 'Leurs fenêtres garnies de visages curieux ou indifférents, pâles, fuligineux, rendus comme irréels à la fois par la vitesse à laquelle ils sont emportés et par le fait qu'ils semblent (comme les poissons derrière les vitres d'un aquarium) appartenir à un monde étranger, aussi différent de celui où ils se trouvent que le feu est à l'eau' (*Les G*, 86). As the train disappears, the collision of realities leaves wisps of dissipating smoke: 'se défaisant, s'affaissant, se dissolvant dans l'air immobile' (*Les G*, 87). The recruits' train in *L'Acacia* also encounters another train carrying not an army being transported for war but a bowling team bound for a tournament. In another episode, the train's movement tracks the mutation the recruits undergo as they are separated from the human community, 'rejetés, exclus, abandonnés' (*A*, 164). The description of a civilian train passing the convoy emphasises the violent impact of two worlds crossing: the mobilised and the non-mobilised, that is, the present and another present which for the young soldiers has hurtled into an inaccessible past. Looking out of the window, the narrator-corporal notices first a family armed with gas masks, then a traveller, a version of his former 'travelling' self. In a mute but telling gesture which deepens the corporal's sense of irremediable abandonment, the man holds up a newspaper with the headline 'MOBILISATION GENERALE'. The shock effect of the encounter enters consciousness directly, traumatically, without any form of defence: 'longtemps par la suite il (le brigadier) devait se rappeler cet homme debout, le journal déployé cachant son visage dont on ne voyait apparaître au-dessus de la manchette que les deux yeux qui le fixaient avec une sorte de fureur, de reproche et de vindicative méchanceté' (*A*, 236). Refusing conventional representations of war, Simon's writing stages the dynamics of phrase universes and spaces, bearing witness to their encounters and ways of traversing one another. In the scene described, no common idiom translates the meaning of general mobilisation for both parties. The 'I' and the 'you' have no common ground or 'we', except the space where incommensurables collide and in which their lack of common measure is registered as trauma in the unconscious.

In *L'Acacia* another paradigmatic scene occurs when the train transporting the narrator and other prisoners of war stops so the soldiers can relieve themselves. As the men stumble down the incline and crouch, they notice a family of (German?) civilians out for an afternoon stroll along the tracks. Apparently, the family does not see them: 'Un couple précédé d'une petite fille habillée en clair, aux longs cheveux, qui court en jouant avec un chien au pelage clair aussi [...] Ils avancent d'un pas tranquille sans paraître remarquer le train et la frange d'hommes accroupis qui le borde' (*A*, 317). The dog's joyful barking reaches the prisoners with a time-lapse, 'comme à travers une opaque épaisseur de temps' (*A*, 318). The incommensurable of war and peace, imprisonment and freedom, is figured here as a shock encounter between two worlds along the fault-lines of violence and terror, and as a failure to perceive a 'frange d'hommes'. Tellingly, the contact between the two realities is apprehended in terms of time, an anachronistic meeting that while coterminous in space and time is radically separated, the strolling family being at once part of wartime divisions and the soldiers' pre-war reality, which is now past for them.

These train scenes in *L'Acacia* must be read in connection with another, which details the recruits' irrevocable separation from their civilian reality. In a crowd of people at a train station, the farewell embrace between a young woman and a recruit is slowed down, symbolising their bodies' resistance to separation. Rather than render their farewell in psychological terms, Simon's writing suspends the woman's body, slowing the moments as the train pulls out. A gifted writer of crowds, Simon reinscribes a poetics of crowd movements within an aesthetics of shock, which Walter Benjamin relates to the disintegration of a common social, historical and cultural bond.[24]

In *Les Géorgiques*, the co-existence of incommensurable realities is present in the old lady's attempt to bury the double history of her ancestor the General L.S.M. and his royalist brother. The repressed family archives are described as a 'cadavre enseveli', the hidden documents co-existing within the same space but out of view. Material and archival history constitutes an anamorphic reality, a dimension of the real that people seek to dissimulate but which re-emerges in the course of time. Within the general framework of the clandestine in Simon's novels, both *Les Géorgiques* and *L'Acacia* present the cavalryman's flight, his internal exile in Occupied France and life in a world of parallel realities – legality/illegality, human/animal, freedom/imprisonment, etc. – which should be understood less as oppositions than as incommensurables. Having left the train, the fugitive 'traveller' stands on the apron:

> séparé de la place, des autobus, des bruits eux-mêmes, par une sorte de vitre, une pellicule de fatigue, comme de la cire ou de la paraffine qu'il peut sentir se craqueler sur son visage, coupante le long des rides, comme un moule, comme s'il était recouvert d'une seconde peau l'isolant de l'air frais du matin dans lequel grelotte le reste de son corps, se rendant compte alors qu'il a pensé son voyage en termes de distances alors qu'il s'est agi d'une mutation interne de sa propre personne, parce que ce ne sont pas seulement les lieux qui ont changé mais lui, sa substance' (*Les G*, 265–66).

24 In his writings on Baudelaire and elsewhere, Benjamin identifies an aesthetics of shock in modernity. He locates it in a historical context in which 'various modes of communication have competed with one another', namely narrative, information and sensation. In the conflict between realms, the atrophy of experience appears as an incommensurability between 'what happened', 'meaning fragments' and experience. See Walter Benjamin, 'On Some Motifs in Baudelaire', in *Illuminations*, New York, Schocken Books, 1969, p. 159.

The soldier's experience of flight is described as a metamorphosis in which notions of legality and illegality, even an individual's bodily integrity and identity, fade in the presence of pure force. In other words, what determines the site of the human or the non-human (man or rat), legality or illegality, lies in the exercise of power determining their different, unstable positions with respect to each other. A fugitive from the occupying power, the soldier hides his identity and pretends to be a 'tourist' within his own country. He is arrested briefly before escaping once more. Although arrests, including those of Jews, are clandestine they occur in full view of passers-by in a parallel reality of incommunicable universes: 'à arrêter les gens en plein jour mais en quelque sorte toujours clandestinement, les passants, les témoins de la scène, continuant leur chemin, comme sans rien voir, sans s'arrêter ni s'attrouper, ni même détourner la tête, sourds et aveugles aurait-on dit'; they manage to circumvent 'l'invisible voiture ou l'invisible camionnette arrêtée et le groupe de ses invisibles occupants autour de l'invisible prisonnier qu'on poussait dedans' (*Les G*, 274). The power to undermine and eliminate common ground between people determines the parameters of invisible visibility, turning seeing into not seeing and making not witnessing complicit with evil.

A major site of incommensurability in Simon appears in the semantics of melancholia. Not only do shock encounters precipitate a profound sense of disjunction and disorientation in time, space and language, they are experienced as a traumatic loss of faculties. The progression from infancy to adulthood is violently derailed, with the adult becoming first an animal and then a living organism. *L'Acacia* tracks the regaining of faculties which painfully recapitulates the stages from elementary organism to instinctual animal survival to childhood and then adulthood. Within the narrator's recuperated (but not restored) sense of consciousness, an unspeakable void or wound remains from which the subject is never again free. As a result, melancholic memory is regression to a state anterior even to childhood and is itself a rupture coeval with the event as well as its reconstruction. The corporal's attempt to remember the site of his virtual death, an anamorphic dimension of the real, brings him back into contact with 'fear' and a nameless realm beyond fear, 'quelque chose comme une déchirante mélancolie, une déchirante agonie' (*A*, 304). On his return to occupied southwest France, he considers himself and other fugitives as creatures of another species, yet he gradually relearns the daily rituals of 'normal' civilian life, in which, ironically echoing Baudelaire, 'tout était paisible, intact, inchangé'.[25] Critics have commented on the narrator's return to drawing, reading and, finally, to the vocation of writing. But the importance of an aesthetic of detail and *tabula rasa* in Simon might be thought of not as a return to an elemental or foundational 'real', but as an obstinate questioning of the very possibility of reinventing a 'measure' for things in the aftermath of the incommensurable.

An aesthetics of collision[26]

Simon's recent work, *Le Jardin des Plantes*, takes its title from the famous institution in Paris whose garden, zoo and museum emblematise knowledge, history, culture and narrative. His novel expands that site and emblem of scientific ordering and classification across continents, histories, public spaces and spaces of intimacy and memory. It also takes up the incommensurable in ways that expand its scope into new areas.

The first epigraph is from Montaigne: 'aucun ne fait certain dessain de sa vie, et n'en délibérons qu'à parcelles. [...] Nous sommes tous de lopins et d'une contexture si informe et diverse, que chaque pièce, chaque momant faict son jeu.' Minute pieces such as 'parcelles' (fractions, fragments), 'lopins', along with attributes such as 'informe' and 'diverse', suggest a model of life in which no mastery or universal 'dessain' is conceivable. 'Contexture', with its older meaning of composition of a work and the arrangement of its parts, is here applied to the 'nous', the 'we' in whom each part and moment has its own space of 'play'. From the outset, the novel presents a vibrant encounter of sensations, places and moments as discrete parts play in combination with and against one another. Throughout Part I, for instance, these encounters may be read in the graphic layout of disparate fragments of texts, which are placed in double columns or divided (brought together) diagonally across the page. The novel's motifs of travel, art, the state, war and torture combine to produce a new series of references to the incommensurable in Simon's work.

As S. attempts to convey to the journalist interviewing him the

25 Charles Baudelaire, *Oeuvres Complètes*, Paris, Gallimard, 1961. Simon's words resonate with those of the prose poem 'L'Invitation au voyage': 'où tout est beau, riche, tranquille, honnête' (p. 253) and 'où tout est riche, propre et luisant, comme une belle conscience' (p. 254).
26 The 'postmodern' architect, Frank O. Gehry, used the term 'collision architecture' to refer to the ways in which a diversity of volumes, forms, materials and dimensions 'collide' in his work.

absolute incompatibility between the calm opulence of the spring countryside in May 1940 and its violent shattering by the bombing of his regiment, the reader becomes aware of the play between the various contexts in which S. is speaking. The gap between the site of enunciation (the space of the interview) and the realities of war continues to grow as S.'s attempts to express the unpresentable are repeatedly interrupted, for instance by the journalist's obsession with the recorder and street noises from outside S.'s apartment. A distance opens up between the journalist's crisp, modern-day professionalism and S.'s memory, as well as between that memory and his recollection of a time and space of radical alterity (filth, hunger and depression). Different realities of history, generation and space together occupy the site of enunciation, with an emphasis, however, on their insuperable separation and distance: 'Même pour moi c'était maintenant comme quelque chose d'étranger, sans réalité. Je savais que je perdais mon temps, que c'était comme si je lui parlais dans une langue inconnue. Mais j'ai quand même essayé de lui décrire ça' (*JP*, 83). In what may be read as a reflexive commentary on the situation of the writer and the reader, the familiar Simonian motif of a disconnection between language and experience, words and things, is present here, but the gap is not so much a condition of language as such as a manifestation of the fundamental lack of common measure between parallel realities. Referring to the word 'fear', the narrator continues: 'Il a dit: Oui je comprends je... J'ai dit: Non Vous ne comprenez pas Vous ne pouvez tout simplement pas C'est absolument impossible mais disons que la peur alors c'est comme la chemise crasseuse et puante que vous portez [...] mais voilà c'est votre chemise et... A ce moment il a levé la main en disant Arrêtez arrêtez! ...' (*JP*, 97). Imagination (writing) is called upon to bridge the gap between different universes of phrases and the countervailing aims in understanding they possess. In *Le Jardin des Plantes*, the incommensurable lies within and between events, but it is resituated here within a further dimension of the incommensurable, between experiencing war and describing it. As the narrator does in *L'Acacia*, S. calls upon the word 'melancholy' to describe his experience of radical loss and traumatic memory, evoking also the melancholic gaze of the condemned in Dostoievski, the melancholy of illness and its perceptual acuity.[27]

---

27 See Julia Kristeva, *Soleil noir: dépression et mélancolie*, Paris, Gallimard, 1987, for a discussion of the traces of melancholia in language, from which a poetics can emerge.

One of the sites from which traumatic memories, 'enkysté en lui', burst forth involves new material describing S.'s life in Paris during the Occupation. While attending a clandestine performance of a play-reading, he recalls a scene of African soldiers sitting in a covered vehicle, which is then juxtaposed with the devastating scene of their annihilation by a bombing raid. The soldiers become burned into S.'s memory, so to speak: 'Il pense: Pauvres bougres, pauvres bougres, pauvres bougres, pauvres bougres...' (JP, 345). Simon's writing embeds a series of shifting memories: one memory (of the performance) contains another (the soldiers' vehicle), distancing S. from the performance, which then in turn contains another (the soldiers' killing).[28] Spaces and occasions of remembrance are themselves reinscribed as being remembered in a writing that bears witness not only to memory but to its condition of incommensurability as well.

Le Jardin des Plantes contains several series of emblematic scenes highlighting a lack of commensurability between the artist and the state and which, in a further development, Simon recounts as one artist's response to the experience of the Holocaust. One series uses the report of an interrogation of Josef Brodski by a state-appointed judge who, refusing to recognise poetry as a profession, has the power to deny Brodski the identity of a legitimate, productive member of Soviet society. The scene of interrogation may itself be understood as precisely the regime of phrases performing censorship as a speech act. Power severs imaginative, creative and critical uses of language from those that are authorised as legitimate social acts.

Another, extensive series relating to the artist and the incommensurable as art is devoted to Gastone Novelli, a friend whom Simon mentions in interviews as one of those artists who, after the Holocaust, returned to a degré zéro, the source and the concrete.[29] Without being 'represented' mimetically, Novelli's experience of torture and trauma in the concentration camps is delineated in his paintings, which consist of an overlay of grids, numbered breasts (without bodies), letters A (without the alphabet), that is, an entire memory

28 See Duffy, who identifies the play as Le Désir attrapé par la queue which 'Picasso wrote in January 1941 and which had its first public reading in Michel and Zette Leiris' appartment in 1944, with Camus as the producer and Sartre and Simone de Beauvoir reading the parts of "Le Bout rond" and "La Cousine"' ('Artistic Biographies and Aesthetic Coherence in Claude Simon's Jardin des Plantes', Forum for Modern Language Studies, vol. 35, no. 2, 1999, p. 183).
29 Interview with Claude Duverlie, 'The Crossing of the Image', Substance, vol. 8, 1974, pp. 47–58.

archive, as the title of one painting (ARCHIVO PER LA MEMORIA) has it (*JP*, 23). In Part I of the novel, the letter A appears to be graphically perceptible in the diagonal line of blanks separating as well as linking two texts: the first evocation of Novelli wedged alongside S.'s wartime memories (*JP*, 23–25). Yet the graphic meanings of the paintings only emerge once they are overlaid with other contexts. At a certain point (*JP*, 235–45), Novelli breaks ties with so-called civilised people and, having become lost in the Amazon, uses his concentration camp experience to negotiate his space and survive once again. When the Indians, whom he does not see, erect a palisade of arrows around his camp, he invents symbolic ways of communicating with them from the ground up, to so speak, by placing fresh fish on the arrows daily. He turns a situation of potential conflict and death into one of encounter and an exchange of signs, which he later refigures in his painting. It is undoubtedly tempting to treat communication with the Indians in the Amazon as a triumph of humanity counterbalancing the concentration camp's mass-produced dehumanisation. But the different encounters with the incommensurable continue to haunt his painting precisely as witness to incommensurability. Novelli's art and his experiences of the limit combine to illustrate the epigraph from Lyotard: 'we are not *in* a context, but the context is in our ability to link'. The condition of possibility of art and literature may itself be thought of as that fragile and paradoxical (un)common ground of incommensurability as such.

In a world where communication may be threatened by an excess of standardised information from limited sources, Simon's writing explores the conditions for heterological and polyphonic languages and writing. Without relying on a universal subject and its experience, Simon invents resistances to forms of closure that eliminate the diversity and complexity of the world and their phrasing. By presenting in his work the uniformisation of image production, media, consumerism and political discourse, he resists its effects by re-materialising the diversity, visibility and sensation of a vast, complex and heterological world. His art of writing is one of 'révolte' in the sense used by Kristeva, for whom a revolt against the uniformisation of language and hence the repression of creative affect must be countered by an aesthetics of *ré-volte*, or the capacity of art to turn perception and representation around.[30] Simon succeeds in turning writing and reading away from

---

30 Kristeva, *Sens et non-sens de la révolte.*

automatisms of language and representation to a multiplicity of heterological sites, which are at once those of contemporary culture, geography, history and individual memory.

The problematics of the incommensurable as it emerges in Simon's writing cannot be understood simply as a static form of disconnection or fragmentation. And, while it is difficult to make absolute distinctions between his practice in *Le Jardin des Plantes* and in the other works I have discussed, his recent work, including *Le Tramway*, certainly infuses the incommensurable with an exceptionally acute sense of space, place and movement. His writing is attentive to the qualities of language which 'happen' in the encounter between distant and incommensurable spaces, times and languages. Thus, as *La Bataille de Pharsale* suggests in evoking Nicolas Poussin and Baroque art's 'movement into space', any discussion of Simon's work taken as a whole needs to consider the importance of movement together with the complexities of the dimensions of travelling with which his writing engages.

Simon's writing has long been concerned with issues of 'contact zones' and 'travelling cultures', whose significance has recently been highlighted by theorists of culture such as Mary-Louise Pratt and James Clifford.[31] Thus, the expression 'traveller-fellow' (*JP*, 26) which Simon uses may be understood not as a translation error reversing the term 'fellow-traveller', but precisely as a formulation naming the importance of travelling for S. *Le Jardin des Plantes* contains many scenes showing S. with a variety of 'traveller-fellows', including named, unnamed and abbreviated names, such as Gastone Novelli, women, the fifteen guests in the Soviet Union, Roger C. (Caillois) and Antoine V. (Vitez). Indeed, most of the novel's sites are those of transit, transition, displacement and movement. The numerous descriptions of bathrooms, meeting rooms, roads, trains and views from planes suggest an opening on to travel and movement world-wide. Among the many distant places mentioned are Colorado, Siberia, Kazakhstan, Japan, New York, Valparaiso, Anchorage, the Andes, Abu Dhabi, New Delhi, Calcutta, Moscow, Cerisy, Goteborg, Egypt, Cairo, St Petersburg and Dallas. Other spaces, only apparently closer to 'home', are the war-torn Flanders road, Proust editing his *oeuvre* or torturing rats, Rommel's self-aggrandising wartime notebooks, the college of S.'s youth, military archives (*Le Journal de marche*) and the interview.

31 Mary-Louise Pratt, *Imperial Eyes: Travel Writing and Transculturation*, London and New York, Routledge, 1992; James Clifford, *Routes: Travel and Translation in the Late Twentieth Century*, Cambridge, MA, Harvard University Press, 1997.

Because Novelli's art and life are poised between extremes, namely Europe and the Holocaust during the war, on the one hand, and the post-war years and the depths of the Amazonian jungle, on the other, they come to emblematise the text's shifting and linked contexts.

In *Le Jardin des Plantes*, Simon emphasises the material specificity of places and people, showing them to be diversely linked in the context of global culture. Spaces appearing to be closed, such as the college, turn out to be connected with a variety of rituals and ideologies, such as those of heroism and war, which the institution re-symbolises as religious iconography ('biblique ravissement', *JP*, 190). The college produces its pupils as subjects with the help of 'vers latins, des tirades raciniennes et des formules algébriques' (*JP*, 194). The college also disciplines its pupils by having them copy masks, which themselves condense education's capacity to appropriate and incorporate the diversity of the world: 'Toute l'histoire du monde, le fracas des armes, les discours des rhéteurs et les larmes de Bérénice avaient pêle-mêle abouti là, fondus avec le temps dans cette unique et même matière plâtreuse sous l'aspect d'une foule de têtes décapitées, vidées de leur contenu' (*JP*, 195). The college is, therefore, a mobile site connecting a series of 'lines of escape' or 'lines of flight', as Gilles Deleuze calls them, linking its charges directly into the war through theological and ideological iconographies of nation and heroism. In Simon's writing, the college unfolds as an open space of sensation, of remembrance (from which S. journeys by train, learning of his mother's death from his uncle as they are simultaneously carried away from and towards her), and of convergence between visual and verbal representations. It thereby becomes another 'jardin des plantes', an institution for cultivating, conserving and reproducing values and ideologies by way of the youth it disciplines. Pupils receive the 'measure' of their culture, and what they are taught supposedly prepares them for serving their god and nation. It is no small irony that horse-riding, an extra-curricular option for the wealthier among them, causes S. to be assigned to a cavalry regiment that ultimately falls into a death-trap in the Second World War.

In seeking convergence, S. seems instead to find numerous confirmations of the reality of the shock encounter of the incommensurable. In Rommel's notebooks (and photographs) of his Flanders campaign, he finds a one-sided heroic universe of phrases, a closed series of images and texts. In the archived military report or *Journal de marche*, characterised by statements of event, statistics and proper names, he finds regimes of phrases at once distancing themselves from the immediacy of traumatising events and yet confirming S.'s experience of them. In its 'accounting' of the attacks, the *Journal* cannot avoid allowing the reality of war and its regimes of phrases – hunger, blood and exhaustion – to enter the discourses designed to frame and contain them. An unbridgeable gap nevertheless separates the military archive genre, dictated by its officers and intended for posterity, from the brutal experience of war at its most traumatic and unpresentable. The final scenes of *Le Jardin des Plantes* describe sequentially and in symbolic fashion S.'s ordering of 'les cadrages, les divers mouvements de la caméra et les angles de prises de vues' of a film presenting a variety of episodes from this as well as other Simon novels. In these frames and mock-ups, disparate wartime events on the Flanders road ultimately converge in the camera, which itself also occupies the position of the machine-gun shooting at the soldiers. The cinematic apparatus is here being called upon not only to re-present the incommensurable, but is itself located at the impossible point of encounter of the incommensurable. Moreover, the cinematic representation of war itself takes place within an aporia of film whereby the 'truth' of the soldiers' attempts to camouflage themselves 'pourrait, au cinéma, sembler l'oeuvre maladroite d'un accessoiriste afin de faire plus "vrai". Il vaudra mieux s'en abstenir' (*JP*, 378). Rather than oppose the 'truth of the event' to the 'fiction of its re-presentation', these scenes reflect on the very limits of any apparatus or regime of phrases to effect a convergence of what remains without common measure and whose very necessity rests on the impossibility of overcoming the incommensurable in modernity.

Conclusion

Simon's work is unique in its aesthetic of writing the incommensurable and the childhood of the event. He has an extraordinarily acute feeling for the dynamics of separation and proximity, distance and shock encounters. In his writing, multiple realities, diverse histories and cultural spaces become possibilities for unfolding the movements coiled within the incommensurable. Simon does not presume to teach us the correct measure of things, nor the criteria for judging according to any common measure. Instead, he invents a writing that is eminently mobile, open-sited and multi-dimensional as it delves into the loss of shared sites, languages and experiences. From within the experience of unreality and the melancholy it enfolds, he invents a writing from within disaster itself. In this sense his work offers a powerful counterbalance to the new aesthetics of 'déprimisme' and narcissistic disaffection whose continued reliance on conventional notions of subjectivity, space and temporality effaces singularities and blocks access to 'l'enfance de la rencontre'. In the widespread haste to embrace models of space and pure speed, which simulate new forms of 'travelling cultures' in technological terms, there occurs a loss in the outward and inward movements of the unconscious, perception and memory.

Simon's writing offers a serious and creative account of the incommensurable which he locates in the shock encounter of different realities, spaces, times and existences. Rather than remain within novelistic practices with predictably familiar narrative limits, he generates a movement that transgresses limits in person, word and thing. In the process, he invents possibilities of linking, which for his readers open up new practices in the movement of reading. The movement of linking traverses all the dimensions of his writing from the letter to consonances and dissonances of word, phrase, sentence, paragraph and volume. Linking (with) the incommensurable in Simon means not allowing the tears in the cultural, social, historical and economic fabric to be dissimulated or elided; or, as Lyotard insists, not permitting the 'cicatrisation de l'événement' to take place.[32] Instead, this linking invents the conditions for a mobile and flexible writing process in which a particularly modern experience of subjectivity, memory, history, context and singularity co-exists with an increasingly linked but abstracted world.

32 Lyotard, *Le Postmoderne expliqué aux enfants,* p. 142.

3

Instant Replays: The Reintegration of Traumatic Experience in *Le Jardin des Plantes*

Celia Britton

Running through the first three parts of *Le Jardin des Plantes* is a recurring episode in which S. is interviewed by a journalist about his experiences in the war, and in particular about the key incident of his war experience, defined here as: 'ce qu'il éprouva pendant l'heure durant laquelle il suivit ce colonel, vraisemblablement devenu fou, sur la route de Solre-le-Château à Avesnes, le 17 mai 1940, avec la certitude d'être tué dans la seconde qui allait suivre' (*JP*, 223).

The war scene[1] has already figured, sometimes centrally, sometimes more tangentially, in previous texts, and *Le Jardin des Plantes* recalls some of these earlier versions in brief allusions to the other novels. From *La Route des Flandres*, for instance, we can recognise the 'rideau de paon' (*JP*, 216), the episode where the colonel stops to buy the men beer in a farmyard (*JP*, 281), and the depiction of the country bistro in which Georges, having escaped pursuit by the enemy, gets extremely drunk (*JP*, 289). Another reference to eating cans of fruit in an abandoned house (*JP*, 270) refers back to *Leçon de choses*, and the reiterated emphasis on the lush, 'opulent' green of the countryside is familiar from the version given in *Les Géorgiques*.

However, its re-presentation in *Le Jardin des Plantes* is significantly different. In the first place it is for the first time seen explicitly as *traumatic*: 'le seul véritable traumatisme qu'il est conscient d'avoir subi et à la suite duquel sans aucun doute son psychisme et son comportement général dans la vie se trouvèrent profondément modifiés' (*JP*, 223). A traumatic experience, in Freudian terms, is one which is so intensely disturbing that it cannot be 'processed' by the normal means whereby the psyche regains and maintains its equilibrium. Freud's

---

1 For convenience, I shall refer to the two above-mentioned scenes as, respectively, the 'interview scene' and the 'war scene'.

definition stresses both the suddenness and singularity of the event, and the persistence of its after-effects – 'une expérience vécue qui apporte, en l'espace de peu de temps, un si fort accroissement d'excitation à la vie psychique que sa liquidation ou son élaboration par les moyens normaux et habituels échoue, ce qui ne peut manquer d'entraîner des troubles durables dans le fonctionnement énergétique'[2] – and both of these aspects are clearly evident in Simon's representations of the war scene.

From this point of view, we can see the repetition of versions of the war scene throughout Simon's fiction as *compulsive*, as driven by the traumatic nature of the original experience, and the constant unsuccessful attempts to reduce it to 'normal' proportions. A major aspect of such normality is intelligibility; the trauma is impossible to express. S. repeatedly tells the journalist that he has already described the incident in question many times in the past – 'Mais j'ai déjà raconté tout ça' (*JP*, 79) – but also that none of these rewritings has been adequate to really communicate to the reader what it was like: 'Alors j'ai sans doute mal raconté tout ça et il faudrait reprendre: heure, état des lieux, personnages, bruits, actions...' (*JP*, 101).[3] Hence the quotation from Conrad that forms the epigraph to Part III of *Le Jardin des Plantes* applies particularly to the war scene (and the connection that Conrad makes with dreaming accords with the unconscious dimension of the traumatic experience): 'Non, c'est impossible: il est impossible de communiquer la sensation vivante d'aucune époque donnée de son existence – ce qui fait sa vérité, son sens – sa subtile et pénétrante essence. C'est impossible. Nous vivons comme nous rêvons – seuls' (*JP*, 219). The 'liquidation' of the trauma, in Freud's terms, therefore, also involves breaking down its resistance to verbal articulation, and the repetition compulsion is also determined by a desire to find the words that will adequately convey the unique quality of the experience; the novels return to the war scene in a series of attempts to make it intelligible, both to others, and equally to S. himself, since for

2 Sigmund Freud, *Introduction à la psychanalyse*, Paris, Payot, 1951, p. 389. This is the French translation of *Vorlesungen zur Einführung in die Psychoanalyse*, written in 1916–1917; the original text appears in the *Gesammelte Werke*, vol. 11, p. 284.
3 Through the workings of this textualised repetition compulsion, in other words, the instant is replayed again and again and the replays themselves build up into the kind of 'mémoire textuelle' defined by Pascal Mougin. See Part IV of *Lecture de l'Acacia de Claude Simon. L'imaginaire biographique, Archives des lettres modernes*, no. 267, 1997, pp. 97–118.

him too it represents an area of experience that resists meaning.[4]

As trauma, its uniqueness is such that it has not been blurred or distorted by the effect of memory – and yet it retains a quality of unreality which, far from weakening its impact, makes it all the more vivid and precise: 'Non, ce n'était pas, comme le journaliste pourrait le penser, l'effet du temps plus de cinquante ans maintenant le brouillage de la mémoire, qu'au contraire il (S.) garde de toute cette affaire un souvenir très précis et que ce qui est précis c'est justement cette irréalité dans laquelle tout semblait se dérouler (*JP*, 262). Its 'unreality' marks it off from all other memories and gives it a sharpness and distinctiveness different from everything else, with the result that it cannot be integrated with the rest of his life.

Here, though, *Le Jardin des Plantes* marks a very significant break with all Simon's previous texts. In this novel, written fifty years after the original event, the war scene is presented in a way that at least begins to work towards its liquidation. That is, it is defined initially as a unique moment of trauma, but one that is then gradually recast in a way that moves towards *opening out* the closed, cut-off moment of the trauma and integrating it with other memories. In other words, the 'instant' that has already been obsessively 'replayed' as repetition compulsion is here given a final replay that, so to speak, spreads it out, dilutes its unmanageable intensity and reconnects it to the continuum of the writer's memories. This process operates along a number of different axes. In the first place, the war scene is inserted into two

---

4   In her discussion of the Freudian concept of trauma, Cathy Caruth sees the subject's inability to consciously know or understand the experience at the time at which it occurs as central to the enigmatic significance of trauma, and as determining its persistence as psychic disturbance. She writes: 'Ever since its emergence at the turn of the century in the work of Freud and Pierre Janet, the notion of trauma has confronted us not only with a simple pathology but also with a fundamental enigma concerning the psyche's relation to reality. In its general definition, trauma is defined as the response to an unexpected or overwhelming violent event or events that are not fully grasped as they occur, but return later in repeated flashbacks, nightmares, and other repetitive phenomena. Traumatic experience, beyond the psychological dimension of suffering it involves, suggests a certain paradox: that the most direct seeing of a violent event may occur as an absolute inability to know it; that immediacy, paradoxically, may take the form of belatedness' (Cathy Caruth, *Unclaimed Experience: Trauma, Narrative, and History*, Baltimore, MD, and London, Johns Hopkins University Press, 1996, pp. 91–92). Simon's experience in the war scene could be said to lack the unexpectedness of the classic traumatic event – indeed, in a sense, there *was* no event involving him personally – but its intense singularity and isolation from all his other memories produce the same effects of unintelligibility and compulsively repeated attempts to assimilate it.

binary oppositions that give it a more elaborated structural framework.

The first of these is spatial. The memory is of riding along a road in open countryside, that is, of being out of doors, unprotected and visually *exposed* to the enemy. The particular terror caused by being the helpless object of vision of an invisible enemy is already striking in the version of the scene given in *La Route des Flandres*, with its emphasis on the spectacular visibility of De Reixach as the target of the hidden sniper (*RF*, 313). And the visibility, and hence the fear, is exacerbated by the brilliant light of midday; the fact that it takes place on a sunny spring day makes it more, rather than less, terrifying: 'le "grand air" où se déroulait la marche des quatre cavaliers (l'éclatant soleil, la paisible campagne, le pépiement d'oiseaux) rendait au contraire la chose disons... infiniment plus disons... insupportable qu'elle ne l'aurait été si tout cela s'était passé de nuit' (*JP*, 297–8).

The setting of the interview scene in the present exactly reverses this situation. It takes place indoors, in an upstairs room from which S. can look down on the street below, seeing people who cannot see him. He, in other words, now occupies the protected position of the voyeur, and the text regularly juxtaposes his description of the war scene with references to him looking out of the window. This reversal, moreover, is reinforced by the fact that what he sees from the window is entirely ordinary and unthreatening. The contrast with the dramatic nature of the war scene is accentuated by a stress on the everyday that extends to the recognised formal features of its representation: the text here adopts characteristic techniques used by those writers – Georges Perec, for instance – who systematically record 'le quotidien'. The most prominent is the deliberately simple and monotonous listing of categories of items; for instance, all the shops on the square: 'Après le tabac il y a un magasin de produits de beauté puis un autre café mais moins clinquant puis une boutique de plats à emporter puis un cordonnier puis un marchand de légumes En face une banque un confiseur puis une bonneterie puis un boulanger puis un magasin en faillite...' (*JP*, 98). The 'outside' of the present scene, which consists of sound as well as vision coming in through the window, is described as 'suspect' but 'reassuring'. It is 'real' in a very ordinary sense, and its contrast with the traumatic memory is made quite explicit: 'Du dehors, quoique les fenêtres soient maintenant toutes deux fermées, parvient, étouffée mais toujours présente, continue, la sourde rumeur de la ville, ce grondement silencieux, étale, à la fois rassurant et suspect, tandis que S. essaie de raconter quelque chose qui, même à lui, semble maintenant irréel' (*JP*, 270).

The second binary opposition within which the war scene is now positioned is a temporal one, and it takes two different but related forms. In the first place there is a straightforward contrast between past and present. All of the previous versions of the war scene have of course also been evoked retrospectively, as memory, but the difference in *Le Jardin des Plantes* is that the point in the present *from which* the experience is being remembered is far more firmly established. It is itself a definite, singular 'scene', and the solidity of this present context also perhaps helps to assimilate the traumatic memory to the rest of the subject's experience. Similarly, we know that exactly fifty years separate the war scene and the interview scene. This fact is mentioned several times, as is the coincidence that both take place in the month of May. In itself, the coincidence might seem to underline, rather than reduce, the opposition; but it also acts as a platform for other coincidences, so that eventually the reader has as strong a sense of the equivalences between the two scenes as of their differences. For instance, the presence in both scenes of spring sunshine, trees, leaves and birds is mentioned repeatedly. One typical example enacts a transition from present to past which starts with the magpies S. sees on the square and moves very smoothly into a recollection of the war scene:

> J'ai vu une des pies arriver [...] battre rapidement des ailes comme pour reprendre son équilibre et disparaître dans l'épais feuillage de l'arbre où elles ont leur nid. Le mâle sans doute. Je suppose que la femelle devait couver. De nouveau je pensai qu'alors c'était aussi le printemps. La campagne verte, les fleurs dans les prés, l'ombre fraîche des forêts, les oiseaux. Et là-dedans, les cavaliers, ahuris, exténués. (*JP*, 99–100)

However, this ambiguous opposition/coincidence between past and present is less prominent overall than a more important contrast between two kinds of time. The *singularity* of the traumatic event, a precisely delineated and unique 'instant' of time – 'l'heure durant laquelle il suivit ce colonel' (*JP*, 223) – is counterpointed with an emphasis on *duration* and *repetition* in the present time of the interview. For example, as we have already seen, the sounds of everyday life coming in through the window of S.'s room are 'étouffée mais *toujours présente, continue*' (*JP*, 270, my italics). Almost everything he sees from his window stresses the continuity and regularity of 'le quotidien' – the rush hour traffic; the magpies who have returned as usual to nest in the same tree as they always do ('La même chose se répète tous les ans', *JP*, 79); and the market:

> Le marché se tient trois fois par semaine: le dimanche, le mercredi et le vendredi. Les employés mettent en place les supports et les tentes le samedi après-midi, ils les démontent le lundi, les remettent en place le mardi, les démontent encore une fois le mercredi et les remettent de nouveau en place le jeudi pour les démonter le vendredi après-midi et ainsi de suite. (*JP*, 306)

Equally, the interview scene as a whole is structured by patterns of repetition. There is a regular alternation between S. looking out of the window, then back to journalist. This is often motivated by the journalist's use of a tape recorder; when the tape runs out and the journalist suspends the interview in order to change it, S. has to stop talking, and so he goes over to the window.

But the tape recorder has another, more important function. It records S.'s spoken description of the war scene and, in so doing, confers on this past traumatic experience a different kind of time: it makes the 'instant' both *durational* and infinitely *repeatable*. That is, the tape carries, and preserves, the continuous flow of S.'s words. References to it stress the length of time that he has been talking: 'Peut-être le journaliste se fatigue-t-il d'entendre S. monologuer ou peut-être s'inquiète-t-il de la longueur encore restante de la bande enregistreuse' (*JP*, 269). Through the tape recorder, in other words, speech is materialised as time passing – as duration. Moreover, the fact that S. has to keep stopping for the journalist to put in a new tape means that the tape recorder is actually structuring and in a sense predetermining the duration of speech. The instant of trauma is converted into, and played out as, a certain stretch of speech-time.

Equally, the tape is infinitely repeatable. The notion of cyclical time is, of course, a recurrent one in Simon's fiction, especially in *L'Herbe* and *Le Palace*, and it appears most obviously here in the description of the journalist's watch:

> Comme il allongeait le bras pour saisir le petit magnétophone sa manche est remontée, découvrant complètement cette grosse montre-bracelet avec ses cadrans pour les secondes, les minutes, les heures, dont les aiguilles tournaient en rond. Comme si le temps n'avançait pas, tournait sur lui-même, repassait toujours par les mêmes endroits, faisait pour ainsi dire du sur-place. (*JP*, 82)

But the watch is almost always mentioned in conjunction with the tape recorder, as here, and on the following page we are told that, while the watch may *symbolise* repeatable time, it is only the tape recorder that can actually go back to the beginning and start again: 'Puisque aucune montre ne peut revenir en arrière. Il y avait seulement le magnétophone qui pouvait' (*JP*, 83). It is the tape recorder, therefore, that provides the central image for the idea of 'replaying the instant': giving the unique traumatic instant duration and a fixed structure, and the possibility of replaying it exactly any number of times.

The reason for the presence of the tape recorder is of course that S. is being interviewed, and this in itself constitutes another major difference from the earlier representations of the war scene. Here it is recalled in speech rather than writing, and within a dialogue with another person, not as monologue. This dialogue is not, however, the kind of therapeutic human contact that might stereotypically help an individual to come to terms with a painful memory. His partner in the dialogue is not particularly understanding or sympathetic. More importantly, though, S. is not *exactly* speaking *to* him: since it is an interview, the answers he gives to the journalist's questions serve to provide the material for a text which will be written up – not by S., but by the journalist – and published. Therefore, the words S. is speaking are aimed as it were *past* the journalist, to a wider public audience. Similarly, the fact that he is speaking rather than writing does not mean that this is a more spontaneous, immediate or authentic expression of his feelings; we are given to understand that it is less close to himself and, paradoxically, more public and distanced than the fictionalised written accounts he has previously published. Here again the tape recorder supplies an image for this very particular distancing from one's own speech: 'J'ai entendu ma voix en sortir – ou plutôt pas exactement: une voix métallique, timbrée, qui n'est pas la mienne ou du moins celle que j'entends quand je parle' (*JP*, 82). The intervention of the tape recorder puts S. in the position of hearing himself speak as though he were someone else. A voice that is not exactly S.'s is speaking to someone who is not exactly the person he is speaking to; and the ultimate effect of this double displacement, and double mediation, is that S. hears what the war scene sounds like to *someone else*. This results in another type of distancing and hence also another way of reducing the traumatic intensity of the experience.

As dialogue, the interview scene also engages in a curious intertextual relation with Simon's earlier novels. Unlike the other allusions I have mentioned, this one is not directly relevant to the war scene, but it has a more profound effect than they do in terms of 'liquidating the trauma'. In almost all of Simon's novels there is an important relationship between a younger and an older man: Georges and Pierre in *L'Herbe* and *La Route des Flandres*, Georges and De Reixach in *La*

Route des Flandres, the student and the American in *Le Palace*, Simon and his father in *L'Acacia*, and, finally, the narrator and his uncle Charles in *Histoire*, *La Bataille de Pharsale* and *Les Géorgiques*. All of these relationships are close but antagonistic, or at least ambivalent. In all cases, the older man is a father or father substitute; he is invested with authority that is resented but nevertheless acknowledged by the younger man; and his authority is based on his superior knowledge. In all of them, also, it is the younger man's point of view which the text adopts.

But in *Le Jardin des Plantes* it is the other way around; S. is in his seventies or eighties (since we know that the interview took place in the 1990s), and therefore much older than the journalist, who is a relatively young man in his forties (*JP*, 76). The older–younger man relationship is thus now seen from the point of view of the older man. Equally, though, the older man here does not have the authority that was invested in his earlier counterparts; he is slightly at a loss in the situation, dominated and interrogated by the younger man. It is the journalist who at least at first seems to be in the position of authority; he is initially described as powerful, expensively dressed, efficient and in control: 'habillé plutôt comme un homme d'affaires que comme un journaliste […] Il avait l'air efficace, précis' (*JP*, 76). His spectacles give him the air of a doctor: 'Derrière les verres rectangulaires de ses lunettes à monture dorée elles aussi il me regardait d'un oeil attentif, professionnel, neutre, comme un médecin' (*JP*, 76).

There is one very particular point of contact between the S.–journalist pair, and the narrator–Charles pair, and it is based on the spectacles that I have just cited. At one point in the interview, on page 83, S. notices that he cannot see the other man's eyes because the lenses of his glasses are reflecting the light from the window. This detail recalls a moment in *La Bataille de Pharsale*, in which Charles's glasses are also reflecting the light so that the narrator cannot see his eyes. It occurs during an episode in which Charles is helping the narrator with his Latin homework. There are a number of curious parallels, but also divergences, between this episode and the passage on page 83 in *Le Jardin des Plantes*, and their juxtaposition reveals a significant change in the positioning of the S. figure in relation to the war scene itself.

The relevant passage from *La Bataille de Pharsale* is the following:

La voix de O. hésite. Elle s'interrompt presque entre chaque mot et O. jette alors un regard rapide sur le visage maigre dont il ne peut voir les yeux cachés par un reflet sur les lunettes. O. dit: noster equitatus – notre cavalerie – non tulit – ne supporta pas, ne soutint pas – impetuum quorum – le choc desquels. A ce moment O. s'arrête et regarde de nouveau le visage maigre. La main qui tient le petit cigare s'élève jusqu'à la bouche [...] En même temps qu'elle rejette la fumée la bouche dit: Continue. O. baisse à nouveau les yeux sur son cahier et dit: sed – mais – motus loco – partant, s'en allant de l'endroit – cessit – elle recula – paulum – peu à peu. O. se tait. Dans un nouveau nuage de fumée la voix dit: Eh bien tu vois que quand tu veux bien faire un effort ce n'est pas si difficile. (*BP*, 220–21)

And this can be compared with the following extract from the interview scene in *Le Jardin des Plantes*:

Assis comme il l'était sur le divan face aux fenêtres, le plus souvent la lumière se reflétait sur les verres de ses lunettes et je ne pouvais pas voir son regard. Comme si j'étais en train de parler à un aveugle. De nouveau je me demandais ce que tout ce que je lui racontais là pouvait bien représenter pour lui. [...] Je savais que je perdais mon temps, que c'était comme si je lui parlais dans une langue inconnue. (*JP*, 83)

Thus Charles's 'visage maigre dont il ne peut voir les yeux cachés par un reflet sur les lunettes' is repeated in 'la lumière se reflétait sur les verres de ses lunettes et je ne pouvais pas voir son regard'. But another parallel is the theme of translation: 'O.' struggling to translate Latin into French in *La Bataille de Pharsale* becomes S. struggling to describe the war scene, and thinking that he might as well be speaking an unknown foreign language. Equally, the specific content of the translation passage in *La Bataille de Pharsale* reminds us of the war scene – the cavalry unable to sustain the shock of the enemy engagement retreats – and this parallel alerts us to another, less explicit one. As we have seen, a crucial aspect of the war scene is the terror of being visually exposed: seen by the enemy, but not being able to see the enemy oneself, as in the key example of the hidden sniper who kills Reixach in *La Route des Flandres*. The image of the glasses reflecting the light evokes precisely the same fear, but with strikingly different implications in the two passages. In *La Bataille de Pharsale*, Charles is in the dominant position: the narrator knows that Charles is looking at him, but cannot actually see his eyes, therefore cannot *see Charles seeing him*. He is intimidated: his voice falters, he looks up at Charles furtively, but can only respond to the depersonalised instructions of 'la voix'. Not being able to see his uncle's eyes has the effect of turning the latter into a slightly sinister collection of separate body parts: 'la main', 'la bouche', 'la voix'. In other words, the invisibility of Charles's eyes gives him the power of the hidden sniper in the war scene, and O.

is trapped in the position of Georges in *La Route des Flandres*: seen but unseeing. In *Le Jardin des Plantes*, on the other hand, exactly the same phenomenon is given the opposite significance. In this case, the fact that S. cannot see the journalist's eyes is interpreted as the journalist *not having any eyes* – as his being blind: 'Comme si j'étais en train de parler à un aveugle'. The same image is made to mean, this time, that the journalist cannot see S. seeing him. The result is to reverse the situation in the war scene, and to enable S. to assume the position of the sniper: the powerful hidden voyeur. By the same token, it also reverses the power relations between the subject as translator and his listener; Charles's superior command of Latin is replaced by the journalist's inability to understand.

I have examined this particular intertextual connection in detail because it illustrates the very small-scale, subtle and indirect ways in which the representation of the war scene in *Le Jardin des Plantes* works towards overcoming the traumatic nature of the memory by reworking and transforming earlier textual versions, not only of the scene itself, but also of other incidents that are related to it on a less obvious level. There is also, however, a much larger scale version of this same process, one which involves the way in which the whole interview scene is structured in relation to the rest of *Le Jardin des Plantes*.

The interview scene does not form a single continuous sequence.[5] Rather, it is broken up into sections which appear from time to time in the course of the first three parts. Most of these are between five and ten pages long – pp. 75–84, 95–101, 209–17, 259–64 – but there are three shorter ones, and a few very brief allusions of just a few words.

---

5 Its recurrent and discontinuous presentation can be seen as another form of the process of re-writing that, in relation to the war scene, I have described as operating across all of Simon's novels. There are several occurrences of it in Parts I and II of the book, written in the first person; but then in Part III it is reintroduced as though it were something completely new, and the protagonist is referred to – by the inital S. – in the third person. Thus the initial reference to the scene on page 35 – 'Des années plus tard un journaliste m'a demandé comment on faisait pour vivre avec la peur' – is paralleled by the reintroduction of the scene, as though it had not been mentioned before, on page 221 in Part III, as: 'Au cours de l'entretien qu'il eut au mois de mai 199... avec un journaliste venu le questionner', which is in turn followed by a recapitulation of the whole interview a few pages later: 'Le journaliste et S. sont assis de part et d'autre d'une table basse sur le coin de laquelle est posé un magnétophone. Il y a déjà un moment qu'ils parlent. Le journaliste a demandé à S. comment on faisait pour vivre avec la peur' (*JP*, 259). Rather than a single account, therefore, the interview scene itself is a series of overlapping versions, covering the same ground more than once, and also repeating some of the words and phrases previously used.

They are clearly separated from what precedes and follows them, both by spaces in the text and by the lack of any connection on the level of the subject matter. Within each section, dialogue between S. and the journalist alternates with S.'s interior monologue. Each of these influences the other; S.'s thoughts are sometimes a reaction to the journalist, or to the memories that the interview is evoking in him, but equally they may be caused by something that he sees from the window, which sparks off another memory, which is then in turn incorporated into the dialogue. For instance, a reference to a 'Un long camion de déménagement' (*JP*, 97) that he sees trying to turn into the square outside, while he is talking about the war, generates a reference to a contingent of African soldiers whom he saw, in 1940, in a 'camionnette'; an apparent non sequitur in the interview is explained by the purely textual link between two similar words: 'Le camion avait fini ses manoeuvres et s'engageait sur la chaussée. J'ai refermé la fenêtre, j'ai dit Mais ce n'étaient pas des Maliens Il a dit Des Maliens qui ça? J'ai dit Un convoi de camionnettes, la nuit, qui s'est arrêté, perdu dans la forêt' (*JP*, 99). Thus a variety of different kinds of link between observation and memory determine the way in which the text moves forward. What remains constant, however – with one important exception, to which I will return later – is that the interior monologue contains nothing that is extraneous to the present situation – nothing, that is, that does not belong either to the interview scene or the war scene.

But towards the end of Part III, the pattern of organisation changes. The passages of dialogue with the journalist become much shorter (about half a page), and they are interspersed with descriptions, based on memory, mainly of other places but including one or two of S.'s childhood and adolescence. After each of these, the dialogue carries on from exactly where it left off, sometimes even picking up in mid-sentence. For instance, on page 292 a page of dialogue in which S. reveals that the colonel had *asked* him if he was willing to continue along the road ends with 'Mais avant ça j'obéissais: c'était sur son ordre que je l'avais suivi, que…' This is followed by a short paragraph describing a scene in India, which is in turn followed by a new paragraph beginning: '… que j'avais eu à affronter cette chose, cette comment dire: ordalie?' (*JP*, 293). This new pattern occurs from page 284 to page 305. Within this span there are nine pieces of dialogue, broken up by memories of a very large number of other places – New York, Saint Petersburg, London, Greece, New Orleans, India, Valparaiso,

Dallas, Cambridge, Bologna, the prison camp, Las Vegas, Japan and the Andes – all separated by spaces in the text.

There are two possible ways of interpreting this. It could be seen as an alternating series of switches in and out of the interview scene; in other words, simply an acceleration of the previous rhythm whereby the scene was so to speak cut up into segments which were interspersed with other, unconnected, sequences of textual material. Or one could see it as an alternation between dialogue and interior monologue *within* the interview scene itself – which would imply that the interruptions to the dialogue (the apparently arbitrary recollections of New York, and so on) are 'happening' within the interview scene: that is, S. is remembering New York, etc., *while* he is talking to the journalist. The ambiguity is impossible to resolve with certainty, but there are some textual clues that would seem to support the second interpretation. One is that the phenomenon of the interview scene generating a memory of something other than the war scene has in fact happened already, albeit only once and far more fleetingly. S. is looking out of the window while the journalist changes the tape, and he sees the 'éboueurs' sweeping the square:

> Après le marché qui se tient trois fois par semaine ils nettoient la place à l'aide de longs balais aux crins apparemment en matière plastique, du même vert que leurs combinaisons. S. se souvient d'avoir vu à Calcutta une montagne d'ordures à peu près de la hauteur d'un deuxième étage et sur laquelle des enfants à moitié nus disputaient des choses à des corbeaux et des vautours. On appelle là-bas ces derniers 'les éboueurs' et on compte sur eux pour le nettoyage des villes. Tour à Bombay au sommet de laquelle on dépose les morts pour qu'ils s'en nourrissent. Mais sur cette route il n'y avaient pas de vautours. Seulement les pillards et, à un endroit, un essaim de grosses mouches qui tournoyaient autour des naseaux d'un cheval tué. (JP, 276–77)

The chain of associations here proceeds from the Parisian streetsweepers to the idea of rubbish, to a rubbish tip in Calcutta with vultures hovering over it, to vultures feeding on dead bodies in Bombay, and then to 'cette route', which the reader cannot place until the mention of the dead horse, famous from *La Route des Flandres*, identifies it as the road in the war scene. The passage as a whole, then, moves from the present situation of the scene viewed from the window to a recollection of the war scene, but with the crucial difference that this time it does so *via* a memory of something completely unconnected with either. Thus this passage is the first, very discreet, indication that the traumatic isolation of the experience of the war scene is beginning to break down.

And, despite the different layout on the page (with spaces between the paragraphs) we can see a similar process operating on a much larger scale in the final series of representations of the interview, on pages 284–305. For instance, at one point S. talks to the journalist about Stendhal's account of Julien Sorel's feelings on the day of his execution, comparing it with how he himself felt about the imminent certainty of his death on the road. This is interrupted, mid-sentence, by a reference to visiting Dallas and the scene of Kennedy's assassination; and this too serves to bring him back to the war scene, as he compares Kennedy's vulnerability in the slowly moving car to his own even greater vulnerability on the slowly moving horse: 'et dans une voiture en marche, pas très très vite bien sûr, mais enfin plus vite qu'un cheval au pas…' (*JP*, 298) – which is then immediately followed by a return to the interrupted dialogue.

A more elaborate example occurs a little later, where, having come up with the word 'mélancolie' to describe his state of mind in the war scene (*JP*, 301), he tells the journalist how the prospect of imminent violent death provoked in him a furious desire to live and a heightened awareness of the external world, and says: 'jamais je n'avais regardé avec tant d'*avidité*, d'émerveillement, le ciel, les nuages, les prés, les haies…' (*JP*, 303, my italics). The text then breaks off and switches into its already established sequence of 'places in America', with a passage about Las Vegas and the gambling at Caesar's Palace. This is followed by a paragraph about Dostoievsky gambling (*JP*, 304), then Dostoievsky's account of watching a public execution in Paris (echoing the reference to Julien Sorel six pages earlier), and then a description of Dostoievsky's own experience of thinking he was going to be executed:

> Lui-même a connu les sensations qu'éprouve un homme à la perspective imminente d'une mort violente lorsqu'il a été victime de ce simulacre d'exécution auquel a été conduit un groupe de prétendus conspirateurs dont il faisait partie. Il décrit cette déchirante et *mélancolique avidité* avec laquelle le condamné regarde autour de lui le monde (le reflet du soleil sur le bulbe doré d'une église, les maisons, les gens) qui va continuer d'exister alors que dans quelques instants lui-même ne sera plus rien. (*JP*, 305, my italics)

Here, in other words, 'mélancolique' and 'avidité' echo his own description, three pages earlier, of himself in the war scene. The apparently extraneous allusion to Dostoievsky is finally rationalised by its relevance to his own experience: the 'mélancolique avidité' with which both men gaze at the physical world around them at the moment of imminent death. In fact Dostoievsky's version of it provides a fuller explanation of the shared experience: the intensity of the gaze is motivated by the thought that the physical world 'va continuer d'exister alors que dans quelques instants lui-même ne sera plus rien'. But the comparison between the two men does not annul the particularity of Dostoievsky's situation: unlike S., he is victim of a sadistically planned fake execution, and the 'world' that he sees is distinctively Russian ('le bulbe doré d'une église'). The point here is less that Dostoievsky leads back into S.'s own memory of the war experience, than that the link between the two is extremely circuitous, taking in Las Vegas, gambling and public executions before it arrives at its metaphorical destination. This is significantly different from the earlier direct transitions between present (interview) and past (war scene); it means that the dialogue with the journalist is now generating memories not only of the war scene, but of a whole range of very diverse other things as well: other periods of S.'s life, and the published experiences of other people, real (Dostoievsky) or fictional (Julian Sorel). All of this demonstrates how the traumatic moment is opening out, losing its sealed-off character, and becoming spread out and diluted among other memories.

There may even be a sense in which, during this final stage of the interview scene, S.'s production of the word 'mélancolie' to define his state of mind in the war scene, represents some kind of, albeit relative, success in the attempt to give verbal articulation and meaning to the trauma. 'Mélancolie' replaces the journalist's initial term, 'peur' , and his other suggestions:

> Le journaliste disant Mais enfin si ce n'était ni désespoir, ni renoncement, ni abdication, ni…, et S. disant que Non ce n'était rien de tout ça, qu'il y aurait peut-être un mot, mais qu'on lui donne en général un sens qui… Hésitant de nouveau (et pendant un moment il peut de nouveau percevoir ce même indifférent et menaçant *grondement*, cette espèce de bruit de fond, *cette rumeur étale*, sans plus de consistance qu'une faible et unique vibration dans quoi vient se confondre toute l'agitation du dehors, se neutraliser toute la violence, les passions, les désirs, les peines, les terreurs), et à la fin il dit Mélancolie, le journaliste s'exclamant Mélancolie! (*JP*, 299, my italics)

Moreover, this crucial discovery of the 'right' word is accompanied by the 'rumeur étale' of the everyday city noises coming through the window. This echoes the earlier description on page 270 that I have already cited, but again with some significant differences. The first occurrence made a point of separating the present everyday situation from the past trauma: 'Du dehors, quoique les fenêtres soient maintenant toutes deux fermées, parvient, étouffée mais toujours présente, continue, la sourde *rumeur de la ville*, ce *grondement* silencieux, *étale*, à la fois rassurant et suspect, tandis que S. essaie de raconter quelque chose qui, même à lui, semble maintenant irréel' (*JP*, 270, my italics). The closed windows isolated the traumatic memories being discussed within the room from the normality of the city outside, and the 'rumeur' was attributed specifically to 'la ville'. On page 299, in contrast, there is no mention of the windows, and the 'rumeur' itself is far more inclusive; rather than being contrastively everyday it now encompasses the violence and terror that were a feature of the war scene, thus once again bringing together traumatic past and everyday present and 'neutralising' the difference between them.

The last evocation of the interview scene occurs on pages 305–08. But there is one further fleeting reference to the journalist – and to 'mélancolie' – a few pages later: 'Mélancolie. S. pense qu'il aurait dû dire au journaliste que c'était comme quand le chirurgien…' (*JP*, 312). This develops into a memory of his period of illness with tuberculosis, in which he was lying in bed, looking out of a different window but seeing trees like those on the square, and those on the road in the war scene. It ends as follows: 'avec cette différence qu'alors, sur votre cheval, vous n'aviez pas trente-neuf de fièvre, que l'air léger entrait et sortait de vos poumons sans que vous en ayez même conscience et que votre corps était plein de vie' (*JP*, 312). In other words, the word 'mélancolie' here allows him to make another link, with *another* memory of being near to death in a very different situation, and the end result of the comparison is to redefine himself in the *war scene* – and this is the last reference to it in the whole of *Le Jardin des Plantes* – far more positively than he has ever done before, as, paradoxically, 'plein de vie'. The resonance of the war scene thus extends beyond the end of the interview scene; it has been 'opened out' also in the sense that, as it reaches the end of the whole sequence, it can itself be mobilised to generate a different memory.

In conclusion, then, I have argued that the 'traumatic instant' of the war scene has already been replayed, as a form of repetition compulsion, throughout S.'s fictional and autobiographical texts; but that its final replay in *Le Jardin des Plantes* is of a very different nature.

Here its textual presentation moves towards a fuller integration of the traumatic 'instant' with all S.'s other memories. From being cut off, unique and 'unreal', it is given a kind of structure and articulation which make it relatively more homogeneous with the rest of his life.

4

The Dynamics of Conflict in the Novels of Claude Simon

J. A. E. Loubère

When, in the 1960s, theorists of the New Novel, led by Alain Robbe-Grillet and then Jean Ricardou, undertook a complete spring-cleaning of the fusty conventions governing fiction, they enthusiastically dismantled and discarded previous notions of intrigue, characterisation, psychology, orderly thematic development in time, spatial co-ordination, plot resolution and closure, recognising fiction only as *facture*, that is, primarily the use and manipulation of words in a text. In this, they were themselves developing ideas inherent in the work of predecessors such as Jarry, Roussel, Valéry, Proust, Joyce, Borges and various Surrealists, but their theoretical approach demolished far more systematically the existing canons of literature. Words and tropes formed by words were henceforth to be the origin and generators of all fictional production, and theme and subject matter were demoted into being merely another element of the text.

A difficulty arises here that has been the source of many disputes and divisions of opinion. Words used by the writer of fiction do not come to the reader pure and unencumbered, but inevitably, in some way, charged and contaminated with our thoughts and feelings about what is 'real', and by our propensity to impose cognitive patterns on experience. Problems concerning logic, time, belief, perception and representation in literature all stem from this contamination. New Novelists, in consequence, all tread the slippery line between mere ludism, or word-play, or even 'oulipism', on the one hand, and a relapse into convention on the other. As a result, thematics were a constant source of contention among devotees of the new writing, for whom theme and 'subject' were the product of language, and not to be privileged in any way. For purists such as Jean Ricardou a battle had constantly to be fought to restore the primacy of the text itself.

The innovative work of the novelist, Claude Simon, provided

Ricardou with an excellent opportunity for demonstrating his theories. However, resistance to Ricardou's rigidity soon developed, typified by Denis de Saint Jacques's intervention, 'L'Obstination réaliste', at the Colloque de Cerisy in 1974,[1] and by the comments of participants in the New York colloquium on the New Novel in 1982.[2] Simon's writing is still at the centre of the debate, as Ralph Sarkonak emphasises in the Claude Simon series of the *Revue des lettres modernes* inaugurated in 1994. 'Un épineux problème', says Sarkonak in his introduction, '"hante" les simoniens depuis longtemps: celui du référent.'[3] In effect, critics have found it impossible to ignore the wealth of referential and thematic material in Simon's writing. This material constantly calls for further exploration, particularly its active role in the productive process, and the manner in which it contributes to the motility of his work.

No one has examined more thoroughly than Claude Simon the difficulties of the balancing act between theme and execution, through the very process of writing. His early attempts at conventional fiction soon revealed to him the extent of the problem, and directed him towards increasingly complex experiments in search of a solution. *Le Sacre du printemps* questions fictional 'truth'. *Le Vent* reveals the spuriousness of any pretence of completeness in story-telling. *L'Herbe* tackles the problems of time and personality. In *La Route des Flandres*, Simon gathers these elements together by means of an all-embracing and predominant theme: the experience of war, specifically, the debacle of the French cavalry in the Second World War. Through this theme, he mirrors the disintegration and ineffectiveness of the old rules of conflict in a novel that exemplifies the disintegration and ineffectiveness of the old rules of composition, and so doing, propels his text productively towards a new understanding of the act of writing, and a dynamic resulting from a constant interchange between diegetics and praxis.

There can be no doubt that the emergence of a dominant 'war theme' is a vital factor in Simon's development as a novelist. Although suspicion of fictional 'truth' is fully expressed in earlier novels, it is in *La Route des Flandres* that he attempts to come to terms (a significant phrase) with the irreducible opposition between words and raw

1   Denis Saint-Jacques, 'L'Obstination réaliste', in Jean Ricardou (ed.), *Claude Simon: Colloque de Cerisy*, Paris, Union Générale d'Editions, 1975, pp. 223–47.
2   See Lois Oppenheim (ed.), *Three Decades of the French New Novel*, Urbana/Chicago, IL, Illinois University Press, 1986.
3   Ralph Sarkonak (ed.), introduction to *A la recherche du référent*, *Revue des lettres modernes*, Série Claude Simon 1, 1994, p. iv.

reality. Between the need to say and the impossibility of saying, Simon's work is shaped by the struggle to take charge of his writing and the constant disintegration of the resulting text. The more conflict there is in the thematic material, the greater are the effects of rupture and fragmentation in the act of writing.

Of all sources of conflict, war is the great destroyer of established structures, material, psychological, ethical or semantic. The novels using this theme show the highest degree of textual rupture and fragmentation. As Simon himself observes in *Le Jardin des Plantes*, 'les facultés de perception du monde extérieur aussi bien qu'intérieur se trouvent sans doute fortement altérées' when the whole being, including the brain, finds itself in extraordinary circumstances (*JP*, 270). In Simon's work, the acuity of the artist's senses is allied to the intensity of his experience. As Jean Duffy points out, 'the disorienting situations in which Simon's characters so often find themselves – physical danger, emotional trauma, drunkenness, illness, exhaustion – impair their capacity to function rationally, render them unusually reliant upon perceptual co-ordinates and make them acutely sensitive to the sights, sounds, scents and textures of their immediate surroundings'.[4] It can be no accident that such situations are the preferred material of so much of Simon's work.

War, and her sister, Revolution, in their many manifestations in Simon's novels – the Second World War, first and foremost, the First World War, the Spanish Civil War, the Revolutionary and Napoleonic wars, Caesar's wars – are prime agents of disorientation. War shatters our relationship with conventional habits, physical, psychological and moral, and it is this breakage, once the war theme supervenes, that is marked in *La Route des Flandres*, on all levels of the text. Many have tried to write convincingly about the horrors of war, but few have achieved that concurrence of theme and execution that occurs in this novel. In *Le Jardin des Plantes*, S., although protesting to a journalistic inquirer that he wrote about many other things, admits later that 'le seul véritable traumatisme qu'il est conscient d'avoir subi et à la suite duquel sans aucun doute son psychisme et son comportement général dans la vie se trouvèrent profondément modifiés fut [...] ce qu'il éprouva pendant l'heure durant laquelle il suivit ce colonel [...] le 17 mai 1940', that is to say, at the culmination of his eight days of terror at the outset of the Second World War (*JP*, 223). In sequence

---

4 Jean H. Duffy, *Reading Between the Lines: Claude Simon and the Visual Arts*, Liverpool, Liverpool University Press, 1998, p. 321.

after sequence, novel after novel, Simon returns to this experience, while stressing the impossibility of communicating any part of it: 'Ce qui est précis, c'est justement cette irréalité dans laquelle tout semblait se dérouler' (*JP*, 262). Wherever the war theme appears in his work, there is a corresponding stress and dislocation in the writing. But, as we shall see, the theme itself attracts further developments, sucking into itself, as it were, like a black hole, similar events in time and space.

La Corde raide, *Le Sacre du printemps*, and *L'Herbe* all refer to war and its effects, but discursively and indirectly. In *L'Herbe*, old Marie rides through the ruined countryside in a decrepit train 'tandis que autour d'elle un pays entier se débandait, s'effondrait, s'abîmait dans un fracas de vociférations et de métal' (*L'H*, 221). It is in *La Route des Flandres*, however, that the monstrous and meaningless destructivity of war is most forcefully conveyed, even though later novels expand and develop the theme extensively in time and space. The material havoc is, of course, very visible (*RF*, 108), but it is not merely the material that disintegrates in war. The Army, that monumental construct of national pride, is revealed to be a paragon of inefficiency, snobbery and prejudice, its 'directives à peu près aussi utiles que [...] celles données pendant la même période par les stratèges d'un café de province' (*RF*, 213). Its disintegration is figured by the recurring sequence of the four men on horseback – all that remains of two cavalry regiments sent to face German tanks – riding blindly into an ambush, one of them to instant death, the others into the hell of prisoners' camp, while the general commits suicide because 'plus rien n'avait de sens, de raison d'être' (*RF*, 214). The defence of the Nation, that hallowed entity, is shown to be run by bureaucrats and incompetents: 'des soldats [...] se trouvaient coupés de toute formation régulière et dans l'ignorance de ce qu'ils devaient faire [...] parce que [...] (le capitaine) n'avait reçu aucune directive' (*RF*, 300). The esprit de corps that is supposed to cement armies together disappears in the face of defeat, along with common humanity, when the captain refuses to let a fugitive soldier mount a spare horse (*RF*, 227), when the soldiers in trucks will not stop for their comrades (*RF*, 211), and in the prison train and the prisoners' camp, where only the fittest and slyest can hope to survive (*RF*, 216–217). There is mental and moral disintegration, 'cette espèce de diarrhée morale [...] impossible à contenir, irraisonnée' (*RF*, 193). There are outbursts of frustrated anger among the soldiers and a madman in the prison camp. The combatants are reduced to a degree zero of communication, and their conversation, directly rendered, is a compound of obscenities or protests that dismally fail to convey the slightest sense of their predicament. Newspapers, supposed to carry information, are reduced to a blur, 'à peine une tache, une ombre un peu plus grise sur la grisaille du papier' (RF, 37).

Only the individual remains, and he himself is in pieces, beyond exhaustion, dazed and bewildered, no longer knowing how his body functions or his brain works: 'au milieu de cette espèce de décomposition de tout comme si non pas une armée mais le monde lui-même tout entier et non pas seulement dans sa réalité physique, mais encore dans la représentation que peut s'en faire l'esprit [...] était en train de se dépiauter se désagréger s'en aller en morceaux en eau en rien' (RF, 16–17). Odd objects capture his attention: the legs and clothing of the woman who gives them a drink in a farmyard; a pink shirt on a hedge; a henhouse; a bird singing in a wood; the head of the dead horse seen from different angles; 'des chiffons, des loques, des draps déchirés ou tordus, dispersés, étirés, comme des bandes, de la charpie, sur la face verdoyante de la terre' (RF, 29). The effect of disintegration is extended far beyond immediate experience. Caught between the boredom and monotony that precedes action, and the sudden violence that follows, Georges perceives that all that has constituted his life has been shattered, his family feeling, his trust in words, his conception of society and history, his sexual emotions, even the sense of his own personality, all lost in a state of confusion and fatigue.

The war theme challenges the writer to describe the progress from order to disorder, to render chaos without succumbing to banality, disorder or illegibility. Simon fully accepts the challenge by attacking that final monument, that source of national pride, the supposed 'rules' governing 'good' writing in French. The internal manoeuvres with which Simon achieves his ends, the circling movement of motifs and themes, the structural, semantic and syntactical innovations, the accumulation of participles and parentheses, the recourse to myth and speculation are all elements which, as Jacques Neefs observes, propel the reader towards 'la plongée dans la confusion qu'est la guerre', which 'avec Claude Simon, devient une approche rythmique, plus qu'une description, un battement verbal d'images qui sera comme le retour mimétique d'un inqualifiable désordre, qui devra permettre de distinguer dans l'indistinction.'[5]

5 Jacques Neefs, 'La Grandeur de l'histoire', in Mireille Calle (ed.), Claude Simon. Chemins de la mémoire, Sainte-Foy, Québec, Editions Le Griffon d'argile, 1993, p. 106.

There is, however, another aspect to this rhythm. The reader/
collaborator of the text, as Simon himself recognises, approaches the
work in a linear fashion, from left to right and according to pagination,
drawn forward by the flow of language, expectant of development.
The ear is also attuned to continuity. In this view, rupture can only be
achieved syntactically, through paragraphing, incompletion, variations in typography and visible breaks on the page, devices of which
Simon makes ample use. In *La Route des Flandres* the primary effect of
disintegration, the scattering of attention from one object to another,
from one event to the next, in disparate zones of time and space, is an
impression of ungoverned, restless movement, an energy let loose in
numerous conflicting directions. The diegetics of forward movement,
the advance towards disaster, is thus rendered episodic, rather like the
dislocated movements of the early films which often appear in Simon's
text. As Maureen DiLonardo Troiano observes, 'The disposition of
objects [...] may [...] be said to delay the forward movement of
fictional time'.[6] Yet this is contradicted by the almost uninterrupted,
unpunctuated flow of prose on the page, incorporating even conversation ('Et Georges [...] et Wack [...] Georges répétant [...] et Martin [...]
et Blum [...] et Wack [...] et Blum [...] et Georges [...] et Blum [...] et
Georges [...] ' (*RF*, 65)), like the steady trot of the horses in the night,
'le martellement monotone et multiple des sabots sur la route' (*RF*, 30),
or the relentless drumming of the rain, until broken abruptly, as Jean
Rousset[7] points out, by the brief flurry of ambush, only to settle back
again into the monotony of the prison camp. At the same time, the
rhythm is further disrupted by intervals of recollection and speculation about past or imaginary events. This, together with the multiplication of textual connections on metaphoric and semantic levels,
creates a conflict of opposing forces, setting up the dual 'tension/
attention' via 'distress/stress' through which the text becomes the
mirror of itself, its own *mise en abyme*.

Pre-existing stresses and tensions irrupt into the text as soon as
attention is captured by recognised signs, such as a sabre, a horse, a
newspaper or a pink rag. These tensions emerge from settings as alien
to conflict as the smiling countryside is to war: the father/son
confrontation about words takes place in a garden kiosk near a farmer
tilling his fields (*RF*, 33–37); Georges's embarrassed hostility to his

6   Maureen DiLonardo Troiano, *New Physics and the Modern French Novel: An
    Investigation of Interdisciplinary Discourse*, New York, Peter Lang, 1995, p. 90.
7   Jean Rousset, 'Le Récit de guerre selon Claude Simon', *Archipel*, no. 8, février 1994, p. 56.

mother's snobbish preoccupation with family and class sees her at home amid piles of dusty documents relating to the Reixach connection and the ancestral tragedy (*RF*, 52–59); Georges's sexual tension and his anxiety about the connection between Corinne and the jockey evoke the brilliant colours and bustle of the racetrack and the transparent pink dress worn by Corinne in Georges's imagination (*RF*, 48–52). Such episodes break into and deflect the war narrative, jolting it off course, much as sudden halts and obstacles, enemy attacks, ambushes and flight deflect the cavalryman's ride to certain disaster. Yet the forward thrust of the narration incorporates the rhythms of other times and places concealed within it and invests them with its own urgency, just as the ordinary rhythms of our lives are transformed and quickened under the conditions of wartime. If, as Georges Raillard says, 'le rythme est un mode de la forme'[8] then the overt and hidden rhythms of *La Route des Flandres* respond most accurately to the exigencies of the theme. Ralph Sarkonak has commented on 'la carence de toute critique (thématique) en ce qui concerne une "écriture en abîme"'.[9] In the case of *La Route des Flandres* theme and realisation become almost one, reflecting one another so that no separating critique could be possible.

All these effects are concentrated in *La Route des Flandres* by the nature of the subject, but they are extended and developed by Simon throughout almost his entire opus, and it is their very nature that dictates the movement of the text, through the tangle of emotions, memories and perceptions into the complexities of textual production, in a kind of constant spiralling motion in which the writer attempts to match the unmatchable qualities of experience. Only in the absence or downgrading of such themes is a completely different pace observed.

Le Palace deals essentially with the same problems but at a remove, action stilled and stalled from the point of view of a narrator who is both there in the past and here as one looking back on that past. As a consequence its dynamic is less that of immediate apprehension of events than an attempt at fusing the two aspects of perception. But the seesaw motion is due to the same elements: a war that is somehow not a war, a world that is filled with disparate objects that are constantly displaced or destroyed, an inefficient bureaucracy and conflict among

8   Georges Raillard, 'Le Rythme des choses', *Critique*, vol. 37, no. 414, 1981, pp. 1167–80.
9   Ralph Sarkonak, *Claude Simon: les carrefours du texte*, Toronto, Editions Paratexte, 1986, p. 76.

leaders, time that seems distorted, and the suffocating atmosphere of defeat. The seeming dryness of the narration contrasts strongly with the flow of *La Route des Flandres*, but it has the same bitterness of tone that corresponds to the futility of the 'student's' involvement in a losing cause. If the rhythm of the previous novel resembles the journey on horseback through the night, the movement in *Le Palace* is like the endless circling of the tramcars, with stops figuring the static quality of the student's useless waiting for some kind of happening, during which he realises that what he is fighting is 'l'introuvable ennemi [...] cette chose qui n'avait pas de nom, pas de visage, pas d'apparence' (*P*, 224). This is a novel of absence, absence of missing furniture, people, purpose and ideals, but above all, absence of progress. Communication, made stranger by a foreign tongue, is stilted, 'comme si [...] une sorte d'idiot, de bègue, de perroquet imbécile nous devançait chaque fois que nous ouvrons la bouche' (*P*, 131), reduced to the mouthing of dead slogans, interspersed by diatribes, words corrupted by the rot that is devouring the city. If *La Route des Flandres* is propelled by the anguish of a young man desperate to understand what is happening to him, *Le Palace* is the paralysis of one bogged down in despair.

The tension, then, in this novel has a hallucinatory quality, the contrast motion/immobility stretched to the breaking point. The revolutionaries rush madly through the city in what seems like suspended animation (*P*, 80). The assassin has the illusion that time and movement have slowed to a crawl: 'tout allait à la fois très vite et très lentement ' (*P*, 90). The horses in the funeral procession 'semblaient ne pas avancer' (*P*, 104). The counter-revolution has died at birth (*P*, 230). The most powerful effect of *Le Palace* is that, despite descriptions of attempted activity, of displacement and search, nothing is happening, nothing will ever happen. In the long flow of words, the text continues inexorably to describe in detail the lack of action. This work, in which the protagonist waits in vain for movement reverses the dynamic of *La Route des Flandres*, in which the protagonist is precipitated into events over which he has no control.

This underlying principle of double tension runs through the succeeding texts like an underground wire, so that at any moment the slightest reference in the discourse may halt the advance of narrative events and trigger the return to the wartime trauma, sometimes by what seems almost insignificant, or at best, irrelevant. In *Histoire* it is the apparently unrelated stress caused by commercial exchange which constantly brings to the surface the images of past conflict. Money concerns are of course a source of tension but do not normally evoke war, except indirectly. In the case of the narrator in this novel, ostensibly occupied in selling off a piece of land and a number of objects from an ancestral home, it takes very little for the old memories to come back, piecemeal but obsessive. In fact, the bank where the transaction is taking place is already a throwback to the bank which has arisen on the site of the former Palace, and it is the clicking of the tape machine that reminds the narrator of the hoofbeats of horses once used for communication, thence to the Baron de Reixach, Corinne, the cavalry of the Second World War and the 'plaines des Flandres monotones' (*H*, 100), and then via a maze of associations to the Russian Revolution as described by Reed, to the uncle who prods the narrator to talk about his foray into the Spanish Civil War (the same uncle who has a picture of Barcelona on the wall, and who harasses the unfortunate student of Caesar's wars). Even a mention of food brings on further reflections about Spain, de Reixach... and back to money (*H*, 170–203). Money distributed by Uncle Charles also connects with Caesar's wars and a demand for understanding 'what happened' and, with the resurgence of the war theme, a renewal of tension between the forward pull of narrative and the regressive drag of memory.

Further stress caused by the dismemberment of the family inheritance, compounded by the closely associated anguish that assimilates the deaths or betrayals of important female characters (lover/ mother), produces similar effects. At any moment, a sudden stimulus, oral, visual, mobile, will cause the text to home back to the essential theme of conflict, as though drawn by a magnet, thus determining the arrival of the following sequence.

If, as Simon says in the preface to *Orion aveugle*, an initial image begins the whole process of writing, that image, however far it may appear to be from the theme of war, will often generate others that lead back inevitably to images of conflict. In *La Bataille de Pharsale* the flight of a bird resembling an arrow triggers the return to the battle between memory and writing, the famous 'battle of the phrase'.[10] *La Bataille de Pharsale* can be read as a 'recensement', a journey through established themes and methods, with frequent stops and starts to re-examine ways of approach to material and writing, leading to an ordering of events, a 'lexicon' and a 'chronology'. Ostensibly, the narration

10 Jean Ricardou, 'La Bataille de la phrase', *Critique*, vol. 26, no. 274, 1970, pp. 226–56.

concerns a search for the site of the ancient battle of Pharsalus, but the narrative is constantly pierced and broken up by recollections of battles of all varieties, which fuse and combine in uncompleted phrases and paragraphs, freed of grammatical constraints, pausing and starting up again at the slightest stimulus, a football game, an open-mouthed clown, paintings, mosaics, sex, a redhead, pigeons, archers (*BP*, 72–77), returning inexorably to the spectacle of war. This fragmentary construction parallels the broken mosaic in the House of the Faun in Pompeii (*BP*, 79), but the theme is anything but an inert memory. In an uneven but irresistible fashion, the text is driven towards a culmination in the section entitled 'Bataille', which becomes a rush of images unleashed by descriptions of battle paintings. Here, all attempts at an expository tone are shattered by constant incursions of memory, which no longer allow pauses between fragments. Something as innocent as a fine day full of green leaves and white clouds suddenly slips into a scene from *La Route des Flandres* (*BP*, 102). Discussion of weather and light in a painting is abruptly obscured by a nightmarish experience from the Second World War (*BP*, 106). War-related words – 'arrière-garde', 'projectile', 'des armes brisées', 'sous-bois' – are sufficient to start the dizzying return to the past, the 'moi au centre' spinning at the heart of this movement, which continues at an unbroken, almost breathless pace, through a series of 'maintenant […] maintenant […] maintenant', toward a moment of stunned oblivion, as annihilating as the culmination of sex.

In conventional writing, a major theme carries the narration steadily forward. Here, in Simon's writing, on the contrary, it is disruptive, shattering the discourse into unequal parts, 'l'action se fractionnant en une multitude d'affrontements singuliers' (*BP*, 103), denying logical development with its excursions into the past, disturbing the expository tone of the segment with an extra emotional charge.

However, critics have noted a radical change of tone in the final section of *La Bataille de Pharsale*. There is what might be called a strategic withdrawal from personal recollections of the war, motivated in part by Simon's involvement with theoreticians of the new novel. In the place of the participator, we have the observer, even the observer of the observer, as the narrator distances himself from the narration by the device of O. (signifying the observer/everyone/no one) who inserts a space between himself and what is related. This distancing has the effect of chopping up the text into shorter, expository sentences, giving equal value to all the themes, military, sexual, descriptive, passing from one to the other by various scriptural devices, none of which is privileged by sentiment: 'O. fait un pas en avant. Le cheval prend le trot. O. se met à courir et touche de nouveau du bout du doigt les rênes flottantes. Le cheval prend le galop. O. essaye d'attraper l'un des étriers qui bat contre le flanc du cheval. L'étrier lui échappe. Le cheval s'éloigne en ruant. O. se met à courir sur le ballast, alourdi par le poids de son équipement' (*BP*, 224).

This new choppiness changes completely the rhythm of Simon's writing and presages the disappearance of the disturbing war theme altogether. It is rather like the substitution of the officers' ordnance map, with its lines of direction and intersection points, in the place of what is actually happening on the front. The writer/protagonist is now eliminating the emotional charge by taking control of language and its rhythms in a deliberate, almost military or mathematical style. We shall see that whenever this brief expository style appears, the sense of conflict and disorder is replaced by a drier tone that admits of no emotional resonance. The conflictual themes are obscured, as in the next three novels, and the movement in the text results primarily from scriptural elements.

In *Les Corps conducteurs* which follows, war is absent, but there is conflict, exemplified in the struggle between man and his own body, that is, man versus 'la grande folie de la nature' (*CC*, 136). This is made clear in the passages that link the suffering of a sick man directly to the sequences relating to the Spanish army struggling helplessly through the jungle (*CC*, 111–12, 127–28), while these in turn relate to the struggle of the invalid through the jungle of the city. The perceptions of the invalid are fragmented; time is stretched or annihilated; objects and people seen through a fog of pain are disproportionately emphasised; metamorphosed movement is slowed, precipitated, abrupt and irregular. However, the 'moi au centre' has been dismissed; O. has become 'il', emotional resonance is dulled, and the conflict is rendered rather by juxtaposition of images in an intricate series of interconnections. The text on the page appears even and uninterrupted; the sentences are short and declarative, highlighted only by typographical devices that serve to emphasise the insufficiency of any text in the face of violence: 'continuant à proposer sans espoir des fragments de mots, d'images, arrachés à un monde violent, déclamatoire' (*CC*, 159).

As the tide of personal reflections withdraws, there is a corresponding simplification of structure and syntax, deceptive, however, in that the writing tightens and compresses the diegetic material into an ever-closer weave of imagery. It is possible to read into this text the unifying experience of one subject, the sick man, a feature that Jean Ricardou has criticised as a weakness,[11] although others, such as Michael Evans, disagree.[12] We may consider *Les Corps conducteurs* as a transition, a movement of writing towards the pure consideration of itself, certifying a change in momentum in the evolution of Simon's work.

In the two novels that follow *Les Corps conducteurs*, extreme stress and conflict as cause of fragmentation are made subservient to the intricacies of writing in a new style which Simon is exploring uniquely from the point of view of the innate qualities of language. This exploration leads to the technical masterpiece, *Triptyque*, in which all emotional charge is absent, the narration absolutely neutral, relying for its movement on the manipulation of literal devices that demonstrate the illusory qualities of straight diegetics, refusing to allow the reader any investment in any of the 'stories' it offers and withdraws.[13] This text turns on itself, appearing static, offering 'the flatness of an unchanging present', as Alastair Duncan observes,[14] despite the 'dramas' it supposedly recounts. It is clear that none of the thematic materials are sufficiently 'loaded' to disturb the even tenor of the text; ruptures in the sequences are brought about by sudden cinematic changes of focus, not by syntactic or metaphoric breakage. The only conflict is with the reader's tendency to add affect or to want completion and closure, which are never granted. It seems, therefore, that the proponents of scriptural dynamics have won their case.

Leçon de choses appears to repeat this achievement, but a closer examination reveals a denser weave in the text of motifs from many of the preceding novels, and from extratextual sources. These motifs add an extra weight to the novel, the more so as the war theme returns both as part of the scriptural texture, and separately in two 'Divertissements', which are both humorous and demotic transformations of scenes recalling *La Route des Flandres*. Despite their 'cocasserie', these 'Divertissements' are loaded with recollections of things past, and

---

11 Jean Ricardou, 'Claude Simon, textuellement', in Jean Ricardou (ed.), *Claude Simon: Colloque de Cerisy*, Paris, U.G.E., 1975, p. 19.
12 Compare Michael Evans, *Claude Simon and the Transgressions of Modern Art*, Basingstoke and London, Macmillan, 1988, pp. 135–36.
13 Compare Mária Minich Brewer, *Claude Simon: Narrativities without Narrative*, Lincoln, NE, and London, University of Nebraska Press, 1995, pp. 104–05.
14 Alastair Duncan, 'Hierarchy and Coherence in Simon's Novels from *La Bataille de Pharsale* to *Leçon de choses*', in Alastair B. Duncan (ed.), *Claude Simon: New Directions*, Edinburgh, Scottish Academic Press, 1985, p. 78.

together with the sequences relating to the isolation and despair of the soldiers holed up in the farmhouse, introduce a certain imbalance into the text and disturb the neutrality of the narration.

Imagery from the war scenes radiates into the accompanying sequences. Through the windows of the farmhouse where the soldiers are hidden can be seen landscapes that reappear inside the room as reproductions of paintings by Renoir and Boudin. These in turn generate the seaside and adultery segments and are regenerated by them. Even the waves in the Impressionist paintings 'ressemblent aux rangées de tentes alignées et basses d'un camp militaire' (LC, 75). On the semantic and metaphoric levels, the army language resonates throughout; an exploding bomb is an orgasm; the vulgar 'vache' in soldiers' parlance is omnipresent; the bottled plums that the hungry soldiers swallow become the swollen tip of a penis; a 'pruneau' is a bullet; the 'ponceau' or small bridge that they watch has the shape of a woman's genitals. Even the masons, who provide the basic 'leçon' of the novel, that of de-con-struction, have their military connection, the older being in fact the voice of the 'Divertissements', the younger having a Spanish/Catalan name that recalls Barcelona and hence Le Palace. The text is saturated with military connotations, and the anguish of the trapped soldiers is given an explicit voice: 'Plus que véhémente: indignée, et plus qu'indignée: martyrisée' (LC, 156).

This voice retells in common language events we have previously encountered. But no language will do. As soon as personal stress is reintroduced, the precipitate tone and failures of communication reappear. 'Estime-toi heureux que j'aie rien entendu,' shouts the captain (LC,129). 'Pour qui tu parles qu'i me dit fais gaffe de Pour personne' (LC,130), answers the soldier. Leçon de choses is therefore a hybrid, combining the precipitous emotional tone of La Route des Flandres with the terser phrases and technical imbrications of Triptyque. This hybridisation is continued in the three succeeding novels to a far greater degree.

In Les Géorgiques, a new force is added to the mix. The war theme now acts less as a fragmenter than as an attractor, drawing to itself, via the newly discovered memoirs of a Revolutionary General, L.S.M., material from other wars, the Revolutionary and the Napoleonic conflicts, the Spanish Civil War from Orwell's point of view, and the icy prelude to the Second World War. The narrator begins in a business-like way to describe what he reads in the short, choppy sentences of the uninvolved reporter: 'Il a cinquante ans. Il est général en chef de l'artillerie de l'armée d'Italie. Il réside à Milan' (*Les G*, 21). But the General is already in pieces, as the introductory sketch shows, and as is demonstrated in the achronic narrative: 'Il voit des points noirs. Le soir il sera mort. Il a trente ans. Il est capitaine. Il va à l'opéra' (*Les G*, 21). His papers are scattered and his story falls into disorder very rapidly, victim to the obsessive memories of the narrator that invade the text. As Jean Rousset observes: 'les deux rythmes fondamentaux sont représentés [...] selon la position des acteurs-narrateurs: il y a l'optique surplombante de qui raconte à distance [...] et l'optique rapprochée de qui subit le choc ultrarapide du combat et le perçoit de si près que le récit semble impossible.'[15]

However, there is more than a simple alternation of points of view, but a subtle melding of the two forms of narrative into a third, presenting the more reflective stance of the older writer. By page 22 the narrative drifts imperceptibly back into the Second World War, the shift only becoming evident with the appearance of words such as 'camionnette-radio' and 'parachutistes' in a text that otherwise might as easily refer to the General's army as to a modern one, and which links the two by the unlikely sounds of Gluck's *Orfeo e Euridice*. Entwined with these elements are glancing references to the scriptor, to the Spanish Civil War (*Les G*, 43, 51), and an ironic comment on the writer's previous attempts to record his experience (*Les G*, 52).

The fragments of the narrative become so densely interwoven that they overlap, and the sense of oscillation in time and space is increased by the use of italics for passages quoted from the General's documents. Further dislocation occurs in the final section of Part I: the narrator seems slyly hidden in the personage of the General, with the observation, 'La mort a une couleur de salissure, gris fer, charbonneuse et noirâtre dans le vert tendre', (*Les G*, 57), which recalls the words of the narrator of *La Bataille de Pharsale*: 'la mort même sanglante [...] avait aussi cette couleur grisâtre sale les bourgeons du printemps commençaient à éclater' (*BP*, 34). The writer emerges to comment on the task he has undertaken and its fragility: 'On dirait que les mots assemblés, les phrases, les traces laissées sur le papier par les mouvements de troupes, les combats, les intrigues, les discours, s'écaillent, s'effritent et

15 Rousset, 'Le Récit de guerre selon Claude Simon', p. 57. We may also refer to a recent dissertation by Laurent Ditmann, 'La Guerre et ses mots: problématique et pratique du roman de guerre chez Julien Gracq, Robert Merle et Claude Simon', Ann Arbor, MI, Dissertation Abstracts International, 1992, Mar. 52:9, 3304A DAI no. DA9204846.

tombent en poussière' (*Les G*, 76). If we add the glimpse of the writer's hand pausing on the page, we now have a condensation of at least five temporal moments impinging on one another, imparting a swirling movement to the text.

It seems then that there will be a return to the complexities of *La Route des Flandres*, with additional extensions in historical time. However, Section II (*Les G*, 79–139) offers a reversal by providing an almost straightforward account of the days of the cavalry regiment preceding the debacle of the Second World War. It is as though one thread had been pulled out of the tangle in Part I and developed in a traditional manner. Part III (*Les G*, 143–256) returns to the original mode, combining an explanation of the concealment and discovery of the General's papers with a visit to his ruined estate and the tomb of Marie Anne, with segments from his letters, and a glimpse of the 'vieille dame', his descendant, who had hidden the documents for shame behind the wallpaper, together with sudden excursions back to the Second World War and the prison camp – bizarrely evoked by the memory of the squalor of the gypsies in the cinema of the narrator's youth – as well as an attempt by the 'visitor' to locate the heavy marble bust of the General. Towards the end of the segment a mention of the General's spell of exile in Barcelona will lead into the fourth section, which is again a (relatively) conventional discussion of the miseries of the Spanish Civil War, and a fusion of the common experiences of the narrator and O. (George Orwell), a narrative slowed down by reflections on Orwell's background and the omissions and lack of honesty in his accounts.

The fifth section offers a long meditation on disintegration, of the General's body, of his ideals, of his property, of his writing, of his family, of France, of Europe, of an entire civilisation: 'un état de choses établi depuis des millénaires, condamné, balayé' (*Les G*, 371), interspersed with segments from the papers, leading into a headlong description of the General's later career and his downfall and exile in his own home, to contemplate his betrayal and the decaying tomb of his beloved first wife. The breakdown of the French Revolution into warring factions, the corruption of a nation parallels the dissolution of the body in the tomb – is it an accident that her name was Marie Anne? – and has intra- and intertextual echoes throughout the entire opus.

The momentum of this novel depends, then, on the equilibrium established between two types of narrative, the swirling patterns of Parts I and III, and the more regular, expository sections, II and IV, which come together in V, where meditation gives way to descriptive (but imaginary) passages of action, interspersed with transcriptions of the General's papers. The use of italics here seems ironic, since the transcriptions are generally in that script, while the suppositions of the narrator are in regular print, yet we learn '*Tout ce qui est en romain dans ce Précis, exprime un fait certain ou le texte d'une loi*' (*Les G*, 410).

What is new here is the vastly increased use of speculation, which allows the narrator to reinvent the thoughts and actions of others mirroring (< speculum) his own. Speculation has already been in use in *Le Vent* and *L'Herbe*, and also in the musings of Georges in *La Route des Flandres* that lead him to imagine the relationships between the jockey and Corinne, and to reconstruct the actions and death of an ancestor whose portrait 'bleeds' in the family home. The writer, who long ago decided that he could not 'invent' characters and plots, nevertheless uses projections stemming from available material to recreate events and thoughts of which he could have had no cognisance, and in *Les Géorgiques* uses them to a far greater degree than ever before. These projections are not, however, attributed to another character within the text, as with Georges or Louise in *L'Herbe*, but are presented as recorded experiences, for example, the probable feelings of the faithful Batti, or the struggles of Jean-Marie caught in the bog (*Les G*, 422–424), only a sprinkling of 'peut-être', or 'probablement', and the disconcerting italics, revealing the presence of the narrator. The effect is to anchor the narrative more directly in 'real' fiction, and hence to appear more conventional. The novel itself, however, through the critique of Orwell, contests the legitimacy of such reconstructions. Far from being a regression to past methods, the novel is, in fact, a compendium of all the skills acquired by Simon in the course of his work. In his constant experimentation he could say, with the General: '*vous me direz que je ne suis content de rien, et encore une fois croyez-vous que j'aie tant d'années à jeter par les fenêtres?*' (*Les G*, 477).

The attractive force is at work in the next novel, *L'Acacia*, widening still further the speculative domain of the writer, an extension that begins with the mother's search for the father's body, and that incorporates into the narrator's material a long examination and reconstruction of the father's experience in the First World War. Now there is constant exchange between all the examples of conflict known directly or indirectly by the writer: the battles of the ancient world revealed by childhood studies and later, by art; the revolutionary wars of the General; the First World War; the Spanish Civil War and the Russian Revolution; the Second World War. In addition, the reader learns of conflict within the family, the disparity between father's and mother's antecedents which makes the father's courtship like a siege, so that he is seen as 'l'homme qui était entré dans la famille pour ainsi dire par effraction, par ravissement' (*A*, 209). The pre-war travels of the narrator to Germany, Poland and Russia broaden the horizon still further, while the outward sweep of the narrative is matched with a downward plunge back into closer and closer detail of the original debacle, as through a magnifying glass, so that the now well-known accounts of the cavalry rout, the flight of the narrator and the prison train and camp, are brought into even clearer focus (*A*, 87–105, 153–161, 223–260, 283–306, 332–337).

The effect of these extensions in breadth and depth is to slow the pace of the novel, especially since the writer now deliberately divides the narrative into numbered and dated sections, and the effects of fragmentation are less visible because of a sense of willed organisation. The long, sweeping narratives now proceed with fewer interruptions, the mosaic being formed rather by the assemblage of different, lengthier sections. Violence is there, however, in the diegetics, as powerfully as ever, in the picture of a Europe geared for disaster twice over, in the expressed feelings of anger and helplessness of the participants in History's farce (*A*, 235), whose victims are sacrificial 'goats' (*A*, 348) delivered to the wolves of greed and stupidity.

The expository mode becomes even more marked in the later novel, *Le Jardin des Plantes*, in which the narrator, S., attempts to convey to a persistent journalist the feelings associated with the now famous debacle and imprisonment. The analysis of these feelings, and a recapitulation of the events, brings no more clarity than before, since language will be forever inadequate to represent the incredulity, the anger and the distress caused by the brute stupidity of war. The conflict lies deep within the self that wants and does not want to know what happened, and can never take control of an experience that was a denial of humanity, and consequently impervious to all definition. At best, S. will call it 'melancholy', at the cost of redefining melancholy itself.

Le Jardin des Plantes is a remarkable gathering of all the themes chosen by Simon, which now include his visit to Russia to attend a colloquium, and the Nobel prize-giving in Stockholm, comments on the work of the Italian painter, Gastone Novelli, Simon's trips to the far and middle East and the United States, and, of course, the layout of the Jardin des Plantes, part classical order, part artful 'nature', at the heart of the book, typifying the eclectic use of material both old and new. All these themes circle about the renewed investigation of forms of conflict, as experienced by the writer and, at a remove, as reported by others as well known as Rommel and Churchill, by Josef Brodski, the poet persecuted by the Soviets, by Trotsky, by the artist Novelli in a concentration camp. The text, often fragmented in original ways on the page to impede superficial reading, is inevitably drawn back, as though sucked in by an eddy, to the essential problem of writing what refuses to be written.

This eddying motion has often been remarked upon, in the first place by Simon himself, who compares it to the swarms of insects whirling on the summer air. It is figured also in many images of swirling water, 'faisant naître à la surface plane de l'eau de faibles ondulations rides se propageant concentriques s'agrandissant [...] ondulant au passage comme montant et descendant' (JP, 20). What has been less observed is the force that sets the movement going, the heart of the eddy, the series of persistent attacks on the flat surface of reality. This force in Simon's work is almost always the experience and memory of war.

If we follow the long trail of war and conflict throughout this work, we find that the energy that wells up at every appearance of the theme diversifies and expands, producing at the outset a concentrated attempt to seize on the elements of one core experience, followed by the ever-widening embrace of many related contingencies. Correspondingly, the writing also widens, becomes less closely packed, although still fragmented and dense with connections, the language less charged with destructive emotion, smoothed by the passage of years. Simon's writing about war, nevertheless, can be compared to a wounded man's efforts to dislodge a deeply embedded missile which 'demeure comme un traumatisme maintenant pour ainsi dire enkysté en lui à la façon d'un corps étranger, installé pour toujours' (JP, 337). The efforts are at first violent and frenetic, but eventually the foreign body is absorbed and, paradoxically, becomes part of the body.

Mention must be made of another and equal force of conflict, so closely linked to the war theme that it is inseparable from it: the sexual theme. It is an accepted dictum that the sexual urge becomes most pressing in the face of death, and that the soldier in the field, deprived of female company, thinks of sex incessantly, wishing for 'la petite mort' in place of the final version. This is certainly true of

Simon's narrator(s). In his texts the theme of sex follows almost immediately upon any sequence referring to war. Indeed, the first necessity of the escaped prisoner in *L'Acacia* on his return home is a prolonged indulgence in paid sex. The common soldier's vocabulary is filled with sexual terminology, even when he is not thinking explicitly of sex. The opening pages of *Le Jardin des Plantes* are remarkably organised to set the two themes side by side or diagonally on the same page, thus forcing the reader to connect them even more closely.

That sex can be and is destructive, being a form of violence, is not in doubt. (After all, was not Orion blinded for having been guilty of rape?) There are, in fact, few sexual sequences in Simon's work that represent it otherwise: the brief ecstasy of the narrator's mother, the 'primitif Eden' (*A*, 146), soon ended, and the devotion of the General to his first wife offer the most positive version. Generally, sex appears as a kind of physical one-to-one combat, as partners grapple and become definable only by their parts, female breasts, male and female genitals, described in close detail, the rest of the participants cut off and subordinated to the aggressiveness of lust. In the heat of sexual struggle, the actors are intensely aware of one another's bodies as objects unconnected with anything beyond their own desire. Sex is often presented as a spectacle, in conjunction with a circus, or a boxing match or other form of sport. If Georges in *La Route des Flandres* is interested in Corinne as he explores her body, it is only to find the answers to his own curiosity about women, about de Reixach and the jockey, not from any concern about her, as she clearly recognises.

Sexual appendages provide some of the most arresting images in Simon's writing. They appear almost as separate *objets d'art*, the male organ most obviously as an arrow, a shaft, a mechanism, a bud, a branch, the female as a mossy plant, a marine animal, an eye, a 'petit pertuis', and an object of worship, 'calice', 'hostie' (*JP*, 93). They seem to act independently of their owners, or rather, own their owners during consummation, and their symbols can crop up anywhere, on a barn door in Greece (*BP*, 39) or between the legs of an assassin, disguised as a gun (*P*, 99).

If feelings do intervene in the joust between Eros and Thanatos, they are even more destructive. Jealousy and desire make Charles/the narrator in *Histoire* so acutely conscious of detail as he stands in the corridor knocking at the door, behind which he suspects the model is betraying him, that he notices each drip of a leaky faucet and the patterns of decay on the wall, and hammers so hard on the door that he damages his hand. The disintegration of his self-control is such that he attracts the disapproving attention of neighbours, and he is willing to let his infatuation finally destroy his marriage, which in turn disintegrates and ends in tragic death. Similarly, the 'student' in *Le Palace* loses touch with reality as he fantasises about the American and a supposed lover. In *Les Corps conducteurs* there seems to be a connection between sickness and a failed relationship.

As a consequence of the intertwining of war and sexual themes, we may expect to find flashpoints in the text where the two meet, dragging the narrative back to (generally unhappy) encounters. In the segment from 'Bataille' mentioned above, we find just such flashpoints. The Dutchman in *Histoire* is notable for his red beard, and his image appears every so often to reawaken the jealousy of the narrator. So, on page 110 of *La Bataille de Pharsale*, inserted in a passage concerning the battle painting in which the combatants' faces are hidden by visors, there is a sudden eruption – 'me demandant où il pouvait bien fourrer cette barbe rousse enfant de putain' – and little by little this underground suggestion rises to the surface at the end of the section as the narrator looks at the position of the bodies depicted on the ground (*BP*, 122).

The sexual theme now becomes more and more insistent in the following pages, interrupting any attempt either to return to the discussion of painting or to observation of the scene before the writer, the latter containing elements of red which fatally drag back the narration to the love-making. The final paragraph of the segment combines the two irresistible elements: 'maintenant elle ne fait plus que crier mais je ne l'entends pas crier presque tous ont la bouche ouverte sans doute crient-ils aussi les uns de douleur les autres pour s'exciter au combat le tumulte est à ce point où l'on n'entend plus rien' (*BP*, 122). The calm artistic discourse has finally given way to the double excitement of combat on the field and in the bed. This combat is felt as dangerous as any on the battlefield, for, as Alastair Duncan and Celia Britton[16] have noted, it carries with it a basic male dread: that of castration. The sword plunged into the body is lethal to both partners in the sexual act.

Jealousy has its counterpart in infidelity, which, on the diegetic level, is a fertile theme in the novels. We need only think of the father of Montès in *Le Vent*, of Louise and Georges, and Pierre in *L'Herbe*, of

16 Duncan, 'Hierarchy and Coherence in Simon's Novels', p. 85; Celia Britton, *Claude Simon: Writing the Visible*, Cambridge, Cambridge University Press, 1987, p. 135.

the narrator/Uncle Charles in *Histoire*, of Corinne, the ancestor's wife and the peasant woman in *La Route des Flandres*, of the newly wed husband in *Triptyque*, of the lovers in *Leçon de choses*, even of the General during his campaigns. Without sexual infidelity, the text would lack impetus, and one of the characteristics of the jealousy it inspires is that it is self-nourishing, the fount of unceasing retelling of the same story, with additions and variations ad infinitum. The text itself is conflictual, like memory unfaithful to what it is saying because of the impossibility of telling, and consequently endlessly (re)productive, proliferating into new and extended versions of the narrative.

The sexual theme is, therefore, like war, an energiser, stirring up the text and breaking it apart, filling it with exotic references, treacherously ready to reappear in the middle of the most sober discussions. Like war, its language is also fragmented, reduced to incoherent cries, or to desperate unfinished sentences. Jealousy and remorse can only utter incoherent phrases: '*je souffrais images quelque chose absolument différent de ce que peut être pour toute autre personne une dame en gris un pourboire une douche altérées en leur matière même je ne les voyais pas*' (*BP*, 171); '*je souffrais comme...*' (*BP*, 46, 59, 75, 158, 168); '*je voudrais je voudrais je voudrais si je pouvais l'enlever l'arracher de moi retrouver la fraîcheur l'oubli Déjanire*' (*H*, 365); '*Oh Bon Dieu Bon Dieu Bon Dieu...*' (*H*, 374). Like war, sex is a physical experience that defies the efforts of language, yet challenges the user of language to try again and again to say what that experience was.

At this point it is necessary to recall another, completely different and contradictory, function of war. It has often been said that in wartime the creative faculties of humankind are stimulated to an exceptional degree, as much in the realm of technology as in the sexual and generative sense. Many of our most useful technological advances have come as a result of conflict. In *Leçon de choses* the masons have to pull down the house in order to reconstruct it, and although the reconstruction is never finished, it is always about to begin. In a similar way, the theme of the destruction of war is infinitely prolific as a productive source in writing, since it provides the stimulus for endless developments in every kind of scriptural device, from the extension of semantic links to the de/construction of the text. Ordinary terms are transformed by the military connection. In *La Route des Flandres* the innocent word 'vierge' takes on military as well as erotic connotations (*RF*, 10, 13) and the horse becomes the emblem of war and death (*RF*, 29). In *La Bataille de Pharsale* the humble pigeon is assimilated to a weapon of war (*BP*, 9). In *Leçon de choses* the common cow is both observer of the sexual struggle (*LC*, 102, 105) and victim of the conflict (*LC*, 22, 141), while the simple construction materials that the masons are demolishing – stone, mortar, plaster, wallpaper – are the same materials that are protecting the soldiers but that can come crashing down on their heads (*LC*, 44–45). In *Histoire* wine – 'frascati' – brings up a vision of soldiers drinking in a bistro (*H*, 336); the bank calculating machine simulates cavalry hoofbeats (*H*, 100); red cherries (*H*,154) link with an infinity of sexual connotations and by extension with Corinne, sex, blood, war, Barcelona and the death of de Reixach. Alastair Duncan points out the resonance in *Leçon de choses* of words like 'tireur', 'tire' and 'retirer', 'charge', 'chargeur' and by implication 'se décharger'.[17] Metaphoric connections are equally abundant, and although it is true that Simon has written about a great many other things besides war, it is often the case that those 'other things' eventually lead back to this obsessive theme.

It may be argued that conflict in one form or another is the natural basis of all types of fiction. Few writers, however, have attempted to make it the basis of the actual writing of the text, and even fewer have as effectively as Simon rendered the disorder, distress and disintegration that typify it. The true conflict in Simon is in any case taking place between the writer and the language that resists, with all the force of academic tradition, all attempts to demonstrate its inadequacies vis-à-vis the real. Simon's desire is towards his text and every one of his 'failures' is the pretext for further pursuit, like Georges's pursuit of Corinne, of the elusive, impossible ideal. In this sense, Simon is a romantic in the lineage of the Flaubert of *Education sentimentale*.

Second, we may seem to belabour the obvious by asserting the importance of the war theme in Simon's work. Yet its importance lies not only in its ubiquity, but in the impulse such a theme gives to the expansion of the entire panoply of the writer's art, and the insights it offers into the nagging problems of re-presentation, as well as into the metafictional notions of History and Truth. War is more than an obsession, it is a constant stimulus throughout the opus, interacting with the language that cannot 'say', yet cannot stop trying to say. Certainly Simon writes about 'other things'. It is notable, however, that conflictual themes are almost always dominant, and when they are not, there is a distinct modification of pace. In the later novels,

17 Duncan, 'Hierarchy and Coherence in Simon's Novels', p. 82.

Simon combines and alternates the two modes of writing, assembling them in varying degrees, expanding their use into a third form that allows for a more deliberate and reflective approach to the problem that he never ceases to address. The reader should be aware how the theme works in and on the text, imposing not only language and metaphor, but also its own rhythms, so that it is not merely the 'subject' but becomes the writing itself. As Simon himself reminds us, 'Pour moi, forme et fond ne sont qu'une seule et même chose',[18] and his work is a constant demonstration of how tight that bonding can be.

---

18 M. Chapsal, 'Entretien avec Claude Simon: "Il n'y a pas d'art realiste"', *La Quinzaine littéraire*, 15–31 décembre 1975, pp. 4–5.

5

Satire, Burlesque and Comedy
in Claude Simon

Alastair Duncan

Satire, burlesque and comedy are not primary characteristics of Simon's work. The subject matter of his novels derives not least from the trials and traumas of personal experience: the absence of his father, killed at the Front in 1914; the death of his mother when he was still a boy; early rejection of the Catholic faith in which he was brought up and of its secularised substitute, Marxism, which seduced so many young intellectuals of the inter-war years; above all, his personal experience of the debacle of 1940: eight days advancing then retreating on horseback before the German tanks, the annihilation of the regiment, the death in ambush of its colonel, Simon's own unaccountable survival. Hence flow many of the themes that dominate his fiction: war, death, grief and grieving, disillusionment, the meaning – if there is one – of history, and the fragmentary, haunting survival of experience in memory. Yet there is another side to Simon's work. The tragic tone of his novels is relieved not just by recurring delight in the sounds, smells, tastes and, above all, sights which the world offers in varied abundance. There are also moments of scrutiny of others and of the self, when judgements are passed, severe or clement, or when, from a distanced perspective, irony or humour lighten the load of history.

Since the publication of *Les Géorgiques* and *L'Invitation* critics have increasingly commented on Simon's sometimes stinging critique of linguistic usages, aesthetic principles, monolithic ideologies of progress and their flawed champions.[1] Not until the mid-1990s, however,

---

1 For example, Jean Duffy studied Simon's critique of the ideology of school textbooks in 'The Subversion of Historical Representation in Claude Simon', *French Studies*, vol. 41, no. 4, 1987, pp. 421–37; Cora Reitsma-La Brujeere, in *Passé et présent dans 'Les Géorgiques' de Claude Simon*, Amsterdam, Rodopi, 1992, pp. 63–106, analysed and reviewed other analyses of *Les Géorgiques* as in part a critical rewriting of Orwell's *Homage to Catalonia*; Pascal Mougin commented on Simon's 'ironie grinçante' in *L'Effet d'image. Essai sur Claude Simon*, Paris, L'Harmattan, 1997, p. 69.

did critical reflection begin to respond to Stuart Sykes's plea for a 'developed essay on parody, satire and irony'.[2] Mária Minich Brewer set parody in the context of postmodernism, while Pierre Schoentjes studied situational and verbal irony in *Les Géorgiques*.[3] Sykes's own remark that the tone of *La Route des Flandres* is 'à mi-chemin entre la comédie et le tragique'[4] was taken up in two 1997 articles. Alexandre Didier used Bergson and Freud to analyse techniques of irony and humour in *La Route des Flandres*; Nathalie Piégay-Gros studied how parody and competing narrative voices in that novel tip epic into burlesque.[5] Simon's own comments on this approach to his work have been few and relatively discouraging. He has expressed a distaste for verbal irony which, in the French tradition, as Schoentjes remarks, he tends to associate with the idea of mockery.[6] When asked some years ago about the function of humour in his novels, his reply was uncompromisingly brief: 'Sometimes a distancing function'.[7] *Le Jardin des Plantes*, however, aroused new interest in this topic: humour has been seen both as a general characteristic of this novel and more particularly in 'le portrait hilarant d'un journaliste'.[8] Maurice Roelens has used examples from *Le Jardin des Plantes* to show how Simon

2 S. Sykes. '*Parmi les aveugles le borgne est roi*. A personal survey of Simon criticism', in A. Duncan (ed.), *Claude Simon: New Directions*, Edinburgh, Scottish Academic Press, 1985, p. 151.
3 M. M. Brewer, 'Parody in Postmodernity: Replication and Cultural Critique', in *Claude Simon: Narrativities without Narrative*, Lincoln, NE, and London, Nebraska University Press, 1995, pp. 73–112. P. Schoentjes, 'Sous le signe de l'ironie. Le sort de LSM et celui de l'*Hommage à la Catalogne*', in *Claude Simon par Correspondance*, Geneva, Droz, 1995, pp. 47–70.
4 *Les Romans de Claude Simon*, Paris, Minuit, 1979, p. 12.
5 A. Didier, 'Rire, humour, ironie dans *la Route des Flandres* de Claude Simon', *Littératures contemporaines*, no. 3, 1997, pp. 133–50; N. Piégay-Gros, 'Légendes et affabulations dans *La Routes des Flandres*', *Littératures contemporaines*, no. 3, 1997, pp. 119–31.
6 'Héritier de la tradition française, Simon entend par "ironie" quelque chose d'assez proche de la définition qu'en donnaient Dumarsais et Fontanier et que la définition du Littré illustre parfaitement: "raillerie particulière par laquelle on dit le contraire de ce que l'on veut faire entendre"', *Claude Simon par Correspondance*, p. 58. Schoentjes is commenting on the discussion between Simon and A. C. Pugh, 'Interview with Claude Simon: Autobiography, the Novel, Politics', *Review of Contemporary Fiction*, vol. 5, no. 1, 1985, pp. 4–13.
7 'Interview with Claude Simon', in Duncan (ed.), *Claude Simon: New Directions*, p. 16.
8 B. Leclairc, 'Un Simon, sinon rien', *Le Nouvel Economiste,* 19 septembre 1997. See also, for example, Y. Preumont: 'L'humour enfin n'est pas absent et vient encore renforcer l'admiration qu'on peut avoir pour l'écrivain' ('Claude Simon. *Le Jardin des Plantes*', *Indications*, no. 5, 1997, p. 91); and D. Viart: 'Chez Claude Simon, cela ne va pas sans humour. Un humour dont le journaliste soucieux de son magnétophone fait principalement les frais' ('Remembrances et remembrement: cultiver les friches de la mémoire', *Scherzo*, no. 3, avril–mai 1998, p. 28).

discredits traditional accounts of war through caricature and mockery in popular style.[9] This essay aims to build on some of these perceptions. Starting from *Le Jardin des Plantes* – and finally returning to it – I shall look at Simon in mocking or self-mocking mood and consider where his work may raise a smile or even laughter. My approach is by means of genre. In moving from satire through burlesque to comedy, I seek help along the way from a range of critics and theorists.

Satire

At the beginning of *Le Jardin des Plantes*, the narrator presents himself as a black sheep, the only one of the party of distinguished visitors to the Soviet Union who refuses to sign the final humanitarian declaration. He resents the expectation that he will sing for his supper – the declaration is 'une addition à payer' – and objects to the clichés in which the supposedly collective beliefs are couched: 'Générations futures Récoltes que nous aurons semées. Nous savons tous que nous devons mourir mais nous voudrions que ce soit le plus tard possible' (*JP*, 13). Versions of this situation occur often in Simon's work: an outsider refuses to conform to the expectations, values and language of a group to which he or she might have been expected to belong. It happens twice more in *Le Jardin des Plantes*. S. appears as the provincial, reluctant and critical guest at a play-reading organised by the Paris literary and artistic establishment, united in their self-regard, their salon Marxism and their ignorance of the realities of war. Their beliefs and behaviour ring false when set against the memory that besets S.: the charred bodies of black, colonial troops witnessed at the Front. Twenty-six years later, S. is once more the outsider, this time at a *nouveau roman* colloquium, held at Cerisy in 1971. It appears that the events of his novel *La Route des Flandres* may have some relationship to lived and remembered experience. This runs counter to the prevailing orthodoxy: 'En montrant comment un texte doit être construit à partir des seules combinaisons qu'offre la langue ne se référant qu'à elle-même, Raymond Roussel n'avait-il pas ouvert (prescrit) au roman une voie dont on ne pouvait s'écarter sans retomber dans les erreurs (l'ornière) d'un naturalisme vulgaire?'(*JP*, 355). Simon's use of the 'style indirect libre' reverses the expected answers to these questions and pours scepticism on the defenders of the new creed.

9 M. Roelens, 'Figures de la "gouaille" et de la raillerie dans *Le Jardin des Plantes*', *Cahiers de l'Université de Perpignan*, no. 30, 2000, pp. 57–66.

Frequently in Simon's work, protagonists find themselves thus at odds with the dominant values of the community, among them Montès in *Le Vent*, Louise in *L'Herbe* and Georges in *La Route des Flandres*. Simon exploits this clash of values to satirise those of the dominant group. He seldom castigates vice: there is little moral impetus to his work, but rather the misguided foolishness of systems that attempt to explain or contain life by squeezing it into ordered patterns, whether political, social, religous or literary. Bakhtin may serve in part as a guide to the mode of Simon's satire. In analysing the comic novel, Bakhtin comments on its use of 'the parodic stylisation of generic, professional and other strata of language'. These generic languages embody 'the going point of view and the going value' of such groups; the author 'distances himself from this common language, he steps back and objectifies it, forcing his own intentions to reflect and diffuse themselves through the medium of this common view that has become embodied in language'.[10] To some extent this description corresponds to Simon's satirical practice, as can illustrated, for example, from the solicitor's monologue which begins *Le Vent*:

> 'Un idiot. Voilà tout. Et rien d'autre. Et tout ce qu'on a pu raconter ou inventer, ou essayer de déduire ou d'expliquer, ça ne fait encore que confirmer ce que n'importe qui pouvait voir du premier coup d'œil. Rien qu'un simple idiot. Seulement, lui, avec le droit de se promener en liberté, de parler aux gens, de signer des actes et de déclencher des catastrophes. Parce qu'il paraît que les médecins classent les types comme ça dans les inoffensifs. Très bien. C'est leur affaire. Mais si, au lieu de se contenter de leur avis, on demandait aussi celui des gens comme nous qui en savent peut-être un peu plus long sur l'espèce humaine que tous ces types de la Faculté... Parce que, écoutez-moi: en fait de spécimens humains tout défile ici, vous pouvez me croire, et en ce qui concerne les mobiles auxquels obéissent les gens, si j'ai appris quelque chose pendant les vingt ans que j'ai passés dans cette étude, c'est ceci: qu'il n'en existe qu'un seul et unique: l'intérêt. Et alors voilà ce que je dis...' (*V*, 9)

The solicitor's judgements and values are those of his caste and class, or at least the literary tradition's perception of that class, in a lineage which descends from Balzac to Mauriac.[11] Dismissing expert opinion,

10 M. M. Bahktin, 'Heteroglossia in the Novel', in Simon Dentith (ed.), *Bakhtinian Thought. An Introductory Reader*, London, Routledge, 1995, p. 197.
11 *Le Vent* is the story of a disputed inheritance. As in the many stories of potentially disputed inheritances from *La Rabouilleuse* to *Thérèse Desqueyroux*, members of the bourgeois class and their professional advisers assume that self-interest and, more particularly, the desire for wealth are the motives of all action.

the solicitor appeals to practical experience and common sense to affirm the absolute primacy of self-interest. Thus anyone failing to display that characteristic is excluded from the community of human beings, an idiot. The language of this speech catches the solicitor between two modes: the parataxical rhetoric of the courtroom rubs shoulders with the informal judgementalism of his private office. The very forcefulness of this language and the crudeness of the solicitor's judgements signal the author's distancing, satirical intent. The solicitor's certainties are undermined even before the narrator proceeds on the next page to question what knowledge any of us can have of events, motives, perceptions or feelings.

Elsewhere, Simon draws more explicit critical attention to the use of generic languages. In *La Route des Flandres* he replicates and parodies the speech habits of the officer class, used to mask the brute facts of war. 'Vilaine affaire', remarks de Reixach to an accompanying officer after the massacre of his squadron. Georges explodes: 'j'avais oublié que ce genre de choses s'appellent simplement une affaire [...] allons tant mieux rien n'était encore perdu puisqu'on était toujours entre gens de bonne compagnie dites ne dites pas "l'escadron s'est fait massacré dans une embuscade", mais "nous avons eu une chaude affaire à l'entrée du village de"'(*RF*, 165). In *Histoire*, Lambert scabrously parodies the language of the Mass (*H*, 326), but he is himself subject to ridicule when as a schoolboy he adopts for Uncle Charles's benefit a tone mingling slang with pseudo-sophisticated condescension (*H*, 213–23), and again when his language becomes that of the electioneering politician, promising to defeat 'les kominformistes'(*H*, 332). A much more radical reworking of a particular political language, invaded and transformed by the narrator's satirical intention, is to be found in *Le Jardin des Plantes*, in the reported speech of the Soviet leader:

> j'ai dit Très content de lui déclaré encore son pays ouvert à tout maintenant prolétaires veaux vaches vers de terre cochons ivrognes droit de tout lire tout voir tout entendre livres étrangers revues étrangères journaux étrangers disques films coca-cola et cetera et cetera tout absolument tout Sauf! Il a dit Sauf! Visage tout à coup sévère plus badin du tout plus question humanisme coca-cola intraitable résolu inflexible : Sauf pornographie! Pornographie strengt verboten Comme vodka strictly forbiden pericoloso absolument défendue Les deux Harlem gays très impressionnés respectueux Second mari de la plus belle femme du monde très respectueux aussi Moi déjà brebis galeuse mouton noir cochon Elle était toujours dans la même position amusée incrédule (*JP*, 17–18, quoted without the parallel section of text which sits typographically alongside it in the novel.)

Through the familiar comic technique of the incoherent list, the Soviet leader is charged with flawed values – coca-cola rather than free speech tops his list of permitted Western imports – and, centrally, with hypocrisy: he declares openness while maintaining censorship and controls. The multilingual telegraphese of his speech – possibly derived from the experience of a listener switching channels from one interpreter to another – has the satirical effect of placing much more emphasis on what is forbidden than on the new permissiveness: 'strengt verboten [...] strictly forbiden pericoloso absolument défendue'.[12]

But Simon's satirical use of heteroglossia is not limited to the exaggeration of parody. From *Histoire* onwards, he increasingly incorporates fragments of other texts into his own. Isolated and removed from their original contexts, these fragments often express values that are subverted by their new contexts. Such is the fate of the triumphalism of John Reed's history of the Russian Revolution when repositioned in *Histoire*, or Elie Faure's analysis of German painting in *La Bataille de Pharsale* (*BP*, 238). On a larger scale, *Leçon de choses* rewrites the textbook 'leçon de choses'

> Le tireur peut encore lire facilement le titre du paragraphe imprimé en gras mais il est obligé de rapprocher le livre de la fenêtre pour déchiffrer le texte en fins caractères: Nous n'avons parlé jusqu'à présent que de l'action des eaux continentales sur les pierres et les terrains; mais l'eau des mers peut agir aussi. Le vent soufflant à la surface de la mer produit les vagues, qui viennent parfois se jeter avec violence sur les côtes. La mer entame alors les bords du continent, elle fait effondre les roches et les terres, elle arrache les pierres les plus dures et les roule dans ses eaux. Comme dans le cas des eaux continentales, les roches seront détruites par la mer avec une inégale rapidité, suivant leur plus ou moins grande résistance. Lorsqu'une même roche aura des parties compactes et d'autres qui seront plus molles, les premières, moins vite démolies par les vagues, formeront au milieu de la mer des colonnes ou des piliers. Ainsi à Etretat (fig. 111), à Dieppe, etc [...] Le pourvoyeur pousse le coude du tireur et dit Ho Charlot j'te cause tu m'entends merde c'est le moment de bouquiner kes'tu lis? Il lui arrache le livre des mains, oriente les pages vers la fenêtre et lit le titre en caractères gras: 145. DESTRUCTION DES COTES PAR LES VAGUES. Il dit merde et la destruction des cons comme nous où c'est qu'ils en parlent? Il jette rageusement le livre. (*LC*, 95–96)

12 There is, on occasion, unintentional comedy in Simon's cavalier treatment of some foreign languages: here 'forbiden','strengt' for 'strengst'; later in the same novel (p. 184) a garbled quotation from Rommel which suddenly turns him into a near-illiterate; in *L'Invitation*, the delightful scribbled message from the famous American playwright married to the most beautiful woman in the world: 'They contempt us' (p. 65). Elsewhere in this volume, however, Mária Minich Brewer defends and justifies Simon's coining 'traveller-fellow'. See p. 57.

The satirical force of the passage lies not in the final gesture of rejection, which is almost redundant, but in the incongruities in context and register. The textbook is describing a phenomenon in the natural world that partly parallels the situation of the soldiers: they too are liable to be stormed by an irresistible destructive force. Yet the textbook's serene tone – the authoritative 'Nous', the universalising present and future tenses, the ordered and logical succession of ideas – imply a human mastery of events which is quite alien to the experience of the soldiers. The ammunition server's vernacular brutally disrupts this cosy myth of human control. Readers have been lulled into an expectation that the soldier's speech incongruously challenges, to comic effect.

A more recent example concerns once again Simon's denunciation of censorship in *Le Jardin des Plantes*. He quotes an inscription above the door of the University Library of Salamanca which threatens with excommunication any reader who defaces book, manuscript or document in the collection. But against this he juxtaposes a description of the library's precious copy of the Colloquia of Erasmus; lines, paragraphs and whole pages have been blacked out by none other than the library's guardians, acting as the censors of the Inquisition (*JP*, 33 and 36–37). To this technique of literal juxtaposition might be added Simon's use of implied juxtaposition, a technique that depends on the reader's knowledge of other texts. For example, the title of *Les Géorgiques* invites comparison with Virgil. For some readers the effect is satirical. Mary Orr, for example, sees Simon's novel as an ironic adaptation of Virgil. She illustrates how Simon deflates and undermines the idyllic, lyrical, bucolic and utopian aspects of the earlier *Georgics*.[13]

Bakhtin can no longer guide us, however, when we come to the most exuberantly satirical of Simon's earlier works. The patterns and rhythms of Blum's speeches in *La Route des Flandres* are not those of any professional group; nor are they to be distinguished from those of Georges. Intellectually, however, these two characters represent different responses to the traumatic events they have lived through. The target of Blum's scorn is the understanding of History to which Georges wishes to cling. Blum's contention – and that of the novel – is, first, that history is not an intelligible, rational, ordered sequence of events. Such sequencing arises when history's remains are reconstituted in

---

13 Mary Orr, *Claude Simon. The Intertexual Dimension*, University of Glasgow French and German texts, 1993, pp. 25–33.

language: 'un résidu abusivement confisqué, désinfecté et enfin comestible, à l'usage des manuels scolaires agréés et des familles à pedigree' (*RF*, 188). Taking the paradigm of the debacle of 1940, the novel demonstrates on the contrary that true history as lived and recounted is a matter of confusion, uncertainty and disorder. Second, history is not a matter of the great deeds (or the noble failures) of great men. The death of Georges's ancestor was not necessarily the 'pathétique et noble suicide' of a disillusioned revolutionary idealist defeated in battle; he could equally well have shot himself in reaction to his wife's adultery or been shot down at the bedroom door by his wife's lover.

Blum's imaginings subvert Georges's heroic version of his family history, not least through their verbal inventiveness and comic verve. Here is Blum challenging Georges to explain one of the supposed facts about his ancestor's death:

> Et Blum: «Mais n'as tu pas dit toi-même qu'ils l'avaient trouvé complètement nu? Comment l'expliquer, alors? A moins que ce ne fût l'effet de ses convictions naturistes? De ses émouvantes lectures genevoises? Est ce qu'il – je veux dire ce Suisse mélomane, effusionniste et philosophe dont il avait appris par cœur l'œuvre complète – est-ce qu'il n'était pas aussi un petit peu exhibitionniste? Est-ce que ce n'était pas lui qui avait la douce manie de montrer son derrière aux jeunes f...» (*RF*, 201)

Simon directs Blum's deflationary satire at the presumed source of Reixach's revolutionary ardour: 'ce Suisse mélomane, effusionniste et philosophe [...] un petit peu exhibitionniste'. His satirical weapons are, first, caricature: Rousseau is dispatched in a noun and four adjectives, and his idealism undercut by the earthiness of his 'douce manie'. Second, Simon plays with words: Rousseau did indeed have 'des convictions naturistes', but not in the delightfully anachronistic sense in which Blum applies the phrase to Rousseau and Reixach. Puns spangle Blum's discourse; their ambiguity of reference pours derision on the human desire to pin reality down in language. Finally, facetious hyperbole mocks Reixach: his enthusiasm for Rousseau is magnified and ridiculed by his reputed feat of memory: the complete works, we learn elsewhere in the novel, amounted to twenty-three volumes.

Burlesque

In *La Route des Flandres*, Blum's scepticism counters Georges's persistent, if ultimately defeated tendency to heroicise and idealise the family past. This tension characterises much of Simon's work. His novels are in some ways the reverse of epic. They are not emblematic stories of great heroes. They document the history of a family in decline, a novelist in revolt against what, through Blum, Simon calls a 'flatteuse légende familiale'(*RF*, 90). Yet undoubtedly Simon's work, or some of it, has epic qualities. Ezra Pound famously defined the epic as 'a poem including History'.[14] Although for Simon, history is not the story of great men and great deeds, he does not abandon history. If he debunks the great, he elevates the ordinary: 'si endurer l'Histoire (pas, s'y résigner: l'endurer), c'est la faire, alors la terne existence d'une vieille dame, c'est l'Histoire elle-même, la matière même de l'Histoire' (*L'H*, 36). What is true of an old lady forced to flee her home in May 1940 – the subject matter of *L'Herbe* – is equally so of a cavalryman lost and buffeted at the Front in the same conflict. In his works of the 1980s and 1990s Simon goes even further. He resurrects the family legend in a new form, linking the peasantry of the Jura to the *grand bourgeois* descendants of a Revolutionary general, and, in *L'Acacia*, placing the writer himself as the product and at the apex of this mythical history of France since the Revolution. In addition, many of his works are epic in scale: in their love of digression, their Homeric interest in nature and in observing the world about them. It might appear, then, that in the long battle with Georges, Blum is ultimately the loser – were it not that Blum's questioning spirit constantly dances attendance on the novels. Simon's perspective slides between epic and burlesque.[15]

Conventionally, the burlesque takes two forms: high burlesque, in which a relatively important subject is ludicrously degraded by the style of presentation; low burlesque, in which the style of presentation ludicrously elevates a relatively trifling subject.[16] Simon uses both these forms.

Blum's deflation of Reixach is classic high burlesque: disillusioned idealist becomes cuckolded husband. Later in Blum's account the circumstances veer towards farce: Virginie's valet lover emerges to shoot Reixach from concealment in a wardrobe. When in *Les Géorgiques* Simon next portrays a Revolutionary general, and at much greater

14 Ezra Pound, *ABC of Reading,* London, Faber and Faber, 1961, p. 46.
15 Cf. D. Alexandre: 'Le récit simonien oscille entre le tragique ou l'épique et le guignolesque ou le grotesque' ('Rire, humour et ironie dans *La Route des Flandres* de Claude Simon' *Littératures contemporaines,* no. 3, 1997, p. 135); N. Piégay-Gros: 'le renversement du tragique en comique, de l'épique en burlesque apparaît donc comme une sorte d'arasement des significations' ('Légendes et affabulations dans *La Routes des Flandres*', p. 123.)
16 John D. Jump, *Burlesque*, London, Methuen, 1972, p. 1.

length, both epic and mock epic are similarly present. L.S.M is heroic in stature, in energy, in commitment to the service of the Revolution and the Empire, unflagging into old age in exercising mastery over his possessions and estate. Part 3 of *Les Géorgiques*, however, is largely cast in the mould of the burlesque. The twentieth-century descendant of the General is shown round the ruins of his ancestor's château by a 'baboon-man' and an 'idiot (*Les G*, 152ff.); the General's crest now survives only as brandmark on bottles of a cheap apéritif (*Les G*, 151). The General himself loses will and agency: he figures as a marble bust manhandled round the battlefields of Europe (*Les G*, 243–56). And the narrator visits the last known whereabouts of the bust in vain. He finds only a weasel-faced bankrupt property speculator; the bust, and most of the other furniture in his flat, has been seized and sold to pay his debts (*Les G*, 235–38).

Low burlesque, on the other hand, the ordinary humorously elevated, is to be found in Simon's distinctive use of a characteristic of the epic, the recurrent epithet. Hélène, the pregnant bourgeois matron of *Le Vent* becomes 'la Junon, l'altière déesse de la fécondité' (*V*, 113); Maurice in the same novel is described as 'le Brummel au rabais'(*V*, 133); Sabine in *L'Herbe* is 'la vieille reine de la tragédie' (*L'H*, 93). Blum mocks some of the main actors in the comic peasant subplot in *La Route des Flandres* by calling them Romeo, Othello and Vulcan (*RF*, 127, 128, 282). As with names, so also Simon elevates certain situations and incidents to comic effect: in *L'Herbe* the mock epic search for Sabine's jewellery, tipped accidentally down the pan of a train toilet; the protagonist's visit to a bank in *Histoire*, cast in terms of a consultation with the Sphinx (*H*, 99).

In *Le Vent*, the mingling of genres is highlighted by the running comparison of Montès's story with drama of the Spanish Golden Age, 'un de ces trucs de Calderon ou de Lope de Vega, une de ces comédies-dramas à multiples journées réparties dans, ou plutôt exhumées, émergeant sporadiquement hors d'un temps vague, d'une incertaine durée trouées d'épisodes burlesques ou macaroniques' (*V*, 112). Such episodes include Maurice's attempts to ingratiate himself with Montès, and Hélène's night-time encounter with Jep. The following extract illustrates Simon's burlesque equivalent of the extended Homeric simile – a vaulting elaboration of related images and comparisons. Montès has just been knocked down and out by the gypsy Jep:

Il chercha Thérésa des yeux mais ne la vit pas. Ni Jep. Ni non plus la grosse auto cabossée qui quelques instants auparavant était encore enlisée dans sa litière d'immondices et servait de support à l'extrémité d'une corde à linge. «Parce qu'ils avaient même réussi à la faire partir, me dit-il. Je croyais qu'elle avait pris racine là, qu'ils l'engraissaient à pleins tombereaux d'ordures dans l'espoir peut-être de la voir se mettre à pousser, grandir jusqu'à ce qu'elle soit devenue suffisamment vaste pour y planter une cheminée et y loger une tribu entière, mais ils avaient tout de même réussi à la faire partir.» Ce ne fut qu'au bout d'un moment qu'il s'avisa qu'il n'avait pas encore vu un seul des hommes. Tout d'abord il pensa qu'ils s'étaient peut-être tous attelés à la vieille quarante chevaux pour remplacer ceux-ci, emporter Jep dans une sorte d'apothéose, d'antique triomphe, la cohue des gitans courant sur la route en tirant à grands cris derrière eux la carrosse de vieilles tôles et, dedans, trônant sur les coussins à têtière, leur champion victorieux. Puis il comprit. (*V*, 124)

An old banger metamorphoses into a chariot and a broken-down boxer into a Roman victor. But this instance of low burlesque has been preceded by another transformation with an echo of high burlesque: the car, twentieth-century man's royal mode of transport, lies embedded in rubbish and is being reclaimed for human use through the natural cycle of growth and decay. This is typical Simon of almost any decade except the 1970s, worrying an image, tossing it up and down through various registers and tonalities. The combination of epic with mock epic arises here from the context. Montès's story has elements of farce: these images of metamorphosis are presented as his speculations, incongruous in a man who has just been assaulted. They reinforce his image as a clown-like figure, a scarecrow and punch-bag. But equally and simultaneously, Montès's story has a tragic resonance: his blundering persistence in doing good brings about the death of the woman he loves and his expulsion from the town. Similarly, Pierre and Sabine in *L'Herbe* are not just grotesques, de Reixach in *La Route des Flandres* not just a hollow man. Like L.S.M in *Les Géorgiques*, these characters are victims of History who will not give up: their resilience is both derisory and heroic. Simon views them with irony and admiration. In *Le Jardin des Plantes* Simon refers us to some literary models of this double vision: 'les événements les plus tragiques ont souvent un côté dérisoire et ce dérisoire en augmente le tragique, voir Cervantes, Shakespeare, "mon royaume pour un cheval", sans parler de la Bovary'(*JP*, 260). Burlesque and epic give depth to Simon's portrayal of human beings and their fate.

Comedy

Wolfgang Iser offers a further means of approaching this combination of tragic vision with comic tonality. In an essay devoted to a writer who combines the same characteristics, though not in the same proportions – 'The Art of Failure: the Stifled Laugh in Beckett's Theatre' – Iser invites us to understand comedy by studying 'the relationship of mutual influence between its structures and the acts of human behaviour moulded by these structures', that is to say, laughter. Blending Freud's views with traditional analyses, he argues that the essence of comedy is 'the contradiction, the contrast between imagination and reality, the clash or violation of norms, the nullifying of current values'.[17] And, following Nietzsche and Freud, he argues that laughter is a means of relieving the perplexity and even anxiety of these contradictions.

Clearly, this attempt to define the theatrical essence of comedy through a combination of audience response and internal features – loosely defined as 'structures'– cannot be directly applied to the novel. The effect of theatre on its audience is direct, unmediated; the relief of laughter is a collective experience. On the other hand, the reader of a novel sits alone; the interplay of character and situation to which he or she is exposed is mediated always by the written word and sometimes – in Simon's case frequently – by a narratorial consciousness. Yet that last factor may allow us in part to transpose Iser's way of looking at things from theatre to novel: within the novel itself, a reflecting consciousness can determine perspectives, can choose to perceive events as tragic or comic and thus set a tone for the reader. There is, however, another comment to be made on Iser's thesis, a missing element which comes to light when we consider a remark such as the following: 'the less our mastery of events, the greater the anxiety, the more vehement our physical reactions'.[18] Here Iser is still discussing comedy and laughter. The missing element in this argument can be illuminated from Simon. An absence of mastery, a high pitch of anxiety, the nullifying of current values: all these are archetypal features of Simon's many accounts of the debacle. While the terror of imminent death might of itself be thought sufficient cause for anxiety,

---

17 Wolfgang Iser, 'The Art of Failure: the Stifled Laugh in Beckett's Theatre', in *Prospecting: From Reader Response to Literary Anthropology*, Baltimore, MD, Johns Hopkins University Press, 1989, p. 152.
18 Iser, 'The Art of Failure: the Stifled Laugh in Beckett's Theatre', p. 155.

Simon repeatedly emphasises even more the collapse of all established patterns of order: 'c'était comme si non pas une armée mais le monde tout entier et non pas seulement dans sa réalité physique mais encore dans la représentation que peut s'en faire l'esprit [...] était en train de se dépiauter se désagréger s'en aller en morceaux, en eau, en rien'(*RF*, 16–17). Yet neither Georges nor, following his cue, the reader is inclined to find relief from this discomfiture in laughter. Iser's argument omits the qualification that the comic perspective requires anxiety to be either limited or distanced. Slipping on a banana skin shows how quickly human dignity may fall prey to the contingent; but the consequent disquiet may find relief in laughter only if the victim does not fracture his skull, or if the fracture has now healed, or perhaps if the victim, in self-defence, seeks to make light of his injury.

It is this last case which is first to be found in Simon's work. Montès is self-aware. Caught up in a sequence of events beyond his control, he watches himself, 'assistant impuissant navré et ironique au déroulement de sa propre vie'(*V*, 74). He is characterised by 'une sorte d'humour innocent et étonné'(*V*, 30), a means of survival, of coping with events otherwise too hard to bear. In this response to private catastrophe Montès prefigures later characters in Simon's work who will react similarly to the experience of war. Blum's rampant speculations and word-play, the ribald backchat of soldiers in *La Route des Flandres* and *Leçon de choses* are means of distancing the horror of war or prison camp. The various versions of Georges, the cavalryman of 1940, who appear in the novels from *La Route des Flandres* onwards share Montès's capacity to be both participant and distanced observer. On occasion this distance allows a comic perspective. Fleetingly but recurrently they record their astonishment at war's many violations of established norms while wryly acknowledging the incongruity of that astonishment. The motif is made explicit in *Le Jardin des Plantes* when S. reports his first experience of coming under fire:

> ça y est: la peur. Animale, incontrôlable, aussi incontrôlable que votre cheval emballé dont vous sentez confusément les muscles se tendre et se détendre entre vos cuisses en même temps que, paradoxalement (il y a de quoi rire: c'est vraiment ridicule, puisque vous êtes là précisément pour ça), ... en même temps que vous éprouvez comme une sorte d'indignation scandalisée: Mais sapristi on essaye de me tuer! Sapristi on cherche pour de bon à me tuer! (*JP*, 82)

War nullifies the value normally placed on human life: in a metaphor Simon often uses, the hunter becomes the hunted. However, war can also overturn norms which are less weighty, but as deeply ingrained. In *L'Acacia* the cavalryman is astonished to find that the colonel leading his tiny troop of survivors is riding a draught-horse, even although his batman is leading two saddled mounts. An attempt to explain this affront to convention leads to grotesque speculation:

> pensant A moins que ce ne soit comme au polo quand ils changent de chevaux à chaque arrêt du jeu donc maintenant un percheron, pensant encore Ou peut-être qu'il le conserve comme l'irrécusable témoignage de son honneur sauvegardé [...] pensant encore. Mais peut-être qu'il le garde dans l'intention de se présenter ainsi à la grille du quartier général dans toute sa gloire, ramenant triomphalement avec lui un percheron deux cavaliers et deux cyclistes. (*L'A*, 291, 293)

Elsewhere, perplexed astonishment leads to a switch in codes: in *La Route des Flandres*, when even the norms of war appear to have been breached – there is no more Front (*RF*, 110) – then perhaps History can be understood as farce: successive waves of tanks from the opposing armies appear to be pursuing one another repeatedly through the same village.

Comedy plays a larger part in *Le Jardin des Plantes* than in any previous novel. The prerequisite for that comedy is greater distance from the traumatic events of the past. First, there is distance in time: the novel is set in the 1990s. As the writer, S., flies over Flanders, he can scarcely pick out the battlefields on which he advanced and fled (*JP*, 154); the memories have faded, 'même pour moi, c'était maintenent comme quelque chose d'étranger, sans réalité' (*JP*, 83). There is distance also in that the writer's memories of war have passed through many relays. They are memories of memories and memories of texts, successively fictionalised, refictionalised and to some degree de-fictionalised as the gulf between Claude Simon and his characters narrows here to the paper-thin – yet unbridgeable – gap between the novelist Simon and his fictional counterpart S. This paradoxical closeness yet distance is advertised in the novel by the device of the interviewing journalist. In *Le Jardin des Plantes*, for the first time, the events of 1940 are not reworked directly into a new fiction. Instead S. is forced to return to them by a reader of his novels who wants to get at the facts behind the fiction. His vain and bumbling attempts to do so provide much of the comedy of the work.

The journalist wants to know how S. coped with fear on the Flanders road. What was it like to be shot at, exhausted, sleepless? How long did it all last?

> Il a dit Seulement huit jours? J'ai dit Seulement. Oui. J'ai essayé de prendre un ton de plaisanterie j'ai dit Par contre aux places de choix, aux fauteuils d'orchestre comme on dit dans le jargon du rugby pour les poids lourds de la première ligne Sauf que je n'étais pas catégorie poids lourds mais dans une de ces divisions dites légères que les règles du Service en campagne modèle 1870 veulent qu'on envoie d'abord entamer la conversation prendre langue en quelque sorte et que malheureusement ceux d'en face ne semblaient pas connaître ce manuel 1870 et qu'ils étaient le contraire de légers et que quant à la conversation ils avaient tout de suite commencé par les gros mots Ah ah ah!... Mais il me regardait d'un air réticent, comme gêné, réprobateur même. (JP, 77)

There is a familiar humour in this jocular tone. The profusion of mixed metaphors are a means of self-defence. Through distancing, they seek relief in laughter from the threat that is both imminent death and war's apparent violation of its own norms, in this case ironically defined as the rules laid down in the long-outdated Campaign manual for 1870. More unexpected is the treatment of a theme that Simon first made explicit in *Histoire*: the impossibility of conveying the experience of battle to those who have not experienced it for themselves (*H*, 152). No longer, however, is this theme the source of an anguished sense of the individual's isolation. Although S. fails to communicate his experience to the journalist, thus thwarting our expectation that language will result in communication, our discomfiture is not so serious that we cannot laugh. On the contrary, we laugh with S. at the journalist, who fails completely to grasp that chronological time has no meaning in the context S. describes: eight days can last a lifetime, and take a lifetime to come to terms with. His response to S.'s jocular tone compounds the comedy of misunderstandings: 'Mais il me regardait d'un air réticent, comme gêné, réprobateur même'. In short, the journalist begins here by belittling the novelist's experience – 'seulement huit jours' – and ends by implicitly chiding him for treating it with inappropriate facetiousness.

Elsewhere in *le Jardin des Plantes*, Simon's comedy is multi-layered.

> Mais j'ai déjà raconté tout ça, s'interrompt S., je... Mais le journaliste dit que Non ou plutôt que Oui mais pas comme ça, que S. a mis tout ça est-ce qu'on peut dire à une sauce romanesque si le journaliste peut se permettre, que par exemple S. a fait du conducteur du cheval de main un jockey et que jamais un jockey ne brutaliserait comme ça un cheval, même à bout de nerfs, et que le colonel devenait un simple capitaine, S. inventant toute une combinaison de facteurs psychologiques et d'antécédents comme de laisser entendre une affaire de jalousie Que non, S. ne devait pas prendre ça pour

une critique, le journaliste ne se le permettrait pas et que d'ailleurs c'était très réussi mais que c'était encore plus intéressant d'entendre raconter sans ces enjolivements (que S. ne prenne pas ce mot en mauvaise part) les faits bruts simplement dans leur matérialité. (*JP*, 272)

Here, as in the previous extract, social conventions are flouted: however attenuated by polite disclaimers, one does not tell a distinguished writer to his face that his novels travesty his own experience, that 'il a mis tout ça à une sauce romanesque'. Social ineptitude combines here with theoretical naïvety. Drain off the literary sauce and we would be left with the brute bare facts: this view implies a one-to-one relationship between language and reality that is as erroneous, in Simon's view, as its counterpart at the other end of the spectrum, represented in *Le Jardin de Plantes* by the quotation from the Cerisy colloquium of 1971: that the function of language is not at all to represent experience.

There is, however, a final layer of comedy to be peeled from this extract. The literary naïvety satirised here is not exclusively that of the journalist. What is here distanced, exaggerated and parodied in the journalist is a facet of Simon's own aesthetic. Readers with long memories will recall that Simon himself once spoke about the 'scories' in his works which he successively sought to eliminate.[19] When interviewed by a journalist after publication of *La Route des Flandres*, he defended the narrative gaps and jumps in that novel on the grounds that the work thus more adequately represented lived experience and how memory functions – brought it closer, one might say to 'les faits bruts [...] dans leur matérialité'.[20] From *L'Herbe* onwards he began to rewrite character and events from his earlier fiction, bringing them closer to historical truth. From *Histoire* the family of *L'Herbe* and *La Route des Flandres* were recast to become increasingly fictional equivalents of his own maternal and paternal families. In *Les Géorgiques* for the first time he attributed to a single containing consciousness the hitherto disparate experiences of a pious childhood, the Spanish Civil War, and Flanders in 1940. Despite all this, Simon is not prey to the

---

19 Claude Simon, 'Discussion', following 'La Fiction mot à mot', in Jean Ricardou and Françoise van Rossum-Guyon (eds), *Nouveau roman: hier, aujourd'hui*, Paris, UGE, vol. 2, 1972, p. 107.

20 'Je ne comble pas les vides. Ils demeurent comme autant de fragments. Ces bribes de souvenir, pourquoi chercher de les classer en ordre chronologique? [...] Dans la mémoire tout se situe sur le même plan: le dialogue, l'émotion, la vision coexistent.' (C. Sarraute, 'Avec *La Route des Flandres* Claude Simon affirme sa manière', *Le Monde*, 8 octobre 1960, p. 9.)

illusion of realism, to the belief that you can tell history as it was – or perhaps rather he has left that belief far behind. Yet the urge to strip away literary artifice, to be true to history, memory and personal experience remains one of the recurring motifs and self-imposed challenges of his work. In the portrait of the journalist Simon acknowledges this tendency in his work and the extent to which his aesthetic might consequently seem to border on self-contradiction, apparently both denying representation and seeking it. This gentle, self-directed irony of a writer confident and at ease with himself is one of the many charms of Le Jardin des Plantes.

Conclusion

Kant wrote that 'Laughter is an affection arising from the sudden transformation of a strained expectation into nothing'.[21] In thus linking philosophy to physiology he set the basis for the influential theory that humour arises from a perception of incongruity.[22] Much of Ionesco's theatre, for example, may be taken as a particular illustration of this thesis: laughter arises when reason is disappointed. The perception of incongruity may equally be seen as an essential aspect of Simon's work. Simon repeatedly disrupts the expectation of order or progress. His satire is directed at individuals, groups or discourses that fail to acknowledge the gulf between expectation and reality. The effect can be comic when the act of disruption is, as Kant prescribed, sudden and unexpected, for example, the ammunition server's brutal challenge to the tone and presuppositions of the textbook 'Leçon de choses'. Equally, the effect can be humorous when an individual catches himself out in what is suddenly perceived as an unwarranted expectation of order, such as S. reports of his first experience of coming under fire in Le Jardin des Plantes.

A second crucial idea is that of self-defence. Freud wrote of humour that '[i]ts fending off of the possibility of suffering places it among the great series of methods which the human mind has constructed to evade the compulsion to suffer'.[23] And another Simon, Richard Keller

21 Immanuel Kant, in The Critique of Judgement, quoted in Richard K. Simon, The Labyrinth of the Comic, Talahassee, FL, Florida State University Press, 1985, p. 192
22 See John Morreal (ed.), The Philosophy of Laughter and Humor, Albany, NY, State University of New York Press, 1987, esp. chs 8, 9,17 and 19.
23 Sigmund Freud, 'Humour', in The Complete Psychological Works of Sigmund Freud, trans. J. Strachey, London, Hogarth Press, 1961, vol. 21, p. 163.

Simon, has argued that to see the comic as a 'defense against pain and suffering' became 'the conventional wisdom of the twentieth century'.[24] This psychological aspect of humour is clearly important in Simon. Set in extreme situations, terrified and disorientated, his characters and narrators seek comfort by distancing themselves through humour. The tone varies from the ironic grumbling of the older mason in *Leçon de choses* to the hectic rants of Blum in *La Route des Flandres*.

Lastly, humour cannot be dissociated from the idea of play. R. K. Simon points out that this aesthetic aspect of humour was central to the views of Schiller and the German romantics: 'For all of them, whatever the term, the comic experience was important because it led to the truth of existence, to the contradiction between the most basic of antimonies, and beyond that because it offered a way out, a way of understanding and then living with the human predicament'.[25] This may be the best perspective in which to see the intermingling of genres in Simon, in particular the switching between epic and burlesque. Changing perspectives offer a space for play. In later novels, especially *Le Jardin des Plantes*, that space seems greater. Although anger subsists, pain and suffering recede; there is room for social comedy, for teasing and amused self-deprecation. For Simon, perhaps, pain has been muted and transmuted by sixty years of the hard but profitable labour of playing with words. For Simon's readers, these fluctuating perspectives, including that of the comic, are a measure of the depth of his humanity.

24 Richard K. Simon, *The Labyrinth of the Comic*, p. 209.
25 Richard K. Simon, *The Labyrinth of the Comic*, p. 217.

6

The Garden of Forking Paths: Intertextuality and *Le Jardin des Plantes*

Mary Orr

Although Claude Simon cited Borges in interviews and lectures from the late 1960s onwards,[1] his name is absent from the *Discours de Stockholm*.[2] This is a striking omission given that, in this text, Simon refers in condensed form to the majority of the writers, painters and works of high cultural art of which he had spoken throughout his career as writer. Nor has Borges received much attention from critics as precursor or intertext in Simon's *œuvre* in general,[3] or in *Le Jardin des Plantes* in particular.[4] Yet scrutiny of Borges's *The Garden of Forking Paths* as intertext in *Le Jardin des Plantes* offers key insights into the control of interwoven narratives that is central to highly self-referential writing. The first part of this essay offers a comparative reading of Borges to suggest a form of 'réécriture' which I term an 'espionage' of writing. The second part of this essay then explores some of the more general ways in which *Le Jardin des Plantes* adds to Simon's *œuvre* 'as a paradigm of intertextuality in its many guises, on large and small scales and including self quotation'.[5] My intention is to consider ways

---

1 For example, B. L. Knapp, 'Interview avec Claude Simon', *Kentucky Romance Quarterly*, vol. 16, no. 2, 1969, p. 182; K. Biro-Thierbach, 'Claude Simon sur les sentiers de la création', *Gazette de Lausanne*, 27–28 juin 1970, p. 32; 'Claude Simon: la voie royale du roman', *Le Nouvel Observateur*, 6 février 1982, p. 74.
2 *Discours de Stockholm*, Paris, Minuit, 1986.
3 Even monographs concentrating on intertextuality and Simon (including my own *Claude Simon: the Intertextual Dimension*, Glasgow, French and German Publications, 1993) or on his twentieth-century precursors (for example, Michael Evans, *Claude Simon and the Transgressions of Modern Art*, London, Macmillan Press, 1988) omit Borges as a major figure, concentrating instead on Faulkner or Proust.
4 In her recent monograph, Annie Clément-Perrier uses the same allusion to Borges's 'sentiers qui bifurquent', but only as a metaphor of the writing process; she does not develop any deeper intertextual reverberations between these fictions (*Claude Simon: la fabrique du jardin*, Paris, Nathan, 1998, pp. 31 and 119).
5 Orr, *Claude Simon: the Intertextual Dimension*, p. 203.

in which intertextual self-consciousness is given new authorial twists in *Le Jardin des Plantes*. Not only does Simon reincorporate materials which belong to those early works he assured critics he wanted to forget or deprecated as 'espèces de fourre-tout';[6] the Author as persona (*contra* Barthes) is more alive than ever in *Le Jardin des Plantes* and reveals his hand in this novel in ways which have not been so visible since the incipit of *Orion aveugle*.[7] Claude Simon's novels are all so many ways of establishing a 'final' version from 'scénarios' rewritten from novel to novel, like the many drafts which issued from the pens of a Flaubert or a Proust. As Simon said himself, as early as 1967, 'mes livres sortent les uns des autres comme des tables gigognes. Je n'aurais pu écrire *Histoire* sans avoir écrit *Le Palace*, ni *Le Palace* sans *La Route des Flandres*. En général, c'est avec ce qui n'a su être dit dans les livres précédents que je commence un nouveau roman.'[8] 'La production du texte' then takes on meanings beyond those intended by Ricardou, not least in that critic's own intertextual inclusion in *Le Jardin des Plantes* (*JP*, 356–57). This novel, I will argue, fictionalises what are normally seen to be strictly the domains of the critic: theories of literature, postmodernist critical theories, and, at the pinnacle of close reading and textual hermeneutics, genetic studies. Simon, *self-critic* of Simon, replies in *Le Jardin des Plantes* to the critical enterprise and to his previous works.

Borges and *The Garden of Forking Paths*

Although neglecting Borges, critics have frequently referred to South American motifs (the writers' congress, the Amazon forest) which are seen as textual generators of *Orion aveugle* and *Les Corps conducteurs*. Here, through *bricolage* techniques, Simon experimented more with the spatial form and a geography of the text than with fictional reference. Paradoxically, it is the image of the maze (*Labyrinths* is the title of Borges's collection)[9] and the reference in *Le Jardin des Plantes* to the man-made encyclopedic garden (see Borges's *Tlön, Uqbar, Orbis Tertius* in the same collection) in a Paris that may be visited, that makes the

6 C. Paulhan, 'Claude Simon: "J'ai essayé la peinture, la révolution, puis l'écriture"', *Les Nouvelles littéraires*, 15–21 mars 1984, p. 44.
7 *Orion aveugle*, Geneva, Skira, 1970.
8 T. de Saint Phalle, 'Claude Simon, franc-tireur de la révolution romanesque', *Le Figaro Littéraire*, 6 avril 1967, p. 7.
9 All references to Borges's *The Garden of Forking Paths* are to the story in *Labyrinths*, Harmondsworth, Penguin, 1970.

forgotten Borges intertext, as it were, turn up. Hidden under accumulations of writing, it is the new material in *Le Jardin des Plantes* – namely the war journals of Rommel, the game of cat and mouse between Churchill and the Nazis – that flushes it out. Direct comparison of the two works reveals further thematic reverberations as well as parallel concerns about the ideology of representation.

Borges's *The Garden of Forking Paths* opens with a series of *mises en abyme*, of which the first is a quotation from page 22 of Liddell Hart's *The History of World War I* (an attack against the Serre-Montaubon line by thirteen British divisions).[10] This intertext, repeated, 'dictated, reread and signed by Dr. Yu Tsun, former professor of English at the *Hochschule* at Tsingtao' (*The Garden of Forking Paths*, 44) becomes a cypher for the ensuing murder and high espionage plot of the tale which hinges on the revelation of a name. A riddle written on a body (which is also a text about a maze which is a book and a person) presents the conundrums of signifiers and signifieds, of right meanings and wrong: all these are intensified by the paratextual materials which intrude in these opening paragraphs. The most forceful is the Editor's note, which serves as both hypothesis and 'fact'. To add further zest to the play of narrative 'authorities', two pages of the document are missing, and the whole is one end of a telephone conversation. Simon's earlier *Les Corps conducteurs* is suddenly a *cousin germain* for it bears many such multimedia hallmarks, but without the obvious range of textual interreferentiality that Borges's story and Simon's latest novel illustrate.

In *The Garden of Forking Paths* and *Le Jardin des Plantes*, there are similar cross-pollinations of *topoi*. In Borges's story, the narrator looks through his window from his bed and a bird translates into an aeroplane which triggers the protagonist's military involvements and his visceral terror. In *Le Jardin des Plantes* (for example, pp. 312–13), the convalescent narrator lies in bed and looks out of the window. The theme of indescribable terror also punctuates *Le Jardin des Plantes* (for example, pp. 178, 236). *The Garden of Forking Paths* ends with the narrator's existential weariness; *Le Jardin des Plantes* returns frequently to the fatigue experienced by S. in the war, to the interminable

---

10 In 'Le Renard du Jardin: remarques sur l'insertion du personnage historique dans le récit simonien', Didier Alexandre picks up on the reference to Liddell Hart's military history, but analyses its importance only in the context of Simon's usage of documents to depict Rommel as 'une double victime', not as a fictional intertext used by Borges (*'Le Jardin des Plantes' de Claude Simon*, ed. Jean-Yves Laurichesse, Perpignan, Presses Universitaires de Perpignan, 2000, pp. 70–71).

speechifying during the visit to the USSR (as seen in Simon's earlier novel, *L'Invitation*), and to the tedium imposed by the impossible interviewer in his apartment. Then there is the sinology theme in both works which in different ways introduces otherness – writing, time, culture – and sameness: the Picasso in *Le Jardin des Plantes* boasts that his own Chinese art is as 'Chinese' as the 'authentic' Chinese calligraphy he has been sent (*JP*, 230). The narrator of *The Garden of Forking Paths*, great-grandson of Ts'ui Pên, calligrapher and builder of labyrinth and book, visits sinologist Stephen Albert who has reconstructed the manuscripts of Ts'ui Pên from 'a heap of contradictory drafts' (*The Garden of Forking Paths*, 50). Stephen Albert then discloses a further 'clue', a fragment of a letter on which are the words '*I leave to the various futures (not to all) my garden of forking paths*'. This phrase then opens the discussion about time as circular, simultaneous and multi-layered, thus permitting all the contingencies of the story to converge on the ending, the fatal shooting of the man who is sacrificed, because his name is the same as the name of the secret military site the narrator wishes to convey to his spymasters.

Similarly, in *Le Jardin des Plantes*, there are several mysteries to solve, codes to crack. The story of Novelli in the South American jungle reports the successful negotiation of a series of clues to a conundrum in which the stakes are high: failure to read the signs results in death: 'Il en conclut que ceux qui avaient ainsi planté les flèches ne nourissaient pas contre lui et son compagnon un dessein franchement agressif mais qu'il y avait cependant là un message à décoder, avertissement, menace ou simple signal' (*JP*, 238). This parallels that other leitmotif of Simon's *œuvre*: the mystery concerning the commander who did or did not commit treason/suicide; in *Le Jardin des Plantes* this may be seen as an even more pressing central question. However, neither the new material from Rommel's war journals nor the inclusion of letters and documents to 'validate' possible interpretations, ever the stuff of Simon's works, leads to 'the answer'. Death is still what is at stake, whether there are too many significations or only one remaining when the clues are put together. Although seemingly very different in form, *The Garden of Forking Paths* and *Le Jardin des Plantes* demonstrate their affiliations both with the detective story – in which the crime and its clues work on the premise that there is a solution in the body of the criminal; correct detective work on the part of the reader is second to the cleverer author who keeps his/her hand hidden until the final decoding scene – and with the more sinister spy novel, where death is the ultimate stake if agent-interpreter makes a slip of interpretation.

Although there are many clues set up across the *bricolage* of events in *Le Jardin des Plantes*, it is through comparison with *The Garden of Forking Paths* that espionage, narrative double-agency, is made most visible in both works, not least in the construction of plot. More overt in *The Garden of Forking Paths* (Yu Tsun is pitted against Captain Madden, German Intelligence jousts with British Intelligence), the unease of the events reworked in *Le Jardin des Plantes* from *L'Invitation* hints constantly at hidden political agendas of which the narrator is aware in principle but not in detail. The variation on this theme in *Le Jardin des Plantes* – paralleling the two intelligence services in *The Garden of Forking Paths* – is the inclusion of Rommel's strategies set against Churchill's. The Borgesian opening reference to Liddell Hart's account of a batallion lost in the trenches of the First World War is echoed in Simon's text by reconstructions of previous campaigns, or rather defeats at the heart of inglorious battle (in 1940 and from time immemorial). The less obvious, but no less important 'espionage' is the relationship in both works between controller and reader. Every time the reader gets so far with the 'clues' (that is, identifies a 'clue' and distinguishes it from a non-clue), rumbles the counterfeiting ruses and textual disguises, retraces steps from false trails and dead ends, the controlling narrator or narrative construction will already have set up a further refinement to keep the reader only half-way through the maze of fiction. The *nouveau roman* has frequently been described as the 'école du regard', as specular or voyeuristic. *Le Jardin des Plantes*, through *The Garden of Forking Paths*, allows authorial and narratorial overseeings to become visible. The hidden controller who builds mazes or constructs novels of forking paths is nonetheless always the spider in the centre of the web. Benign to a degree in wanting the reader to gain some access, but malign in the constant thwarting of desire, the espionage of *Le Jardin des Plantes* is nowhere more apparent than in the inclusion of S. in the narrative fabric. Close to Simon the author, he gives 'authoritative' answers to his interviewer in ways to which every critic of Simon can relate. Knowingly caught up in his/ her own agenda and interpretation of the materials, soliciting valida- tion from the Master, the interviewer/critic or even ordinary reader is ever at the mercy of versions of truth with as many heads as a hydra. Fiction in the end, as *Le Jardin des Plantes* concludes, may be more real than that which can be replicated in 'life'. Since the glint of the sun on uniforms and harness was revealing the cavalrymen to the enemy, they spread mud on the offending parts; however, this would not do for a film scenario: 'ce camouflage grossier pourrait, au cinéma, sembler l'œuvre maladroite d'un accessoiriste afin de faire plus "vrai". Il vaudrait donc mieux s'en abstenir' (*JP*, 378). Not only does this come close to a parable of the double agency of life–death tactics of men in war or engaged in high political and international drama to survive; it allows that ultimate 'espionage' between fiction and its external referents to be enacted, where the signature never reveals the body.

Proust and Flaubert

Intertexts drawn from fiction (perhaps especially intratexts or autotexts),[11] because they represent the potentially subversive presence of other and dangerous literary or cultural artefacts, present signals akin to those tactical clues of high espionage that lend or obfuscate 'meaning'. Such a dance with intentionality, with impersonality, with textual objectivity, often associated more with Flaubert criticism, has enormous relevance here. If viewed as the master techniques of the literary spying machine that one might call modernism (and Simon would see himself as inheritor of this literary lineage), the concerns with narrative's own (self-)generation – whether as the challenging play of references within national literary traditions or the *mises en abyme* of writing process *qua* process – are developed and illustrated in *Le Jardin des Plantes* with greater sophistication and complexity than ever before in Simon's *œuvre*. Two new intertextual strategies make their presence felt in *Le Jardin des Plantes*. The first is the development of the use of intertexts from privileged authors who have either been hallmark motifs in his fiction, such as Proust, or have been referred to in interviews but have not hitherto made their way overtly or substantially into a Simon novel, such as Flaubert. This intrinsic play with 'authority' and 'authorship' circumnavigates the author's final word as ultimate 'truth', and reopens debates within theorisation of intertextuality about the role of authors; it links back overtly to the centrality of this game of, and with, authorities in *The Garden of Forking Paths*. The second intertextual function that emerges overtly in *Le Jardin des Plantes* is the critical and self-critical process of fiction through the screen of academic or aesthetic evaluation and how this is (in)formed.

---

11 Both these terms have been used to describe a writer's reuse of his or her own previous writings.

Critics have frequently investigated the generative properties of the Proustian intertexts in Simon's novels from a number of different and enlightening angles.[12] Jean Duffy[13] rightly highlights the 'new' aspect of concerted usage of fragments from *Sodome et Gomorrhe* in *Le Jardin des Plantes*: the theme of sexual perversions in this part of *A la recherche du temps perdu* dovetails with the biographemes of Proust's killing of rats with hatpins (*JP*, 142). But what seems rather more important about the Proustian intertexts peppering *Le Jardin des Plantes* is their dual context. First, Simon emphasises Proust's concern with the role of the Writer, that is to say with the civilising mission of high culture, when a war is raging, in this case the First World War. In contrast with the frequent perception of *A la recherche du temps perdu* as a poetic work, Simon in *La Bataille de Pharsale* already chose to set Proust also in the context of history, evoking, for example, episodes from the Great War in Proust's descriptions of the sinking of the Lusitania.[14] Second, Simon stresses how the literary work is brought to completion, how final corrections or authorial changes are made in the light of valued critical comment.

In *Le Jardin des Plantes*, the Proust intertexts are largely concentrated in the second part of the novel, but triggered by several in the first part. They are introduced by the Simonian response to Proust that emerged through *La Bataille de Pharsale*'s final part: 'Je ne souffrais pas' (*JP*, 129). Then follow two key Proust intertexts in quick succession:

> 'D'autre part mon malheur était un peu consolé par l'idée qu'il etc. Je pense que j'ai dû corriger sur les épreuves', écrit Proust à Berthe Lemarié. 'Si je ne l'ai pas fait il n'y a qu'à remplacer le mot malheur par le mot chagrin en laissant la phrase pareille.' (*JP*, 138)

> Au mois d'octobre 1916, Proust écrit à Gaston Gallimard: 'Et puisque ce mot de guerre est venu "sous ma plume", je crois (mais d'ailleurs c'est sans intérêt pratique, puisque nous ne le pouvons pas) que j'ai eu tort de vouloir attendre la fin de la guerre pour paraître (...). Mais (mes raisons) maintenant que j'y ai pensé (et encore une fois c'est toujours théorique) sont qu'en ce moment où (pas moi mais presque tout le monde) on s'est habitué

---

12 See, for example, Françoise van Rossum-Guyon, 'De Claude Simon à Proust: un exemple d'intertextualité', *Marche Romane*, vol. 21, 1971, pp. 71–92; Randi Birn, 'Proust, Claude Simon and the Art of the Novel', *Papers on Language and Literature*, Spring, 1977, pp. 168–86; Orr, *Claude Simon: the Intertextual Dimension*, pp. 106–37.

13 J. H. Duffy, '"Ce n'est pas une allégorie, c'est une feuille tout simplement": Text, Intertext and Biography in Claude Simon's *Jardin des Plantes*', *Romanic Review*, vol. 89, no. 4, 1998, pp. 583–609.

14 Orr, *Claude Simon: the Intertextual Dimension*, p. 131.

à la guerre, on ne lit guère que le communiqué et encore, on aimerait quelque chose d'autre, on pourrait s'intéresser à une longue œuvre. Après la guerre, la Paix, la victoire, seront des choses nouvelles, savoureuses, on y pensera, plutôt qu'à lire. Et alors la guerre elle-même déjà rétrospective, deviendra l'objet d'un intérêt d'imagination qu'elle n'excitait pas comme réalité quotidienne et d'un progrès insensible.' (*JP*, 139)

The strategic importance of these passages is that they are author-referential. Behind the magisterial, finished *A la recherche du temps perdu* lies the writer anxious about the intricacies of a creation where every word reverberates with countless others, and for whom the sanctity of Art is also a riposte to the obscenities of war. Proust's concern is that readers are dulled in times of war by reading only newspaper reports, not works of art. *Le Jardin des Plantes* takes up the challenge to readers now dulled by peace in a novel that is the realisation of the final part of the quotation above: an 'objet d'un intérêt d'imagination', but crafted out of other experiences of war including Simon's own.

Part I of *Le Jardin des Plantes* then includes two further responses from Proust concerning editorial or authorial decisions taken in 1918 about the 'final' manuscript, notably highly censorious self-corrections or modifications of style to non-war sections of *A la recherche du temps perdu* (*A l'ombre des jeunes filles en fleurs*, *JP*, 141) and additions to the original and its earliest part, *Du côté de chez Swann*: 'Aussitôt ce fut comme si un mur avait caché une partie de la vie de Gilberte. Dans une langue que nous savons, nous savons substituer à l'opacité des sons la transparence des idées. Mais dans une langue que nous ne savons pas…' (*JP*, 144). Meanings (hyper-symbolised or contingently inter-associative or contradictory) are created neither from individual words nor sounds alone. *Le Jardin des Plantes*, by inference, contemplates the poetry of war, the battles of signification and the author's retrospections on his/her creation at the end of the *œuvre* as manuscript and finished work.

While the fictional intertexts from *A la recherche du temps perdu* about la marquise de Cambremer in *Le Jardin des Plantes* (Part II onwards)[15]

15 The Proust reference to la marquise de Cambremer was also used by Simon in an interview with Philippe Sollers on the publication of *Le Jardin des Plantes*: 'Il y a des phrases de Proust qui sont beaucoup plus poétiques que bien des poèmes. […] Prenez la visite à la marquise de Cambremer, c'est une des choses les plus extraordinaires qu'on ait faites en littérature; cette sensation du temps qui passe, marquée par les changements de couleur des mouettes-nymphéas, c'est prodigieux' ('La Sensation, c'est primordial', *Le Monde*, 19 sept. 1997, pp. I–II). Renée Ventresque

are integrated and transformed by Simon into his own re-writing (and David Ellison's essay in this volume focuses specifically on this Proustian intertext in Simon's hands), the quotations above are largely discrete because it is their author-referentiality that is paramount. This is underpinned by intertexts in the same vein, namely those by Flaubert, which serve as fictional realisations of the 'heap of contradictory drafts' in *The Garden of Forking Paths*. Simon has often commented that Flaubert's 'scénarios' for *Madame Bovary* are more richly evocative than the final version, where much of the heady emotionality and sensation are sacrificed to 'realism'.[16] Similarly, Simon often quotes Flaubert's letter to George Sand on the 'mot juste', whether chosen for its musical qualities or for its capacity to generate 'sens pluriels'.[17] All of these concerns are variations on a Proustian theme and on the 'noeuds de signification' in his own novels to which Simon first called attention in *Orion aveugle*. It is therefore no surprise to see Flaubert intertexts in *Le Jardin des Plantes* in dialogue with Proustian ones to emphasise further the writing process and authorial decision-making in the creation of self-conscious writing.

The Flaubert intertexts are, however, more than accessories to Proust.[18] Simon uses four of them in strategic ways as they unfold in *Le Jardin des Plantes*. Like the many aphorisms on Art and the aesthetic, including references to representation and realism in Flaubert's *Correspondance*, the two Flaubert citations used in *Le Jardin des Plantes* to describe the reader's experience of novels are potentially contradictory. Both are fully sourced as Flaubert's words. In Part I, 'Ceux qui

---

adds to this: 'Claude Simon insère [Proust] dans le texte du *Jardin des Plantes* à la manière de collages [...] Proust est là dans la chair du dernier roman de Claude Simon' (Renée Ventresque (ed.), *Claude Simon: à partir de 'La Route des Flandres': tours et détours*, Montpellier, Service des publications de L'université Paul-Valéry-Montpellier III, 1997, p. 11).

16 See, for example, Orr, *Claude Simon: the Intertextual Dimension*, pp. 97–104.
17 See, for example, Claude Simon, 'Roman, description et action', in P. Hallberg (ed.), *The Feeling for Nature and the Landscape of Man*, Proceedings of the 45th Nobel Symposium held 10–12 September 1978 in Göteborg to celebrate the 200th anniversary of the Royal Society of Arts and Sciences of Göteborg, Göteborg, 1978, p. 91.
18 Among the few critics to discuss Flaubert as intertext of Simon, see Orr, *Claude Simon: the Intertextual Dimension*, pp. 97–104, and more recently, Christine Genin, *L'Expérience du lecteur dans les romans de Claude Simon: lecture studieuse et lecture poignante*, Paris, Honoré Champion, 1997, p. 343, with direct reference to *Le Jardin des Plantes*: 'Il convient de signaler que Simon a si bien assimilé et digéré leurs propos [fragments de Flaubert] qu'il les modifie sans aucun scrupule, les citant, dit-il souvent *de mémoire*' (Genin's emphasis).

lisent un livre pour savoir si la baronne épousera le comte seront dupés' (*JP*, 53) would seem to underpin the truism about Simon's fiction that the reconstruction of a single, coherent version of events is impossible. This Flaubert fragment at the same time is itself only one among others intercalating previous literature with Simon's own, or with his various accounts of travel to conferences.

The parallel aphorism is the epigraph from Flaubert to Part IV of *Le Jardin des Plantes*, the section of the work which has fewest literary intertexts. Here we have a highly poetic, incomplete sentence which will strike Simon readers as a parallel literary formulation to the visual arts intertext, Poussin's *Orion aveugle* in Simon's novel of the same name: 'Avec les pas du temps, avec ses pas gigantesques d'infernal géant' (*JP*, 317). While Flaubert here appears to be shorthand for the aspirations of fiction to frame the rest of Part IV, this section of Simon's novel demonstrates art's entrepreneurial banality and ability to produce copies in other texts or media. Novels provide film scenarios: in this case the self-irony is that the scenario used here is that for the projected film version of Simon's *La Route des Flandres*. There seems to be deliberate distancing of Flaubert as precursor and as antagonist in the paper separation of this paratextual intertext from the ensuing fiction.

This difference, however, is achieved at the same time as recognition that there are affinities with Flaubert that insert Simon and his unfolding *œuvre* into the modernist tradition. An unsourced segment from one of the scenarios of *Madame Bovary*, but used by Simon in interviews as a positive response to Flaubert and to his own lineage in his tradition, appears on page 130 of *Le Jardin des Plantes*. The names 'Rodolphe', 'Emma', 'Yonville' and 'Homais' all more than suffice to signal its original author. This segment has, however, a further auto-critical function, to measure where the writing of *Le Jardin des Plantes* has taken Simon beyond his earlier statements on fiction in the style of Flaubert. This auto-critical stance is equally apparent through negative references to Flaubert (also taken from earlier interviews) such as the ways in which Flaubert, as it were, impaled Emma's heart on his scalpel (*JP*, 276). Literary intertextuality in *Le Jardin des Plantes* therefore now includes references to a medium that would normally be excluded from fictional creation: interviews or journalistic literary criticism. Those auto-citations to Simon the literary critic, churning out so many *idées reçues*, have a self-mocking double edge.[19] The writer

19 See Orr, *Claude Simon: the Intertextual Dimension*, p. 202.

is not a critic, but can come up with authoritative statements about fictional creation on a par with critics whose sole job this is. There is no small authorial jibe here at trite and superficial criticism of his own works and the critical machine that has kept Simon mistrustful of television or unscripted interviews. We will see how other intertextualisations and fictionalisations of critical stances emerge below.

The last Flaubert intertext to note, however, is of none of these kinds and is new to any of Simon's work, fictional or other. It occurs strategically in the highly collaged first part of the novel: '"Amuse-toi bien au pays des cons rasés", écrit Flaubert à Bouilhet qui part pour l'Algérie' (*JP*, 132). The emphasis is on the importance of the correspondent as linchpin of creative process and narrative distance, *accoucheur*, co-accomplice in the narrative process. This one-liner opens up the 'correspondences' of travel in the Middle and Far East which Simon or his ancestor (for example, in *Histoire*) have also undertaken and which are incorporated in *Le Jardin des Plantes*. It also furthers the citational values of correspondence (in the sense of epistolary exchange) as the artist's mode of gaining some viewpoint on self-referentiality in the authorship of the text.

Genetic criticism and self-criticism

In *The Garden of Forking Paths*, Stephen Albert asserts that he has done the proper genetic criticism on the various texts and fragments which constitute the Ts'ui Pên *œuvre*, 'from the heap of fragmentary drafts' (p. 50). This editorial process of revisions is at the centre of intertextual development in *Le Jardin des Plantes*. Here Simon uses documents that had previously been available to his critics in research libraries, but not to general readers of his fictions. The intertexts discussed above demonstrate the importance of the writer or his writing through the inclusion of a published letter to a significant addressee˙ able to comment on that Art. They are recapitulated in Simonian key in the second half of the novel in the reproduction of a letter from a correspondent questioning the 'authenticity' of episodes in *La Route des Flandres*. The Colonel wrote: '*cet épisode est fidèle dans le plus petit détail*' (*JP*, 354). The naïve realism of this response serves as a pendant to Ricardou's critical approach, radical anti-realism.

Reader response, both positive and negative evoked by such letters, is dovetailed with auto-readership not only in the sense that each of Simon's novels 're-reads' its previous one(s). In *Le Jardin des Plantes* this process of fiction 'reading' previous writing (Simon's own 'réécritures' and the deployment of intertexts from others) is given a human form: included in the novel is a *mise en abyme* of the processes of writing, reading and correction of manuscript as illustrated by Rommel:

> A la lecture du récit qu'il en fit plus tard (ou qu'il mit au net pendant cette période où, après sa blessure, convalescent, dans l'attente d'un nouveau commandement ou de son assassinat, il rédigea – ou corrigea – ses carnets (documents que, par la suite, sa veuve et son fils cachèrent avec ses lettres en divers endroits, répartis ici et là par petits paquets [...] échappant aux sauvages recherches de ses assassins, puis des services secrets ennemis [...] le plus gros, malgré tout, découvert à la fin, mis sous scellés, expédié de l'autre côté de l'Atlantique [...] minutieusement étudié par des diplômés aux cheveux coupés en brosse, restitué enfin après des années avec les excuses de courtois diplomates [...]. (*JP*, 186)

Replicating once more the espionage/sabotage of writing in *The Garden of Forking Paths*, and final corrections of Proust discussed above, the writerly aspects of Simon's works are given a new reading: the writer's own and his critics', which also signals that no writing is completely 'new', but rather always an editing or 'correction' of previous manuscripts.

The manuscript aspect of Simon's work has also always been recognised: his use of family papers and postcards, for example, or the way in which previously published fragments re-emerge in expanded form in a later novel. *Le Jardin des Plantes* (pp. 354–55) takes up the previously published fragment called 'Les jardins publics'.[20] The drawing of his own hand in *Orion aveugle* now finds its refictionalisation in the exploration in *Le Jardin des Plantes* of the versions and processes of writing fiction. In the times of a Flaubert or a Proust, manuscripts were the last stages of the many 'brouillons', 'carnets', 'scénarios' and versions, before the final text was established through corrections, correspondence with other writer-friends, or readings before a critical audience. In Flaubert's case there was also the stage of reading the work aloud to himself (the famous 'gueuleoir'). In so many ways, Simon takes these narrative strategies straddling the hidden oral and written elements of any 'definitive' version (most often stabilised by the critical edition and the work of scholars rather than the writer),

---

20 Claude Simon, 'Les jardins publics (extrait)', published in Mireille Calle-Gruber (ed.), *Les Sites de L'écriture: Colloque Claude Simon, Queen's University, Ontario*, Paris, Nizet, 1995, pp. 25–37.

and rewrites them directly (the Flaubert and Proust intertexts above) and in a contemporary key.[21] Part IV of *Le Jardin des Plantes* is the centre of this revisionary incorporation of oral criticism into written correction (or the ignoring of such expert critical advice). The intertextual references to Simon's critics, most notably Ricardou and the Colloque de Cerisy, are more than just another layer of reflexivity on the reflexive novel. I would suggest that they are the new equivalent of the kinds of correspondence that Flaubert or Proust engaged in. Their collections of letters presented as many sidelong glances at the current values in aesthetic production as they did insights into the work currently being written. The Ricardou intertexts taken from the heart of structuralist and post-structuralist theorising on the *nouveau roman* – that avatar of technical virtuosities, especially the non-referentiality of words to things or to the authority of an 'author' – are replayed here fictionally like the tape recording they became of the live, literary critical session. Ricardou now lives on as 'the big bad wolf', essential to the tale of any path through the woods of criticism for unsuspecting but eager critics of Simon. Without the huge impact of this epoch and Simon's place within it, and later on its margins, his current work might not have had that stalking horse necessary to take the famous disintegrating horse corpse into a new version of *La Route des Flandres* at the heart of the *œuvre*.

External and public critical evaluation at Cerisy (like Gallimard's appraisals of Proust) coexists with the private critical response of friends or other interested parties such as Flaubert received from Bouilhet or Alfred le Poittevin. The tedious and persistent journalist interviewer, armed with his equally annoying and disruptive tape recorder, transposes into a modern medium exactly this vital step of turning the text out into the public domain, to fend for itself amid every possible misreading, error or occasional insight. In this is the latent ground of another subsequent work as the critic also furnishes new potential fiction. The 'marmalade' (*JP*, 280) of tenuous impression then takes shape as it is verbalised before an interlocutor. Thus Simon endorses the role of the critic while also mocking such earnestness. The rare flashes of self-conscious humour in Simon's works find a new butt in *Le Jardin des Plantes*: we are this hapless critic persona trying to

21 In answer to questions during the colloquium at which the first version of this paper was read, Madame Réa Simon assured Simon critics of the amanuensis and addressee functions she plays in the production of the text.

establish a Simon text and fit it into a critical edition, critical tradition or research framework.[22]

The last aspect of genetic criticism that *Le Jardin des Plantes* highlights to an unprecedented degree in Simon's *œuvre* is the layout of the page as manuscript.[23] Previously, the parentheses, the lines of dots to mirror separation of textual fragments with no obvious or necessary connection to others on the same sheet, the alternative versions of the one 'event', all replicate the early stages of manuscript production to

22 The publication of *Le Jardin des Plantes* coincided with the 'canonisation' of *La Route des Flandres* in a plethora of critical studies appearing also in 1997, the year before the latter was set as a text for the 'agrégation'. See, for example, Didier Alexandre, *Le Magma et l'horizon. Essai sur 'La Route des Flandres' de Claude Simon*, Paris, Klincksieck, 1997; Alain Cresciucci and Jean Touzot (eds), *Claude Simon: autour de 'La Route des Flandres'*, *Littératures Contemporaines*, no. 3, Paris, Klincksieck, 1997; Sophie Guermès, *L'Echo du dedans: essai sur 'La Route des Flandres' de Claude Simon*, Paris, Klincksieck, 1997; Hubert de Phalèse, *Code de 'La Route des Flandres': examen du roman de Claude Simon*, Paris, Nizet, 1997; Catherine Rannoux, *L'Ecriture du labyrinthe: Claude Simon 'La Route des Flandres'*, Orléans, Paradigme, 1997; Renée Ventresque (ed.), *Claude Simon: à partir de 'La Route des Flandres': tours et détours d'une écriture*; Dominique Viart, *Une mémoire inquiète: 'La Route des Flandres' de Claude Simon*, Paris, PUF, 1997.

23 Clément-Perrier offers two more imaginative interpretations of the layout: 'C'est le principe de simultanéité que tente Simon dans *Le Jardin des Plantes* dont certaines pages (les 75 premières pages, puis les pages 117–19 et 128–29) présentent une composition typographique nouvelle: les espaces blancs traversent les pages en diagonale ou forment un angle droit offrant ainsi une composition semblable à celle d'un jardin [ ] L'effet typographique demande de circuler d'un endroit à un autre, de revenir sur ses pas, puis de continuer sa promenade' (*Claude Simon: la fabrique du jardin*, pp. 32–33); 'Mais c'est dans *Le Jardin des Plantes* et sa typographie singulière que cette notion du labyrinthe est illustrée' (p. 107). A further parallel is the chessboard or concrete poetry as Isabelle Serça notes in '*Le Jardin des Plantes:* une composition de damier', *Littératures*, no. 40, printemps 1999, pp. 60–61. On page 61 she also likens the layout in *Le Jardin des Plantes* to Mallarmé's *Coup de Dés*, in keeping with her reading of the form of the text as a 'jeu'. Closer to my interpretation, but not developed, is Dominique Viart: '[*Le Jardin des Plantes*, pp. 23–25] ne sont d'ailleurs pas sans évoquer les pages manuscrites de Claude Simon, avec leurs lignes fuyantes. Conserver dans le texte imprimé cette disposition, c'est se tenir au plus près des brouillons [...] Cette fidélité produit un autre effet: elle semble instituer le texte comme document' ('Remembrances et remembrements', *Scherzo*, avril 1998, p. 25). In 'Simon et Novelli: l'image de la lettre', Brigitte Ferrato-Combe compares the textual layout of Simon's novel to a Novelli painting (in Laurichesse (ed.), *'Le Jardin des Plantes' de Claude Simon*, p. 104). In the same volume, Jean-Yves Laurichesse describes the layout as 'pavés' of text and photograph transposed from the earlier Simon work to *Le Jardin des Plantes* ('Aux quatre coins du monde: *Le Jardin des Plantes* comme *Album d'un voyageur*', p. 129). The illustration of a page from Simon's manuscript of the latter interleaved between pages 8 and 9 only adds further weight to my interpretation here.

show the writer at work on the text.[24] *Le Jardin des Plantes* has very few of these parenthetical strategies, although they recur notably in that final part, the dialogue with the journalist interviewer. I would suggest that this is because the novel is laying claim to its status of more complete draft than previous novels, and hence is less preoccupied with early ideas, sketches and drafts. What is striking is the greater density of Part I of *Le Jardin des Plantes*, as if it were a page of a Flaubert manuscript. Around the 'main' section are many blocks of ideas in progress, parallel 'bloc notes', shapes of text at odd angles to the main structure. All of these occur in the spatial collages of this vital section of *Le Jardin des Plantes*. Thereafter, the text stabilises into less fragmentary and seemingly less contradictory narrative. There is no visually presented dialogue or dispute between fragments, no contradiction of materials. The illusion of order and coherence, consistency and authorial control are then broken open by the novel as it unfolds in apparently seamless, linear fashion. The text re-disintegrates as fiction and its intertexts to unpack its oral, visual and publicity billboards (such as those found in *Orion aveugle* or *Les Corps conducteurs*) in new guise. The self-publicity by artistic means is also underpinned by the final film scenario: 'success' is no longer gauged by critics within the readerly confines of the colloquium, but is defined also by the values of spectator cinema-goers. Specularity and espionage continue to intertwine from Borges and the 1960s to the late 1990s. Simon's authority comes not least from the consistency of his *œuvre* and the voice-over of its dissemination in a variety of media.[25]

Modern manuscript studies and genetic criticism have much to give and much to learn from *Le Jardin des Plantes* and its intertextual fictionalising of such critical approaches to the word, textual and

24 Critics have often noted Simon's parenthetical style. Raymond Gay-Crosier notes the ironic function of the parenthesis which signals dual and contingent contexts: 'Enfin, outre sa fonction syntaxique traditionnelle, la parenthèse comme procédé narratif rejoint souvent le registre ironique où, au lieu de réduire l'importance de ce qu'elle importe, elle surcode son contenu. Enfin, chez Simon, la pratique de la parenthèse rejoint le procédé intertextuel de la mise en abyme dans la mesure où elle est à la fois séparation et intégration, exclusion et inclusion.' ('De l'intertextualité à la métatextualité: *Les Géorgiques* de Claude Simon', in Raimond Theis and Hans T. Siepe (eds), *Le Plaisir de l'intertexte: formes et fonctions de l'intertextualité*, Berne, Lang, 1985, p. 329). The 'manuscript' version operates in very similar ways in *Le Jardin des Plantes* as *mise en abyme* of the production of the text.
25 '[C]'est l'extrême cohérence de l'œuvre simonienne, *Le Jardin des Plantes* compris, qui a émergé puissamment', as Renée Ventresque wrote in the avant-propos to *Claude Simon: à partir de 'La Route des Flandres'*, p. 7.

authorial. Ever suspicious of theory, Simon nonetheless 'creates' an author-theory (like *auteur*-criticism within Film Studies). This combines *auteur*-criticism and *auteur*-biography in such as way as to prevent critical fashions from having the last word. With criticism itself so much in the foreground, *Le Jardin des Plantes* thus also raises again the question in a new key as to whether Simon's fictions are autobiographies in the first and third persons.[26] Undoubtedly there is a strongly self-referential (and self-critical) base common to the narrator, S., and to the Claude Simon who signs the novel. However, unlike *L'Acacia*, which seemed to get as close to fictional autobiography as is possible, in what I called 'self-resuming artefacts',[27] *Le Jardin des Plantes* turns from the person of the writer to the person of the writing. The new dimensions of the intertext that Simon has employed in *Le Jardin des Plantes* are further convergences of fictional writing persona and writer, as well as, of course, the complete chasm that lies between them. Like the fictional Marcel who shares with Marcel Proust a name and points of reference but who is not the same person, S. and Claude Simon are also not the same. Simon's exploration of how they are not and how they can be distinguished are demonstrated with a new complexity and clarity in *Le Jardin des Plantes*.

Conclusion

As *summa* of Simon's intertextual preoccupations and 'réécritures', *Le Jardin des Plantes* offers an exemplum of Marc Eigeldinger's definition, particularly his horticultural metaphor, of 'le propre de l'intertextualité':

> De construire un univers relationnel, un univers d'alliances et de connexions, favorisant la libre circulation entre les œuvres; elle est le lieu de leur confrontation et de leur cohabitation dans le langage [...] L'intertextualité ne recouvre ainsi pas seulement une opération mémoriale et assimilatrice, elle n'est pas uniquement une transplantation d'un texte dans un autre, mais elle se définit par un travail d'appropriation et de réécriture qui s'applique à recréer le sens, en invitant à une nouvelle lecture.[28]

26   See, for example, Mary Orr, 'Intertextual Bridging: across the Genre Divide in Claude Simon's *Les Géorgiques*', *Forum for Modern Language Studies*, vol. 26, no. 3, 1990, pp. 31–39, or more recently, in respect of *Le Jardin des Plantes*, J. H. Duffy, 'Artistic Biographies and Aesthetic Coherence in Claude Simon's *Le Jardin des Plantes*', *Forum for Modern Language Studies*, vol. 35, no. 2, 1999, pp. 175–92.

27   Orr, *Claude Simon: the Intertextual Dimension*, p. 190.

28   Marc Eigeldinger, *Mythologie et intertextualité*, Geneva, Slatkine, 1987, p. 11.

Inter- and intratextuality, which connect literary production with the process of literary reception (criticism and self-criticism), seem to find no better expression than in *Le Jardin des Plantes* which can be considered also as a fiction of one of Borges's *Parables*, namely *Borges and I*:

> The other one, the one called Borges, is the one things happen to. [...] I know of Borges from the mail and see his name on a list of professors or in a biographical dictionary [...] I live [...] so that Borges may contrive his literature, and this literature justifies me. [...] but those pages cannot save me, perhaps because what is good belongs to no one, not even to him, but rather to language and to tradition. [...] Little by little, I am giving over everything to him, though I am quite aware of his perverse custom of falsifying and magnifying things. [...] I shall remain in Borges, not in myself [...] Thus my life is a flight and I lose everything and everything belongs to oblivion, or to him.
>   I do not know which of us has written this page.[29]

Simon's *Le Jardin des Plantes* not only includes and excludes the mortal Simon of similar preferences in a not-quite-hostile relationship. It includes a tribute to the love–hate relationship of writer and writing with real and fictional critics. In this, *Simonistes* can all claim a part, however small, in the revisioned manuscripting of his wonderful, writerly fiction, a brush-stroke among many in the collage of an Artist who continues to write first and foremost to perfect that illusive 'real', 'final' version. More than ever before, Simon's *Le Jardin des Plantes* laughs at theories of representation à la Ricardou because these ultimately fail to take into account so many forking paths.

---

29 *Labyrinths*, pp. 282–83.

7

A partir du *Jardin des Plantes*: Claude Simon's Recapitulations

David Ellison

Repetition, recapitulation, textual departures

Faithful readers of Claude Simon's extensive fictional *oeuvre* will sense, at first, that they are in familiar territory as they begin to peruse *Le Jardin des Plantes*. Not only does the central traumatic event of the novelist's life – his strange participation/non-participation in the rapid defeat of the French army in the Second World War – occupy centre stage here, as it did in the Reixach cycle, but the overarching theme of order versus disorder inhabits the pages of this 1997 work with the same intensity as in the earlier writings. The liminary quotation for *Le Jardin des Plantes*, taken from Montaigne, seems, at first glance, to be a repetition, with a slight tonal variation, of the liminary passage, taken from Rilke, which frames *Histoire* (1967):

> Aucun ne fait certain dessain de sa vie, et n'en délibérons qu'à parcelles. [...] Nous sommes tous de lopins et d'une contexture si informe et diverse, que chaque pièce, chaque momant faict son jeu.
> Montaigne (Le Jardin des Plantes)

> Cela nous submerge. Nous l'organisons. Cela tombe
> en morceaux.
> Nous l'organisons de nouveau et tombons nous-mêmes
> en morceaux.
> Rilke (Histoire)

In both passages the emphasis is on the difficulty, perhaps even the futility, of finding or creating a 'design' in one's life, of bringing forth some kind of unity out of fragmentation. Montaigne's words 'lopins' and 'parcelles' remind one, inevitably, of Rilke's 'en morceaux', and Montaigne's evocation of the human being's constitution as being fundamentally 'informe et diverse' echoes Rilke's generalisation of our falling to pieces in our very attempt to organise that enigmatic 'cela' which submerges us: in each case, we have difficulty putting both ourselves and that 'cela' exterior to ourselves which we attempt to mould and form, together. There is, in the creative process, a strain towards unity that comes up against our own fragility as humans, our own tendency to (in all senses of this expression) fall apart.

I am suggesting, therefore, that the reading habits we have gained in analysing novels such as *La Route des Flandres*, *Histoire* and *Les Géorgiques*, can be put to good use as we encounter *Le Jardin des Plantes*, that the thematic centrality of the war experience and of the order/disorder polarity as well as the temporal fragmentation and dispersion that characterise Simon's writing in general have as a first effect that of familiarity. We are, or seem to be, in a place we have seen before. A sceptical and unfriendly reader might even object that we have seen these landscapes and these forms so often before in previous novels that *Le Jardin des Plantes* is really nothing but a repetition of the same, a *redite* that adds nothing to what we have already experienced in the previous works. Yet an attentive reading of the 1997 text shows something slightly different from what has gone before in Simon's *oeuvre*; this novel, I shall contend, is both the same and different from the earlier works, both familiar and defamiliarising: as text, it enacts what Freud called *Unheimlichkeit* (in English, *the uncanny*, in French, *l'inquiétante étrangeté*).[1] The effect of the *unheimlich* arises not from the introduction of a radically new content or stylistic experimentation, but from a new framing of pre-existing material, and especially, from what appears to be a reversal in the hierarchy between the fictional and the real, from a transformation in their frames of reference.

Put in the crudest way, one might say that the efforts Simon made to fictionalise his own personal experience (for example, to create the Reixach cycle using a Faulknerian family and geographical nexus in order to transmute the particularity of his life into the universality of human experience) are now turned inside-out. The overall result of the interview sequences in *Le Jardin des Plantes* seems to be a peeling back of fictional disguise towards the brute and unmasked reality which lies at the origin of the writer's imaginary world. The narrator's concern for historical accuracy and verification (the archives in the château de Vincennes), his quoting of tersely worded military communiqués and

---

1 See Sigmund Freud, 'Das Unheimliche', *Gesammelte Werke Chronologisch Geordnet*, vol. 12 (1917–20), London, Imago, 1947, pp. 227–68. The English translation is 'The "Uncanny"', *The Standard Edition*, vol. 17 (1917–19), London, The Hogarth Press, 1955, pp. 217–56.

of Rommel's barebones accounts of battle progress and prowess lend an aura of demystification and demythification to the recent text. It is as if Claude Simon, having mesmerised his readers through the alchemy of fictional transmutation, is now showing us the tricks of his trade, is now revealing to us the unadorned simplicity underlying the literarily achieved complexity we have been admiring for these many years. It is as if, having read and written so much in a life rich in both real experience and literature, Simon were now able to let down his guard and tell us the unguarded truth, a truth that fiction is only able to disguise, and badly. In this regard, the narrator's pointing at Stendhal behind Fabrice (*JP*, 35) and his parenthetical expression 'en satisfaisant aux goûts de Charlus (*en fait*, aux goûts de Proust)' (*JP*, 142; my emphasis) would appear to amount to an authorial/confessional admission concerning the fundamental and primordial position of the real referent as anchor to all fictional transformations. The inclusion of the now-famous letter signed 'colonel C..., ex-colonel au 8e Dragons' in the context of the 1971 Cerisy colloquium, the real letter of congratulation, confirmation and verification that needed to be taken *à la lettre* but that caused consternation among the apostles of literary self-referentiality (*JP*, 354–58) adds to the suspicion we have, as readers of *Le Jardin des Plantes*, that this new text is, in part, the narration of a difficult combat *between* the real and the fictional.[2] This means, then, that the modal identity of the new work is a hybrid one, that we, as readers, are located in the interstices, and that the bland designation of 'roman' underneath the book's title needs (to use 1970s jargon) problematisation.

But the word 'hybrid', now all the rage in the cultural studies movement, is vague as a descriptive term and requires some further comment. If we decide to say, for purposes of provisional clarity, that *Le Jardin des Plantes* is a hybrid work, half-novel, half-autobiography, half-fiction, half-confession, the question becomes: how, in practice

2   For a commentary on the ex-colonel's letter to Simon and on the controversy it caused, see Michelle Labbé, 'Paysages perdus dans *Le Jardin des Plantes* de Claude Simon', *Courrier du Centre International d'Etudes Poétiques*, vol. 217, January–March 1998, p. 23. Labbé's article examines the notion of 'paysage' in Claude Simon's work. She concludes that the construction of landscape(s) in Simon is always impossible and that this impossibility calls into question the very notion of realism: 'Ainsi l'impossible paysage induit l'impossibilité d'un réalisme autre que subjectif, réalisme exprimant seulement la relativité de la vision et la présence au monde d'un sujet. L'homme, dans une relation constamment dialectique avec son univers, ne peut parvenir à la pause et à la lucidité' (p. 35).

(in the *praxis* of Simonian writing), does the real relate to the fictional? I will suggest, as provisional answer to this tough question, that we follow Simon's own phraseology, as it occurs in two crucial contexts in the 'novel', and that we call the act of writing in its fictional modality a *departure from the real*. In French, the real is the *point de départ* for the fictional; the fictional exists in the mode of an *à partir de*. Thus, in an early interview sequence, the somewhat harassed author responds to the persistent journalist:

> Vous savez je n'ai pas beaucoup d'imagination alors à part mes tout premiers bouquins qui n'étaient pas très fameux les suivants ç'a toujours été plus ou moins *à partir de choses que j'ai vécues*, de mes expériences personnelles, ou encore de vieux papiers de famille, tout ça... (*JP*, 76–77; my emphasis)

In the same way, in a passage in Part II to which I shall return in the final section of my essay, when the narrator is describing the parallel events taking place at the same time in the real theatre of war and in the grotesquely theatrical *conciliabule* of important political and military personages theorising, in high abstraction and palatial splendour, about the movements of troops that have already been decimated and lost, we have the phrase: '*A partir de là* vont simultanément se dérouler plusieurs événements qui, en dépit ou peut-être en raison même de leur apparente incohérence, constituent un tout pratiquement homogène et cohérent' (*JP*, 202–03; my emphasis). At the beginning, there is an action or event from reality or nature whose effects are propagated far and wide, forming a pattern of some kind; and this pattern, however bizarre, unsettling or apparently incoherent, does seem to constitute 'un tout'. But what is the nature of this totality? How does one travel (I use this term advisedly) from the central brutal and real *factum* outwards within the convoluted transformations it undergoes as it assumes an aesthetic guise? In the act of travelling out, what frontiers does one cross, what boundaries does one transgress? These questions will be at the centre of the two development sections that follow: the first, on the Jardin des Plantes sequence for which the text is named; the second, on the curious (*unheimlich*) juxtaposition of passages from Proust with the description of the Second World War debacle which structures Part II.

Le Jardin des Plantes or the cultural space of nature

There is, in Paris, a place called Le Jardin des Plantes. It is there to be visited by Parisians and tourists alike and could be called, in Pierre Nora's terminology, a *lieu de mémoire*.[3] It is also Claude Simon's *lieu de remémoration* and, since it gives the title to the novel we are discussing, would seem to stand, minimally, at the thematic crossroads of the work as a whole, or perhaps even, as the generating centre of the text. To understand *Le Jardin des Plantes* as aesthetic totality, then, would require one to begin with the section that describes the garden explicitly (*JP*, 61–63), then depart from it, following the threads that unwind progressively from it as centre: *à partir du Jardin des Plantes*. I am going to assume that all readers, in opening the book, are driven towards finding the sequence within the work that gave it its title. There is something comforting, familiarising, about finding that sequence some sixty pages into the text. Doubly familiarising: first, because we all recognise the place (even those of us who are not of French origin have no doubt been there, probably several times), and second, because we assume that if we read the sequence carefully, we will find ourselves oriented towards the grand design of the novel, towards its multiple meanings. What we find 'in' the sequence, in the textual place of its unfolding, is, however, not all that familiarising, even though the rhetorical mode of the descriptive prose at this spot appears to be declarative, constative in the most reassuring way. I have not yet taught *Le Jardin des Plantes* in a classroom setting, but I can easily imagine that my students would breathe a sigh of relief upon reaching this island of descriptive repose in which the well-articulated (and complete!) sentences contrast strikingly with the carnivalesque fragmentation of the preceding pages. The first part of the sequence sounds as if it could have come from a well-written guidebook; it is essentially the narrator's choice of emphasis on certain details rather than others, his studied *focalisation*, that graft on to these pages the mark of literariness and that cause the reader to ponder what is at stake in the passage, what lies beyond or below its descriptive surface.

3 See the three-volume series, under the direction of Pierre Nora, entitled *Les Lieux de mémoire (I. La République; II. La Nation; III. Les France)*, Paris, Gallimard, 1984–92. The series, in somewhat abbreviated form, is now available in English, edited by Lawrence D. Kritzman and translated by Arthur Goldhammer: *Realms of Memory: The Constructions of the French Past (I: Conflicts and Divisions; II: Traditions; III: Symbols)*, New York, Columbia University Press, 1996–98. For a cogent account of the French and English versions of the text, see Tony Judt, 'A la Recherche du Temps Perdu', *The New York Review of Books*, vol. 45, no. 19, 3 December 1998, pp. 51–58.

   The sequence as a whole is constructed on one of the foundational polarities of Western thought: *physis* versus *techné*, or nature versus culture. The first segment of the passage evokes the 'plan géométrique' of the oldest part of the Jardin and, in alluding to the carefully pruned plane trees bordering the esplanade, generalises about the human tendency to 'domestiquer, asservir la nature' (*JP*, 61), and compares this domestication to the 'pruning' of language that took place in the drama of the classical period. The analogy is clear and straightforward: just as we are driven to tame the abundance of nature, so we seem compelled to tame his own passions by enclosing them in a spare, rigorous, coded form of language. But what is interesting about Le Jardin des Plantes is the fact that, in another part of its domain, at the beginning of the Montagne Sainte-Geneviève, one finds a wild and asymmetrical ensemble of trees and vegetation in the mode of the so-called 'English gardens', so that, in a circumscribed space, it is possible for the Parisian or the tourist to walk from one style to its opposite, from the manifestation of one aesthetic philosophy to its radical other. To the nature–culture dichotomy we now graft the English garden versus French garden opposition, which would seem to be a variation on the same theme: that is, the English mode indicates respect for nature in its unspoiled profusion, whereas the French style is an imposition of cultural norms upon nature, a form of violence done to the natural realm. How logical, then, that the narrator should allude to Jean-Jacques Rousseau and to Bernardin de Saint-Pierre in the context of the English garden description, and that he should choose to describe, at some length, the statues of the latter and of his fictional creations, Paul and Virginie, who are depicted, with consequent *couleur locale*, as playing under banana trees. The passage concludes with the observation that a 'dangerously leaning' pine tree, supported by a steel rod, barely touches the statue of Bernardin de Saint-Pierre, while, on the other side of the walkway one finds a plane tree planted by Jussieu in 1785.

   The passage is, of course, considerably more complicated than this incomplete presentation indicates, especially as concerns the nature–culture relation. At the beginning of his evocation of the French garden style, the narrator says: '*Il apparaît* que l'homme s'est appliqué là à *pour ainsi dire* domestiquer, asservir la nature' (*JP*, 61; my emphasis). These forms of rhetorical prudence should caution the reader against coming to the immediate conclusion that nature can, in fact, be tamed. We think we tame it, so to speak, in a manner of speaking, in appearance only, but the truth of nature does not lie in its apparent 'willingness' to be domesticated, but rather in its *danger*. Unless the pine tree were propped up, it would fall upon the statue of Bernardin de Saint-Pierre; the propping itself is an obvious and not aesthetically pleasing artifice. And the statue itself is oxidised to such a degree that a pale shade of green (the physical manifestation of the passing of time) covers not only the author of *Paul et Virginie* but also the banana tree and the children themselves: this green colour, in the narrator's words, is 'indifféremment étalée' (*JP*, 62) over the author, his fictive creations and the represented banana tree. Time takes on form and colour by levelling all things, by cancelling the distinctions between and among levels of representation. Oxidisation, a natural process, treats the genial author, his fictional characters and his imagined tropical landscape with the same lack of *politesse*, by covering them over, by reducing them to a neutral sameness. There is considerable irony, of course, in the depiction of Bernardin de Saint-Pierre being covered over 'indifferently' by the forces of nature, when it is as disciple of Rousseau and apologist for nature that he gained his notoriety.

If nature is represented in this passage as a dangerous and levelling force that human beings think erroneously of taming, nature is also depicted as something – let us call it Rilke's *cela* – which human beings attempt, without success, to imitate aesthetically. The problem with the French garden versus English garden dichotomy, and with the whole cultural debate surrounding this polarity in the eighteenth century, is that the English garden is not 'more natural' than the French one, but *fake in a different way*. The French garden, in doing violence to natural forms, advertises itself openly as a cultural imposition: no one is going to mistake a pruned plane tree from a plane tree left to its own devices. The English garden is more perverse: it advertises itself as nature, but is, of course, a cleverly disguised artificial imitation of nature, as the narrator reminds us:

> De grands arbres centenaires dont un cèdre au feuillage sombre, y poussent entourés d'une végétation variée et sauvage venue *comme au hasard:* bambous, lierres grimpants, buissons de diverses essences y composent un ensemble conforme à ce goût rêveur de la Nature à la mode vers la fin du XVIIIe siècle et illustré par des écrivains comme Jean-Jacques Rousseau ou Bernardin de Saint-Pierre (*JP*, 62; my emphasis).

Nature *is* 'le hasard' in all its unpredictable brutality, while the English garden exists in the mode of 'as if' – '*comme* au hasard' – that is, in the mode of artifice and fiction. Whereas the disciples of Rousseau (including perhaps Bernardin de Saint-Pierre, who, when not travelling the world, occupied the post of *intendant* in the Jardin des Plantes) and the proponents of the English garden refused to see the contrivance behind natural appearances, Rousseau himself was the first demystifier of this illusion. In the eleventh letter of Part IV of *La Nouvelle Héloïse* (1761), the description of 'Le jardin de Julie', St Preux shows his progressive astonishment as he realises that an exotic, utopian garden that seems to have materialised magically from a distant island is, in fact, an elaborate construction. Before she reveals any of her gardener's secrets to St Preux, Julie prefaces their walk with the sobering words: 'Avancez, et vous comprendrez. Adieu Tinian, adieu Juan-Fernandez, adieu tout l'enchantement! Dans un moment vous allez être de retour du bout du monde'.[4] St Preux is in need of, and receives from Julie, a lesson in recognising the cleverly concealed cultural marks lying among the elaborately composed elements of nature. Most importantly, Julie reveals to her 'pupil' the complex ways in which the irrigation of the garden is hidden from view: the water is led to the garden from an outside source, and it is only because we do not see the connections between the inside domain of the garden and its outside that the illusion of the exotic 'island' in the midst of Wolmar's estate can be maintained (*La Nouvelle Héloïse*, 355–56). What is at stake here is a matter of some narrative importance – namely, that of *framing*. Julie's garden is not only not 'natural' in the pre-Romantic sense of that term, it is also not self-enclosed: its openness, its permeability to the outside undermine its insular compositional integrity.

I mention Julie's garden not because Claude Simon consciously thought of it as an intertext for the Jardin des Plantes sequence of his book, but because the problem of framing that is crucial to Rousseau's novel (the impinging of a certain outside reality on the garden as self-enclosed paradise) is also important in Simon's hybrid text. Indeed, the Jardin des Plantes passage properly speaking (if one can use this term) is interlocked or interlaced with the description of a dinner in Madras in which the narrator (a narrator who is here as much Claude Simon as Charlus is ever Marcel Proust), in the course of evoking the guests, the food and the dining area, pauses to tell us about the artwork displayed on the room's walls. Along with a tourist brochure depicting, somewhat incongruously in Madras, a panoramic view of the Alps, we find also:

---

4 Jean-Jacques Rousseau, *Julie, ou La Nouvelle Héloïse*, Paris, Garnier-Flammarion, 1967, p. 354.

Sur l'un des murs est accrochée une copie maladroite à l'huile de 'Paul et Virginie fuyant l'orage' par Madame Vigée-Lebrun: le jeune garçon s'efforce d'abriter sa compagne sous une sorte de voile que gonfle le vent. Le ciel est noir, le voile jaune. Un lourd cadre doré hérissé de sculptures de style rocaille entoure le tableau. Trop grand pour celui-ci, il laisse un vide entre ses bords et ceux de la peinture (*JP*, 63).

We have here a second artistically transposed representation of Bernardin de Saint-Pierre's imaginary universe, with a slight variation: whereas in the Jardin des Plantes sequence proper, the author and his characters were statues surrounded by an artificially constructed 'nature' in the form of an English garden, in the Madras dinner sequence, an episode from the eighteenth-century novel is badly imitated from the first ('original') imitated version of Madame Vigée-Lebrun. In both cases, we are at least doubly, if not triply, removed from nature, which recedes far into the background of an artfully contrived tableau. What is emphasised in both segments is the defamiliarisation that results from the omnipresence of representational artifice in its varied forms. When read together, it is difficult to determine which segment is more suffused with aesthetic overlay: the Jardin des Plantes passage 'proper', in which oxidised statues of Bernardin de Saint-Pierre and his fictional characters lie underneath real trees which, however, have been grouped together to resemble 'nature'; or the Madras passage, in which a badly executed reproduction of an eighteenth-century painting occupies the same space as elegant Indian women eating food with their hands ('naturally?') while the European guests are provided with the artificial support mechanisms of knives and forks. In both cases, I would suggest, the deconstruction of the natural as such and the multiplication of artificial supports accompany what could be called *le travail textuel de la défamiliarisation, qui est celui de l'inquiétante étrangeté.* The fact that the Jardin des Plantes sequence 'properly speaking' (but what can be said to be 'proper' when there is no original and only an infinite regress of copies?) reflects, in an uncanny light, the Madras dinner scene is accentuated materially by the *mise en page* of the text, where we have a very interesting spectral symmetry. What I have been calling until now the 'proper' scene of the Jardin des Plantes begins, alone, on the second paragraph of p. 61; then, on pages 62 and 63 there is the interlocking effect of which I spoke (fig. 1). And finally, on p. 64, we have the concluding paragraph of the Madras dinner scene, which is the first paragraph of the page. Thus, the passages *frame each other* at their outside borders, but are interwoven in the middle, the

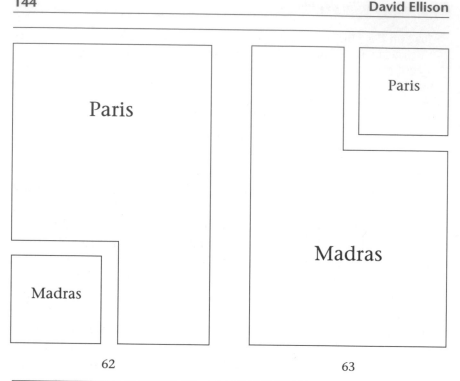

Figure 1

final effect being the negation of any possible prioritising of one sequence over the other.

Thus, the Jardin des Plantes passage 'itself' is not so much a central place to which one can return for hermeneutical reassurance and from which the various pathways and passageways of the novel derive logically and visibly, as it is a utopia in the etymological sense of a 'non-place' which is self-undermining and self-negating in its overlay of artifice and fictionality. A reading of 'this' passage (which means a simultaneous reading of another, perhaps many other uncannily similar passages) does not give us an anchor in nature or in reality, does not provide the kind of solid reference point that the journalist is constantly badgering S. for in other sections of the novel. Between the framed inside and the framing outside there will always be an empti-ness, a *vide*; it is within this space as *non-lieu* that resides the only *point de départ* possible in the novel entitled, perhaps perversely, certainly playfully, *Le Jardin des Plantes*.

The art of uncanny framings: Proust, prophet of war

Although I have taken some pains to demonstrate the reasons why I think it would be unwise to try to find, in the Jardin des Plantes episode, an interpretative key to the mysteries of the novel, it is also clear that the nature–culture combat which inhabits this particular sequence also pervades the text as a whole. I would say, then, that the Jardin des Plantes passage explains nothing, but reverberates everywhere, not just in the immediately adjoining description of the Madras dinner. I would contend, further, that the kind of juxtaposition one finds, microcosmically, in the framing/unframing of the two passages which inscribe the Paul and Virginie story similarly-but-differently is to be found everywhere in Simon's novel. One text conjures up another, and the texts resemble and differ from each other uncannily, according to the peculiar narrative logic of *Unheimlichkeit*. In order to illustrate this last point without being in any way systematic, I should like to turn to Part II of *Le Jardin des Plantes*, in which the apparent opposites of Rommel and Proust, wartime destruction and aesthetic construction, come together despite their 'apparente incohérence' to constitute 'un tout pratiquement homogène et cohérent' (*JP*, 203).

Part II of Simon's novel is composed of some fifty-one segments or fragments, varying in size from two lines to eight pages, nineteen of which are quoted passages from Proust's *A la recherche du temps perdu*, sometimes in isolation, sometimes accompanied by the Simonian narrator's brief remarks. Since the majority of the other segments focus on the Second World War, especially the debacle of May 1940, the first inevitable question for the reader would seem to be: how do the Proust passages and the war sequences relate to each other? What themes or stylistic devices do they share? What, so to speak, is their 'common ground'? On a first reading, there appear to be two possible links, one quite casual or fortuitous, the other strangely disquieting, or uncanny. (1) Casually, fortuitously, the rapid defeat of the French forces and the Proust passages (all of which come from one specific scene during the second stay at Balbec in *Sodome et Gomorrhe*) take place in the month of May, the springtime atmosphere being important both in Proust's depiction of the imagined Norman seaside resort and in Simon's fascination with the enduring beauty of an awakening nature even when sullied by the discarded *matériel* of wartime activity. (2) Strangely, uncannily, Proust seems to have 'prophesied' the Second World War in the sentence, quoted by Simon on page 159 of *Le Jardin des Plantes*: 'On disait qu'à une époque de hâte convenait un art rapide, absolument comme on aurait dit que la guerre future ne pourrait pas durer plus de quinze jours'.[5] With uncanny precision, Proust has evoked, two decades before its actualisation, the rapidity of the German *blitzkrieg*, but has done so, significantly, within a comparison, within a simile that explicitly compares modern art to a possible (twenty years later, real) form of modern warfare. Both art and war are in the domain of *techné*, and both are, in their different but analogous ways, superimposed upon nature, or *physis*. Readers of Claude Simon know the writer's continual obsession, repeated forcefully in *Le Jardin des Plantes*, with the strange dramatic contrast between the explosion of war and the tranquillity of an idyllic springtime countryside. The following is a passage from the beginning of Part II in which Simon, using the future tense in a hypothetical way, compares his own trajectory to the presumed route taken by Rommel on the same day, and in doing so, interjects a note of disruptive violence into a scene that is not without its Proustian resonance:

> Il sera alors environ dix ou onze heures du matin. Il fera très beau et le soleil printanier brillera sur les prés, les haies d'aubépine en fleurs, les vergers, teintant de saumon les fumées qui çà et là s'élèvent parfois de véhicules achevant de se consumer, étincelant sur les toits d'ardoise des fermes. Rommel sera passé là au cours de la nuit à la tête de sa division . . . (*JP*, 160).

The hawthorn hedges which so fascinated the young narrator-protagonist in *Combray*, those hedges which, in the course of modern literary history, have become, one might say, the intellectual property of Proust, appear here, but *framed* by the effects of the lightning warfare which Proust could only imagine but which Claude Simon lived through. The important matter we readers of Simon need to keep in mind, however, is that war (the terrible rapidity of modern warfare) does not, as some cultural critics would have it, negate the aesthetic as such or render it impossibly irrelevant in our contemporary brutalised world. Rather, war, in its Simonian presentation, is a patina, an appendage to nature that, despite its awful human consequences, will eventually disappear from what we call 'the face of the earth', consumed by Time, that most Simonian (and Proustian) of dimensions.

---

5   Marcel Proust, *Sodome et Gomorrhe, A la recherche du temps perdu*, vol. 3, Paris, Gallimard-Pléiade, 1988, p. 210. All further references to Proust will be to the third volume of the second Pléiade edition and to the scene in *Sodome et Gomorrhe* extending from page 200 to page 229. I shall abbreviate *Sodome et Gomorrhe* as *SG*.

The juxtaposition of a scene from Proust that describes, for most of its length, an idle and comical conversation about art on a hotel terrace with the relentless depiction of the absurdity and horror of the Second World War is less brusque, less contrived, than it might seem at first, for one essential reason: Proust's scene, like Simon's musings on war, is concerned with the transitory and vain palimpsest of culture over nature, with the stubborn resistance of nature and natural phenomena to cultural appropriation. In both Simon's novelistic universe and that of Proust, the individual human pursuing his desires and asserting his will-to-power is revealed as fundamentally puny and ineffectual – in short, to use a good Simonian term, *dérisoire*. At this juncture, I should like to examine briefly certain moments of the scene in *Sodome et Gomorrhe* to which Simon alludes repeatedly but fragmentarily in Part II, in order to determine how the Proustian text – not only those parts of it quoted by Simon, but those unquoted parts of it lying outside *Le Jardin des Plantes* qua frame-text – impinges upon Simon's novel and, in a sense, frames *it*: this strange enclosure of the outside by the inside would be the manifestation of what one might call *the textual uncanny*.

The episode in *A la recherche* from which Claude Simon draws his quoted material occurs shortly after the beginning of *Sodome et Gomorrhe* II, 2, and extends some twenty to twenty-five pages, depending upon where the reader decides to establish a logical narrative break (Proust's paragraphing being here, as often, not particularly helpful). The core of the scene, however, is easy enough to disengage from its textual surroundings: it consists of a funny, sometimes outrageously stupid discussion of late nineteenth-century aesthetic trends in the visual arts and music, punctuated occasionally by references to the setting of the sun. The participants are the narrator, Albertine, an unnamed lawyer and dilettante collector of art, Mme de Cambremer *douairière*, and her daughter-in-law, Mme de Cambremer née Legrandin. Most of the conversation focuses on the narrator's sly efforts to mediate between the elderly Mme de Cambremer, who is an outstanding performer of Chopin's piano music but bereft of any form of artistic judgement, and the younger Mme de Cambremer-Legrandin, who adheres to whatever the latest trends dictate, in this case Debussy, whom she considers to have dethroned Chopin and consigned him to the dustbin of history. As was the case with the dinner-table debates in *Un amour de Swann*, the humour of the scene derives, in large part, from a law of inverse proportions familiar to us all: the less a character knows about art, the stronger are his opinions on art. The other Proustian 'law' illuminated in this scene, which must have appealed to Claude Simon as participant in innumerable theoretically oriented colloquia, concerns the tendency of theoretical discourses on art to impose (retroactively) on works of the imagination a rigid and codified armature – dare I say, shades of Jean Ricardou? – whereas the real role of theory should be to ensure the continued productive evolution of artistic forms. In Proust's somewhat Darwinian terms: 'Car les théories et les écoles, comme les microbes et les globules, s'entre-dévorent et assurent, par leur lutte, la continuité de la vie' (*SG*, 210).

Perhaps more important than the moments of high comedy per se (Madame de Cambremer's confusing of seagulls with albatrosses; Albertine's assumption that the phrase 'les Ver Meer' refers to living people) is the matter of the narrator-protagonist's ethical position in this aesthetic discussion. Like Swann, who surrounded all his appreci-ations of art in quotation marks in order never to reveal what he really thought, Marcel, eschewing any form of authenticity in his discourse, does not speak in his own voice but adopts the ultra-romantic tone of Legrandin in order to be better understood by Legrandin's sister. The following is a passage that Claude Simon quotes on pages 161–62 of *Le Jardin des Plantes*:

> Nous regardions la mer calme où des mouettes éparses flottaient comme des corolles blanches. A cause du niveau de simple 'médium' où nous abaisse la conversation mondaine, et aussi notre désir de plaire non à l'aide de nos qualités ignorées de nous-mêmes, mais de ce que nous croyons devoir être prisé par ceux qui sont avec nous, je me mis instinctivement à parler à Mme de Cambremer, née Legrandin, de la façon qu'eût pu faire son frère. 'Elles ont, dis-je, en parlant des mouettes, une immobilité et une blancheur de nymphéas' (*SG*, 203).

Whether the narrator's own description – 'des mouettes éparses flot-taient comme des corolles blanches' – is substantially different from that of the 'ventriloquist' Legrandin is a matter for debate. The impor-tant point, however, is that Marcel *presents himself as insincere* through-out the scene. And this insincerity would appear to be infectious, since, later in the passage, Mlle Legrandin imitates Robert de Saint-Loup's 'dialect' in responding to Marcel for the same reasons Marcel had adopted Legrandin's verbal tics in speaking to her, the only problem being that this very 'dialect' does not originate from Saint-Loup, but derives from Rachel (*SG*, 214). With typical Proustian (or, in a sense, Aristotelian) complexity, we have now not just imitation, but an imitation of an imitation, language imitating language in a disconcerting regressive movement. Not only are the opinions evinced about art suspect in their modish quality, but the language in which these opinions are expressed is itself pure mimicry, ethically null and void. Culture, in this scene, is mere overlay, empty artifice, the expression of fiction as feint or deception.

The extent to which this sense of artifice or fictionality pervades the passage as a whole can be seen in those moments that fascinated Claude Simon – namely, the separated and occasional references to the seagulls on the water and the setting of the sun that provide a rhythmical punctuation to the scene. The problem is that the sunset, that cyclical demonstration of the recurrent and inevitable rhythms of nature, *cannot be seen as such* by the participants in the aesthetic discussion. The sunset, too often depicted in the arts, has become inaccessible to us as natural event. Hence Mme de Cambremer's remark, quoted on page 170 of *Le Jardin des Plantes*: 'j'ai horreur des couchers du soleil, c'est romantique, c'est opéra' (*SG*, 207). Hence also Marcel's observation, near the end of the scene:

> Dans l'ensoleillement qui noyait à l'horizon la côte dorée, habituellement invisible, de Rivebelle, nous discernâmes, à peine séparées du lumineux azur, sortant des eaux, roses, argentines, imperceptibles, les petites cloches de *l'angélus* qui sonnaient aux environs de Féterne. 'Ceci est encore assez *Pelléas*, fis-je remarquer à Mme de Cambremer-Legrandin. Vous savez la scène que je veux dire' (*SG*, 217).

What we know from the world, the 'world around us', is that the rising and setting of the sun provide the framework within which we live. The episode in *Sodome et Gomorrhe*, however, shows how the artefacts and artifice of culture tend to reverse this order and frame nature. This is strikingly and beautifully the case in the final allusion to the seagulls and the sunset within this passage, which Claude Simon quotes and uses to conclude Part II of *Le Jardin des Plantes* (*JP*, 217–18):

> Avant de lui [à Albertine] répondre je la conduisis jusqu'à ma porte. Celle-ci en s'ouvrant fit refluer la lumière rose qui remplissait la chambre et changeait la mousseline blanche des rideaux tendus sur le soir en lampas aurore. J'allai jusqu'à la fenêtre; les mouettes étaient posées de nouveau sur les flots; mais maintenant elles étaient roses (*SG*, 222).

Claude Simon chooses to frame Part II of his novel with a Proustian evocation of the sunset, ending this section on a note of aesthetic completion. The seagulls, seen through the frame of the window, are now rose-coloured; they have composed a beautiful tableau which Marcel and Albertine can contemplate from their privileged perspective. One might be tempted to conclude that the 'Proust-theme' has conquered the 'Rommel theme', that aesthetic form has, at least temporarily, negated the horrors of war. But Claude Simon himself reminds us that the short transition section depicting Marcel and Albertine ascending in the hotel's lift towards the protagonist's room is described, wittily and paradoxically, as a 'parodique descente aux enfers' (*JP*, 202), so that the tone of the Proustian scene, viewed in its complexity, veers from humour (from the *dérisoire* and the *loufoque*) to anguish. Most crucially, the passages immediately preceding and following the aesthetic discussion/sunset scene 'properly speaking' concern Marcel's contentious relationship with Albertine, and notably, his tendency to lie to her, to invent fictitious relationships with Gisèle or Andrée in order to obtain her submission. The entire episode with mesdames de Cambremer was, in fact, parenthetical, an aesthetically charged *intermède* that only temporarily interrupted the labyrinthine descent into cruelty and mendacity that characterises Marcel's 'love' for Albertine. The sentences that lie beyond the frame Simon has imposed on Proust's text and that follow immediately upon the evocation of the rose seagulls are worth reading. I shall quote them as they occur in the Proustian narrative flow:

> J'allai jusqu'à la fenêtre; les mouettes étaient posées de nouveau sur les flots; mais maintenant elles étaient roses. Je le fis remarquer à Albertine: 'Ne détournez pas la conversation, me dit-elle, soyez franc comme moi'. Je mentis. Je lui déclarai qu'il lui fallait écouter un aveu préalable, celui d'une grande passion que j'avais depuis quelque temps pour Andrée, et je le lui fis avec une simplicité et une franchise dignes du théâtre, mais qu'on n'a guère dans la vie que pour les amours qu'on ne ressent pas (*SG*, 222–23).

The 'love' of Marcel for Albertine is as fictional, as artificial, as the theatrical or 'operatic' view of the sunset, whether it be expressed naively by Mme de Cambremer or with some sophistication by Marcel himself. In Proust, the aesthetic is framed by the ethical: the question of Marcel's insincerity and of his cruelty envelop all idle chat on artistic movements and theories. If there is any metaphor one could use to describe the rapports between Proustian lovers, it would have to be that of warfare – of tactics, skirmishes, margins of manoeuvre, feints, surprises, *détournements* and *débordements* of all kinds. The realm of the aesthetic, in Proust, is always entwined with the fundamental violence of human behaviour, with the will to dominate and enslave. Claude

Simon the careful and imaginative reader of Proust knows better than anyone that Proust is not an aesthete; he also knows that the un-imaginable violence of which we are capable, as human beings, which he lived through in May 1940, has its aesthetic character, precisely insofar as it superimposes itself upon nature, turning aside, *per-verting* nature's laws.

We live caught between the aesthetic and the ethical, subject to the contrary pulls of culture and nature. Perhaps the most we can hope, in a universe of the fundamentally *dérisoire*, is that the warring factions of ideas and theories that continue to characterise the intellectual world do not result in the pure chaos and destruction of war *per se*, war in its literality, but that these ideas and theories 'assurent, par leur lutte, la continuité de la vie' (*SG*, 210). Claude Simon's *oeuvre*, in bringing together war as brutal fact and the 'wars' of human conduct, challenges his readers to bring together the literal and the metaphorical, to see the literary text as a locus of convergence-through-dispersal, a place from which, *un lieu à partir duquel*, the reciprocal claims of culture upon nature and of nature upon culture engage in the only kind of war to which the adjective 'productive' can be adjoined.

8

Supplementary Organs: Media and Machinery in the Late Novels of Claude Simon

Wolfram Nitsch

Throughout Claude Simon's novels, technology appears as an important thematic and metaphorical field. Montès, the main character of his early novel *Le Vent*, never parts from his camera, looking through it as through the window of 'une auto, un tramway, un train, un véhicule en marche' (*V*, 197); S., the protagonist and narrator of his 1997 novel *Le Jardin des Plantes*, is equally obsessed by technical media and by machines. In Simon's literary presentation of this field three different but often overlapping perspectives can be discerned. First, numerous references reveal a polemical critique of technology as totally exterior and therefore dangerous to man. This critique echoes the cultural pessimism articulated by Spengler and his romantic forerunners, who warn against man's submission to industrial machinery, claiming that instead of increasing his power, it actually usurps it.[1] Thus, the members of the society in which Montès lives belong to a decadent 'espèce nouvelle', a species unable to survive without technical artefacts:

> sorte de ver blanc et mou de fabrication récente, issu [...] selon toute apparence du coït entre l'automobile et le radiateur de chauffage central, totalement inapte à se mouvoir autrement qu'à l'aide d'un moteur, à se distraire qu'en technicolor et à se concevoir qu'en monnaie-papier (*V*, 104).

Although necessary, these artefacts always threaten to strike back against their inventors and users; in wartime, especially, they take revenge, unveiling 'l'inflexible perfidie des choses créées ou asservies par l'homme' (*RF*, 60). Second, however, a number of passages in Simon point rather to an anthropological assessment of technology as an indispensable

---

1 Oswald Spengler, 'Die Maschine', in *Der Untergang des Abendlandes. Umrisse einer Morphologie der Weltgeschichte*, Munich, Deutscher Taschenbuch Verlag, 1972 [1922], pp. 1183–95. An influential romantic critique of industrial machinery can be found in Michelet, one of Simon's favourite nineteenth-century writers; see Paul Viallaneix: 'Michelet, machines, machinisme', *Romantisme*, no. 2, 1979, pp. 3–15.

extension of man. Parallel to some important trends in modern anthropology, they stress the supplementary character of technical inventions, suggesting that any human experience of the world is always already guided by them.[2] Montès's camera, for example, is compared to a 'troisième œil, un organe supplémentaire' (V, 23); like a third eye it enables insights that would otherwise be impossible. Paradoxically, this crucial role of instruments particularly comes to the fore when they do not work in a perfect way, when their functional ensemble gives play to the parts, for it is only then, as Simon observes, quoting Heidegger, that they attract the attention they ordinarily lack: *'C'est dans ce découvrement de l'inutilisable que soudain l'outil s'impose à l'attention'* (BP, 187). Finally, technology often appears in an aesthetic perspective. Quite frequently, Simon's novels refer to technical innovations that stimulate or illustrate writing; like Proust, whom he admires, and Proust's followers Beckett and Leiris, he uses media and machinery productively by presenting them as powerful motors or models of literary imagination, and sometimes even of literary initiation.[3] This is, however, only brought about through the use of poetic devices, particularly metaphors. In this sense, writing itself resembles 'un organe supplémentaire' (RF, 33, 244). On the one hand, it seems to be just another of those necessary artefacts, very close to technical objects which are culturally less prestigious; on the other hand, it plays the role of a super-medium which opens up aesthetic possibilities far beyond the conventional use of these objects. Simon's threefold presentation of technology as dangerous inorganic exteriority, as indispensible quasi-organic extension and as possible aesthetic stimulus is especially prominent in the three late novels, where media and machinery occupy a central place. Consequently, I

2 This anti-rousseauistic view also chararacterises Gehlen's philosophical anthropology, McLuhan's media theory and the cultural anthropology of Leroi-Gourhan. See Arnold Gehlen, 'Der Mensch und die Technik', in *Anthropologische und sozialpsychologische Untersuchungen*, Reinbek, Rowohlt, 1986 [1957], pp. 147–62; Marshall McLuhan, *Understanding Media. The Extensions of Man*, New York, McGraw-Hill, 1964, especially chapter 4; André Leroi-Gourhan, *Le Geste et la parole*, vol. 1, Paris, Albin Michel, 1964. The last study is an important point of reference for Derrida's theory of writing, which is centred on the concept of the 'supplement'. See Jacques Derrida, *De la grammatologie*, Paris, Minuit, 1967, pp. 207–34.

3 For Proust's aesthetic use of technology, see, for example, Manfred Schneider, *Die erkältete Herzensschrift. Der autobiographische Text im 20. Jahrhundert*, Munich, Hanser, 1986, pp. 93–103, and my study 'Fantasmes d'essence. Les automobiles de Proust à travers l'histoire du texte', in Rainer Warning and Jean Milly (eds), *Marcel Proust. Ecrire sans fin*, Paris, CNRS, 1996, pp. 125–41.

shall confine my remarks to these novels. My principal instances will be the tape recorder in *Le Jardin des Plantes*, the railway in *L'Acacia*, and the cinema in *Les Géorgiques*.

The tape recorder in *Le Jardin des Plantes*

Among the technical instruments observed or used by Simon's protagonists, aural media appear rather late. They are almost completely absent from their worlds until *Les Corps conducteurs*, where the central character listens to lengthy speeches which are distorted by a microphone, and several times uses a telephone, unsuccessfully trying to call his ex-lover (*CC*, 93–118).[4] It is only in *Le Jardin des Plantes* that such an intense confrontation with an acoustic medium recurs. Here, the quasi-autobiographical narrator (who sometimes also calls himself S.) repeatedly remembers bits and pieces of a long interview he gave in the 1990s that was recorded on tape by a young journalist. At the outset of the interview, he declares openly his profound aversion for the medium ('Je n'aime pas beaucoup cet instrument', *JP*, 79), going on to develop a very critical image of the tape recorder which stresses the ways in which it disturbs and distorts speech. First, the taped conversation is always liable to be interrupted by technical contingencies. Several times, S.'s emotional account of his war memories has to be abruptly interrupted because his interviewer must check the recorder (*JP*, 82, 97) or change the tape (*JP*, 99, 276). Second, the recorded voice of the speaker differs so much from the voice he usually hears within himself that he cannot recognise it as his own. Listening again to a part of the interview, S. hears a strange voice that seems to originate from the apparatus itself, 'une voix métallique, timbrée, qui n'est pas la mienne ou du moins celle que j'entends quand je parle' (*JP*, 82). Within a few minutes, he begins to suffer from an aural self-alienation which resembles the experience of Beckett's Krapp, who perceives his own speech on an old tape as the voice of an unknown idiot.[5]

---

4 Before *Les Corps conducteurs*, the microphone appears only in *Histoire* (*H*, 326–30), the telephone only in the comic strip described in *La Bataille de Pharsale* (*BP*, 65–71). For a brief account of Simon's references to the telephone, which are inspired by those in Proust's *Recherche*, see Franc Schuerewegen, 'Orphée au téléphone. Appel et interpellation chez Claude Simon', *Poétique*, no. 76, 1988, pp. 451–61.
5 Samuel Beckett, *La Dernière Bande*, Paris, Minuit, 1959, pp. 17 and 27. Even earlier than in Beckett's drama, however, the voice of the 'idiot' Montès is characterised as a 'voix de phonographe' (*V*, 22). On Simon's general tendency to present the voice as something absent from or exterior to the speaker see Celia Britton, 'Voices, Absence and Presence in the Novels of Claude Simon', *French Studies*, vol. 36, 1982, pp. 445–54.

As the interview goes on, however, S. also begins to feel that his aural perception is being sharpened by the recorder. The longer the conversation takes, the more he becomes aware of the sounds surrounding him. This is because the tape does not distinguish between taped speech and the noise that accompanies it. Shortly after the beginning of the interview, the journalist suddenly stops the recording because the voice of his interlocutor is drowned by a roaring motor, 'un grésillement qui la couvrait presque complètement' (*JP*, 97). Although this loud background noise soon disappears, S. is from now on very attentive to all the other sounds that can be heard in addition to his words, even to the silences that separate them. By the end of the interview he seems to be obsessed by a faint noise that echoes the noise of the motor at the beginning, a 'tenu et tenace bourdonnement (ou plutôt chuintement) d'un moteur au point mort, tournant à vide mais obstiné' (*JP*, 288). It appears to him as a threatening acoustic trace of the world outside, a 'bruit de fond' suggesting terror and violence (*JP*, 299). In this way, the background roar of the metropolitan traffic reminds him of the traumatic war experience he has desperately tried to convey to the journalist. It recalls not only the deafening turmoil of modern war machinery, but also the 'fracas silencieux' (*CC*, 88) which is repeatedly evoked in Simon's novels, the faint sound of time itself that becomes audible between or after battles.[6] Thus, the taped conversation leads to an aural experience of temporality. Wherever S.'s speech is troubled or interrupted, his attention is drawn to what Blanchot calls 'le murmure', an impersonal and uncanny noise inherent in all speech but normally covered by it.[7] But for S. this shift of attention does not merely result, as Blanchot claims, from a poetic use of language foregrounding that murmur. It results rather from the use of an aural medium that reveals verbal communication to be constantly threatened by contingent noise.[8] Just as the 'silencieux fracas' in *Les Corps conducteurs* is revealed by the telephone (*CC*, 93), the 'tenu

---

6 This is especially the case in *La Route des Flandres*, where between the extermination of de Reixach's squadron and his own violent death the 'silence au deuxième degré' of the clatter of the cavalry horses reveals 'le cheminement même du temps' (*RF*, 30), the 'destructeur travail du temps' (*RF*, 314).

7 Maurice Blanchot, 'Mort du dernier écrivain', in *Le Livre à venir*, Paris, Gallimard, 1986 [1959], pp. 296–302. On Simon's familiarity with Blanchot, whom he met on the occasion of the *Manifeste des 121* in 1960, see his interview with Bernard-Henri Lévy, *Les Aventures de la liberté*, Paris, Grasset, 1991, pp. 12–21.

8 For a brilliant, although somewhat deterministic account of the influence of this mediatic experience on modern literature, see Friedrich Kittler, *Grammophon Film Typewriter*, Berlin, Brinkmann & Bose, 1986, pp. 35–173.

et tenace bourdonnement' in *Le Jardin des Plantes* would not have become audible without the tape.

Simon's novel links the imagined perception of time to the reception of technical media; this does not, however, diminish the role of literature as a necessary mediator. This becomes obvious in the end, when S. prepares the scenario for a film version of one of his novels.[9] Here, a long sequence shows the writer's study where the recorded interview took place. Like the earlier description of the interview, the scenario insists on the roar of the traffic: 'au risque même de lasser le spectateur, le grondement des voitures est très violent' (*JP*, 373). Finally, this harassing noise is replaced by the sound of the writer typing, a sound which is itself gradually superseded by the sound of the horses' hooves which serves as a link with the next shot of a scene from S.'s war experiences. The sophisticated soundtrack of S.'s film project leaves no doubt that the tape-guided perception of noise only turns into an experience of time through the mediating power of writing. In a way, this very power has already been demonstrated in the interview scene. For the uncanny noise from outside is not simply stated, it is also performed by the chain of signifiers: 'tenu et tenace bourdonnement (ou plutôt chuintement) d'un moteur au point mort, tournant à vide mais obstiné'. Here the incessant roar is suggested by onomatopoetic expression and phonetic repetition. The alliterating words 'tenu', 'tenace' and 'tournant', together with 'plutôt', 'moteur' and 'obstiné', suggest a mechanical sound, the same 'Ttt' that was used before to express the 'déclic' of the tape recorder (*JP*, 99); the rhyming words 'bourdonnement', 'chuintement' and 'tournant' imitate a monotonous ostinato. This is how the acoustic lesson of the medium is transformed into poetic expression. In this, Simon follows Leiris, to whom he alludes, although somewhat polemically, at the end of the novel.[10] Leiris, in a chapter of his autobiography *La Règle du jeu*,

9 In 1977, Simon himself wrote a script for a screen adaptation of *La Route des Flandres* that was never filmed. See his letter to Jean Dubuffet in their *Correspondance 1970–1984*, Paris, L'Echoppe, 1994, p. 23.

10 He is the dandy-like 'maître de maison au crâne non pas chauve mais tondu comme celui d'un bagnard, au visage torturé de bagnard, tordu ou plutôt convulsé', host of a private theatre première shortly before the liberation of Paris (*JP*, 341); the play alluded to is Picasso's *Le Désir attrapé par la queue*, performed in June 1944 in the presence and, in some cases, with the participation of a group of leading metropolitan intellectuals, including Sartre, Camus, Lacan and – as a still obscure 'cousin de province' (*JP*, 339) – young Simon himself. For evidence of his – rarely declared – admiration for Leiris, the writer, and for *La Règle du jeu*, see Simon's interview with Madeleine Chapsal, *Quinze écrivains*, Paris, Julliard, 1963, p. 169.

describes how the use of the phonograph led him to an early acoustic experience of death, which he evokes by a suggestive word-play on the mythic name of Persephone.[11] In *Le Jardin des Plantes*, the aural medium is used and incorporated in a similar way: with onomatopoetic and other poetic devices S. (re-)creates the sound of time and violence he has learned to discern with the help of the detested tape recorder.

The railway in *L'Acacia*

As the first example has shown, the omnipresent noise revealed by aural media is, in Simon, closely related to the sound of machines. Two types of machinery mainly attract the attention of his characters and narrators. One is agricultural, for instance, the wrecked tractor which is described as a paradigmatic 'machine' in *La Bataille de Pharsale* (*BP*, 147–53); the other and more important type is the railway, present in almost all his novels and almost always connected with war. Simon's trains lead either straight to battlefields or to prison camps, or, at least, to memories thereof.[12] *L'Acacia* offers examples of both types of journey. During the protagonist's railway journey to the Front, other quite similar journeys come to his mind: on his long journey from southern France to Flanders, after the general mobilisation of 1939, he recalls trips to Barcelona in 1936 and Moscow in 1937, and anticipates his transportation to a Saxon camp in 1940. On this occasion, the railway is characterised repeatedly as a pernicious vehicle which triggers or perpetrates violence, an 'assemblage menaçant' (*A*, 165) inspiring an 'instinctive horreur' (*A*, 153). At first, it threatens to hurt the passenger by shaking his body and by jolting his mind.[13] The 'bruyant fracas' of the wheels and the 'chocs réguliers' caused by the joints of the rails

---

11 Michel Leiris, *Biffures*, Paris, Gallimard, 1948, pp. 86–101. The name of Persephone, the goddess of the underworld, is associated with a threatening 'percée' as well as with the 'phonographe' or 'graphophone' whose scratches produce violent aural shocks.

12 See, for example, the train heading for civil war Spain in *Le Palace* (*P*, 44–99), the military train heading for Flanders in *Les Géorgiques* (*Les G*, 79–87), or the prisoners' train heading for Saxony evoked throughout *La Route des Flandres*. See also the post-war railway journey in *La Bataille de Pharsale*, which constantly provokes images of violence (*BP*, 153–81).

13 Both dangers are concisely summarised in *Les Géorgiques*, where the railway passenger suffers a 'choc brutal qui se répercute douloureusement depuis les talons jusque dans la boîte crânienne' (*Les G*, 82). For a historical account of reflection on these dangers, see Wolfgang Schivelbusch, *Geschichte der Eisenbahnreise. Zur Industrialisierung von Raum und Zeit im 19. Jahrhundert*, Frankfurt a. M., Ullstein, 2nd edn, 1984, pp. 106–41.

seem to produce an artificial earthquake (*A*, 169–70), a man-made 'cataclysme' destroying its inventor and user (*A*, 155). Moreover, the railway furthers the formation of large human crowds which swallow up the individual. When the military train leaves, the people on the platform are pressed together until they find themselves reduced to a 'conglomérat humain', an anonymous 'marée humaine' (*A*, 155–56). Later on, the same thing happens inside the train. In the goods wagon bound for the Front, the soldiers are transformed into a wild horde (*A*, 234–35); in the livestock wagon bound for the camp, the prisoners become an 'informe et vague agrégat', closer to a herd of animals than to a human crowd (*A*, 316–17). Ultimately, the railway appears as the central element of the continental war machine. The technical ensemble of powerful locomotives and far-reaching railroads provides an impressive image for the mechanism of modern warfare.[14] Thus, the military train for Flanders is described as

> un de ces trains qui tous ensemble, au même moment, grondaient sur des ponts, s'engouffraient dans des tunnels, franchissaient des fleuves, sifflaient lugubrement, haletaient à travers les plaines d'un continent couturé de cicatrices, cousu et recousu tant bien que mal comme on recoud tant bien que mal le ventre ou le poitrail des chevaux déchirés par les cornes du taureau pour les lui présenter à nouveau (*A*, 190).

The vehicle carrying the protagonist is only one of countless vehicles of the same kind, all running at the same time and thus forming an enormous machine, 'quelque invisible et impitoyable machine' (*A*, 379); their ubiquitous rails resemble the scars of Europe, now no longer 'raped', but lacerated by the mythical bull. Using images like this, Simon's novel points back to the pessimistic nineteenth-century myth of the steam engine as a destructive monster, staged most forcibly in Zola's *Rougon-Macquart*.[15] It is not by chance that all his trains are pulled by rather old locomotives, steaming noisily from one theatre of war to another.

For the traveller in *L'Acacia*, however, the railway is more than an impersonal death machine. On his long journey to the Front, he uses

14 See Schivelbusch, *Geschichte der Eisenbahnreise*, pp. 21–34, and Daniel Pick, *War Machine: The Rationalization of Slaughter in the Modern Age*, New Haven, CT, Yale University Press, 1993, pp. 35–36 and 101–10. The metaphor of industrialised war as a railway-like 'énorme machine' appears as early as *Les Géorgiques* (*Les G*, 131–34).
15 For a detailed reconstruction of this 'mythe littéraire de la machine', see Jacques Noiray, *Le Romancier et la machine. L'image de la machine dans le roman français (1850–1900)*, Paris, Corti, 1981–82, vol. 1, pp. 424–47, and vol. 2, pp. 391–97.

it as a personal vehicle of perception and imagination that offers a particular experience of time and space.[16] First, it permits him to hear things he would otherwise have missed. Lying near the wheels and the rails allows him to imagine the 'inquiétant et inaudible tonnerre' of all the trains crossing the continent, something very similar to the uncanny noise disclosed by the tape recorder (*A*, 170). Second, by accelerating the appearance and disappearance of the objects which flash past, the railway yields a dynamic, sometimes even phantasmagoric vision of the world it traverses.[17] The image of the crowd on the platform, for example, changes rapidly at the departure of the train, the faces becoming 'taches', then 'points', then 'rien qu'un indistinct et sombre agrégat' (*A*, 160); what was presented as the effect of a mechanical compression is now described as the result of a technically modified perception that shatters a static, anthropocentric view of the world. The guards who, during the night, abruptly enter and leave the protagonist's compartment are perceived as spectral apparitions: appearing and disappearing with almost the same speed as things seen through the train window, they seem 'enfantés par la nuit et la guerre' and therefore 'vaguement mythiques et fabuleux' (*A*, 195–99). Thus the modern vehicle gives way to a mythic imagination that traces industrial warfare back to archaic violence. Third, in the same way as aural and visual perception is stimulated by the railway journey, so retrospection is also activated by it. From his compartment, the passenger can see his past 'dans une perspective téléscopique', remembering other railway journeys in the violent world of the late 1930s (*A*, 165). It is only through this that he is able to imagine Europe as a 'continent couturé de cicatrices', torn again and again by military aggression. The train makes him a piece of the rational modern war machine, but in doing so, it also makes him capable of picturing its irrational origins.

Above all, the train stimulates his poetic activity. Right from the beginning of his journey, the protagonist shows a heightened sense of

16 See Maurice Merleau-Ponty's note on the 'temps de la nuit ferroviaire, des wagons' in Simon's novels ('Notes de cours "Sur Claude Simon"' (orig. 1961), *Genesis*, vol. 6, 1994, p. 144). See also Jean Duffy, 'Claude Simon, Merleau-Ponty and Perception', in *French Studies*, vol. 46, no. 1, 1992, pp. 33–52.

17 See Schivelbusch, *Geschichte der Eisenbahnreise*, pp. 51–66. This particular effect was already noted in 1837 by Victor Hugo, to whom the flowers seen from the running train appeared as 'des taches ou plutôt des raies rouges ou blanches' and the linesman near the railroad appeared as 'un spectre debout [qui] paraît et disparaît comme l'éclair'; see his *Œuvres complètes*, vol. 13, ed. Claude Gély, Paris, Laffont, 1987, p. 611.

the suggestive power of language. Shortly after departure, his eye is caught by the headline of a newspaper lying on the carriage floor, which because of the regular jolts of the vehicle he can only read 'machinalement', i.e. paying less attention to the transmitted message than to the printed characters themselves (A, 161). As a result of this, the headline letters cease to be mere conventional symbols and turn into evocative icons for the announced outbreak of war, just like the 'lettres de deuil' of an obituary (A, 239) or the 'caractères monumentaux' carved on a grave (A, 248).[18] The same happens with the name of the station where the traveller watches the guards disappear:

> CULMONT-CHALINDREY, le nom surgissant soudain de la nuit, passant rapidement devant les yeux et de nouveau englouti, comme si, de même que les gardes mobiles, il avait été enfanté, fabriqué tout exprès, par les ténèbres, vaguement menaçant, avec ses lourdes consonances d'enclume et de chuintement de vapeur, pour se trouver là, loin de tout (de la lumière, des mers, des régions habitées) au fond de ce temps sans dimensions où le train continuait à rouler (A, 198).

Observed from the moving train, emerging suddenly like the ghostly soldiers, the place-name presents itself as an iconic sign, the phonetic design of which evokes the martial sounds of an anvil ('*Culm*ont'/ 'en*clum*e') and of a steam engine ('*chalind*rey'/'*chuint*ement'). By reading it 'machinalement', as the train speeds across the country, the passenger effectuates a cratylistic remotivation of the strange-sounding name. Up to this point, he seems to be following the example of the young hero of Proust's *A la recherche du temps perdu*, who, on his railway journey to Balbec, also moves 'd'un nom à un autre nom', interpreting the name of each station as the verbal image of the locality designated by it.[19] The tendency of this remotivation, however, is very different. While Proust's station names evoke desirable, individual places, Simon's 'nom surgissant soudain de la nuit' suggests the noise of a war machine that destroys all individual essences by making all the names, as it were, sound the same.[20] In thus foregrounding the

---

18 For the semiotic distinction between symbolic and iconic signs, which was first made by Peirce, see Arthur W. Burks, 'Icon, index and symbol', *Philosophy and Phenomenological Research*, vol. 9, 1948–49, pp. 673–89.

19 Marcel Proust, *A la recherche du temps perdu*, ed. Jean-Yves Tadié, Paris, Gallimard, 1987–89, vol. 2, p. 5. On Proust's 'cratylisme secondaire', see Gérard Genette, *Mimologiques. Voyage en Cratylie*, Paris, Seuil, 1976, pp. 315–28.

20 A similar cratylistic commentary is triggered by the brand name MAC CORMICK in the description of the tractor in *La Bataille de Pharsale* (BP, 151). For further details, see my study *Sprache und Gewalt bei Claude Simon. Interpretationen zu seinem Romanwerk der sechziger Jahre*, Tübingen, Narr, 1992, pp. 220–23.

evocative potential of words, the protagonist's journey to war is also a journey to writing. Indeed, his violent separation from his southern 'univers normal' (A, 200), his transportation in the 'cordon ombilical' of the train (A, 240), finally lead to a literary initiation that makes him a novelist.[21] As he recalls during his journey, his previous attempts to write a novel were doomed to fail; his early literary efforts seem to have been no less academic than his early paintings, which were influenced by Cubism and its manner of converting all objects into geometrical forms, 'en assemblages de tubes d'acier, de cônes et de sphères' (A, 171, 180). Obviously, this self-critical flashback is also an attack on the uncritical attitude of the earlier avant-garde towards technology and its ingenuous enthusiasm for modern machinery, an enthusiasm shared by the Marxist 'philosophie de la matière' he was studying at the same time (A, 173). It is only after his return from the prison camp that his attempts to write succeed, stimulated as they are by the electrically illuminated acacia in his garden. Now he seems to be guided rather by Proust and the second, surrealist avant-garde, who both offer a darker image of the machine, stressing its destructive potential as well as its productive effects on art. This can also be seen in the mythic metaphor which compares the railway to a network of 'cicatrices' and to the omnipresent trace of a gigantic bull-fight, since the image is clearly inspired by Leiris's *Miroir de la tauromachie*, where the bloody ritual is interpreted as a model for an aesthetic anthropology centred on violence.[22] This is why the military train in *L'Acacia* does not lose its darker connotations when it turns out to be a vehicle of literary creation: even after it has delivered the passenger to his desk, its original terror remains.

The cinema in *Les Géorgiques*

Simon's interest in technology is inextricable from his interest in visual media. Among these, photography occupies the central place. In the course of his fiction, which is accompanied by an important body of photographic work, Simon often evokes the production and reception

21 For a detailed discussion of this initiation process, see Alastair Duncan, *Claude Simon: Adventures in Words*, Manchester, Manchester University Press, 1994, pp. 128–52.
22 Michel Leiris, *Miroir de la tauromachie*, Paris, Fata Morgana, 1984 [1938]. On the influence of this programmatic essay on Simon, see my *Sprache und Gewalt bei Claude Simon*, pp. 13–24.

of photographs.[23] Even more frequently he refers to photography as a model of perception and remembrance, emphasising its affinity with shock and trauma, an affinity already pointed out by Proust.[24] Quite a number of these references, however, reveal a special interest in the moving image (i.e. the image transgressing the technical limits of photography), focusing either on the 'trace fuligineuse' of the blurred shot (*H*, 269) or on auxiliary technologies like the magic lantern (*A*, 315) or chronophotography (*JP*, 30).[25] No wonder, then, that there are also numerous references to cinematography in Simon, especially to the early and rather primitive state of the medium. In the fiction of the 1950s and 1960s references are, by and large, metaphorical. On the literal level, cinema does not appear before *Triptyque*, where various sex-and-crime films are shown in rather marginal and archaic projection contexts, closer to a circus or a peep-show than to a modern film theatre.[26] Another but no less primitive cinematographic experience is evoked in *Les Géorgiques*. There, the protagonist, descendant and biographer of the French Revolutionary general L. S. M., recalls the Sunday afternoons he spent as a schoolboy in the cinema of his small southern town, watching silent films from the same cheap seats as the local gypsies. In the course of his reminiscences, he offers a critical view of cinematography, foregrounding above all the aggressive appeal of the medium. In several respects, this view corresponds to that of Walter Benjamin, who points out the tactile impact of cinema and the ritual character of its reception, but who also warns against the political abuse of these particular features.[27] The tactile element is underlined from the beginning of Simon's description. Before the projection of the film starts, the audience is harassed by aggressive

23 For Simon's own photographic production, see *Album d'un amateur*, Remagen, Rommerskirchen, 1988; *Photographies 1937–1970*, Paris, Maeght, 1992; 'Werkbuch', *du*, no. 691, 1999, pp. 28–73.
24 For a thorough discussion, see Irene Albers, '"The Shock of the Photographs, the Weight of Words": Photographic War Memories in Claude Simon's *La Route des Flandres*', in Thomas Wägenbaur (ed.), *The Poetics of Memory*, Tübingen, 1998, pp. 231–48.
25 See Luc Fraisse, 'La Lentille convexe de Claude Simon', *Poétique*, no. 117, 1999, pp. 40–41.
26 One of the two projections described takes place in a decaying suburban cinema, the other in a barn, the wall of which is papered with circus posters and perforated by a peep-hole; the peep-hole is sometimes used by two boys who at other times examine torn-off film-strips with a magnifying glass. The circus posters evoke the early cinema of Méliès; the film-strips are reminiscent of Edison's kinetoscope, which admits no more than one spectator, thus favouring voyeurism.
27 Walter Benjamin, 'Das Kunstwerk im Zeitalter seiner technischen Reproduzierbarkeit' (orig. 1936), in *Illuminationen*, Frankfurt a. M., Suhrkamp, 1977, pp. 136–69.

advertising, first by the 'tintement harcelant' of the entrance bell, then by the 'agressif rideau de réclames' which covers the screen (*Les G*, 204–08). This violent attack on the senses continues and increases when the showing of the film begins. The shocking discontinuity of the cinematic pictures, due to the 'flou sautillant de la mauvaise projection', strikes the spectator as 'terrifiante et vertigineuse'; even the actress on the screen seems to be violated by the technical medium, 'comme si le projecteur de la cabine l'avait plaquée contre le mur' (*Les G*, 212).[28] Even the frequent interruptions of the projection do not allow the spectator to take breath; when he glances at the floor, he faces the things thrown away by other spectators, 'révélés soudain en gros plan' (*Les G*, 207). In short, cinema confronts him incessantly with an aggressive material world; before, during and after the presentation he suffers the same 'chocs brutaux', the same 'sentiment d'agression' that he endures in a travelling train, when the 'lunette' of the toilet suddenly uncovers the moving picture of the detritus strewn along the railway line (*Les G*, 80). In addition to this, the description also accentuates the ritual element of the cinema situation. The audience seems to be attending 'la célébration de quelque culte barbare', centred on the screen which is 'le lieu d'une mystérieuse et lugubre cérémonie' (*Les G*, 205–07). This impression is especially fostered by the gypsies who gather in the so-called 'places populaires', since they resemble a 'horde barbare' constituted by 'primitives tribus' (*Les G*, 212). Analogous to the train in *L'Acacia*, the cinema in *Les Géorgiques* produces a crowd that regresses from civilisation to barbarism. In order to emphasise this, the description is interrupted by the evocation of a German prison camp where a very similar throng is gathering; there, the searchlight projectors unveil an analogous process of regression, thus repeating the effect of the film projector behind the popular seats (*Les G*, 209–11). This audacious analogy may have been inspired by Sartre, who in *Les Mots* also compares early cinema audiences to the inmates of a prison camp, since both constitute an elementary form of community.[29] However, even if this is really an intertextual citation, it is clearly a polemical one. Sartre praises the

---

28 A comprehensive survey of such effects is offered in *Triptyque*, where film is associated constantly with rupture, destruction and violence. The primitive projection produces continuous visual shocks when the film breaks (*T*, 52, 102), gets jammed (*T*, 129) or burns (*T*, 195), while at the same time the soundtrack is interrupted (*T*, 33) or distorted (*T*, 35, 57) by the noisy equipment and is, consequently, marked by a 'violence du son' (*T*, 139).

29 Jean-Paul Sartre, *Les Mots*, Paris, Gallimard, 1972 [1964], pp. 104–05.

cinema for the absence of any ceremonial, for a free 'présence sans recul de chacun à tous'; Simon, on the contrary, shows that a quasi-barbaric ceremonial is inseparable from the projection of the film.[30]

For all that, the cinema experience recalled shows still another side. The aggressive medium is also presented as a transgressive medium that, in Benjamin's words, effectuates a wholesome alienation between the spectator and his familiar world.[31] On the one hand, the films viewed offer him a poignant model for a new attitude towards history, one which is not guided by old narrative conventions and is therefore opposed to the attitude he criticises in the civil war historian O., alias George Orwell. His experience of the present is marked by discontinuous perceptions that are best illustrated by the cuts or tricks of a film. When he sees someone abruptly emerge from under the tractor at L. S. M.'s farm, he has the impression of a so-called stop trick, 'un de ces truquages de cinéma ou de music-hall, quand une scène déserte se peuple, s'anime tout à coup, comme par magie' (*Les G*, 153); later on, in the empty apartment of an estate agent, he again feels 'comme au cinéma', recalling this magical film effect invented by Méliès (*Les G*, 237). His view of his own past is also characterised by a film-like discontinuity. When, immediately following his account of the cinema visit, he recalls an episode from the war, he compares the transition to a silent picture where two temporally distant scenes are directly juxtaposed, separated only by a brief insert, 'par la brève apparition d'un placard' (*Les G*, 215). When he reconstructs O.'s authentic war reminiscence, which O. has so well concealed in his conventional war chronicle, he evokes the proto-cinematographic effects of a moving train:

> c'était comme s'il se mouvait, engagé ou plutôt aspiré dans une sorte de tunnel, continuant machinalement à agiter ses jambes sous lui, rattrapé, dépassé par l'assourdissant ouragan d'un train express, rejeté par le souffle sur le côté, les lumières rapides des wagons l'extirpant de nouveau, le révélant chaque fois dans l'une des positions successives d'un homme en train de courir, comme dans ces kaléidoscopes où l'on peut voir les petites images fragmentaires d'un athlète immobilisé selon les attitudes décomposées de la course à pied, avec cette différence que le cylindre tournerait à l'envers, de sorte qu'il semblait pour ainsi dire avancer à reculons (*Les G*, 360).

30 On Simon's critical attitude towards Sartre, see Vera Szöllösi-Brenig, *Die 'Ermordung' des Existentialismus oder das letzte Engagement. Künstlerische Selbstfindung im Frühwerk von Claude Simon zwischen Sartre und Merleau-Ponty*, Tübingen, Narr, 1995, esp. pp. 121–32.

31 Walter Benjamin, 'Kleine Geschichte der Photographie' (orig. 1931), in *Angelus Novus*, Frankfurt a. M., Suhrkamp, 1988, p. 240.

The remembered self is fragmented into a discontinous series of instantaneous images, as they appear in the turning cylinder of a kaleidoscope or rather praxinoscope, one of the nineteenth-century forerunners of cinema; this fragmentation is due to the quasi-strobo-scopic effect of a violent historical process, suggested once more by the image of a thundering train. Finally, even the protagonist's view of the collective past finds itself expressed in cinematographical terms. Reconstructing his ancestor's rapidly changing fortunes at the time of the French Revolution, he is reminded of an old slapstick picture, 'un de ces films projetés à l'accéléré, avec ses foules, ses personnages ataxi-ques, aux gestes incohérents, inachevés' (*Les G*, 385). Here, the discon-tinuity proper to early cinema takes on a metahistorical dimension, denying a teleological concept of history. Most of these filmic meta-phors, of course, have already been used in Simon's earlier novels.[32] However, it is not until *Les Géorgiques* that they are metonymically related to the 'eye-opener' of a concrete cinema experience.

This experience is, on the other hand, also one of ecstatic waste. Whereas the aggressive discontinuity of the film transgresses the con-ventions of perception and retrospection, the regressive rituality of its reception transgresses cultural taboos. The 'culte barbare' celebrated in the 'places populaires' may well be promoted for commercial or political ends; yet it gives way to an encounter with the domain of sexual or violent self-sacrifice which once was sacred, but later became repressed with what Leiris calls 'le sacré dans la vie quotidienne'.[33] The schoolboy is irresistibly attracted to the uncomfortable cinema precisely because it constitutes an 'univers interdit' beyond his upper-class background (*Les G*, 204). The sexual dimension of this forbidden world is stressed as soon as he enters, or rather 'penetrates', the dark hall (*Les G*, 205); the implicit genital image becomes explicit with the description of the dark screen as a 'rectangle magique, virginal et impollué' (*Les G*, 207) and the comparison of the smoke, lit by the projection beam, to a 'placenta' floating in the air (*Les G*, 211). Simul-taneously, all that leads to this world is invested with a sacral aura: the

32 There, cinema equally serves as a model of perception (*V*, 48; *H*, 41), remembrance (*CR*, 47; *P*, 20–21) or history (*L'H*, 72).

33 Michel Leiris, 'Le Sacré dans la vie quotidienne' (orig. 1938), in Denis Hollier (ed.), *Le Collège de Sociologie*, Paris, Gallimard, 2nd edn, 1995, pp. 94–119; for further details, see my study 'Besudelte Körper. Transgressive Kreatürlichkeit in Claude Simons *Histoire*', in Rudolf Behrens and Roland Galle (eds), *Menschengestalten. Zur Kodierung des Kreatürlichen im modernen Roman*, Würzburg, Königshausen & Neumann, 1995, pp. 137–50.

decrepit usher appears as a 'personnage aux occultes pouvoirs', and even the characters on the advertising curtain are promoted 'au rôle de tout-puissants gardiens d'un inépuisable trésor' (*Les G*, 205–07). The gypsies are subject to a similar process of promotion. They represent the dimension of violence in the forbidden realm: since they seem to destroy all they touch, including themselves, they are presented as human embodiments of 'la violence à l'état pur' (*Les G*, 215). Yet this is exactly what gives them the halo of archaic 'divinités' and makes them even more fascinating than the stars on the screen (*Les G*, 212–13). It is thus not in spite of, but as a result of the primitive ceremonial that it shelters that the cinema constitutes a sacred place. In this respect, it stands in clear contrast with the theatre and the church, the official sanctuaries that are described later in the text. Seen in the light of the cinema experience, however, these two also turn out to be barbaric places. When, for the first time in his life, he watches a dramatic performance or when he attends the mass on Sunday morning, the young moviegoer discovers further 'rituels à la fois sacrés et barbares' (*Les G*, 224), which are surprisingly close to those he shares on Sunday afternoon. Thus, in his personal experience and in his memories, the cinema always comes first, not last; its particular cult serves him as a guide to other more traditional and prestigious, but ultimately no less barbaric cults.

Of course, this special position of the cinema is itself already an effect which has been prompted by his audacious metaphors. He would not be able to describe cinema as a modern initiation rite without his own initiation to writing which takes place far from the popular seats and is closely related to the discovery of the General's papers.[34] Yet this last and perhaps decisive step in his exhausting passage through history can also be traced back to his encounter with the new medium. It is only after the cinema has opened his eyes to the hidden violence in his own cultural sphere that he decides to question his Uncle Charles about the violent history of his ancestor (*Les G*, 229). This narrative link is underlined by a rhetorical one which results from the double sense of 'placard'. The reference, in his description of the film, to the 'brève apparition d'un placard' (*Les G*, 215) conjures up by association another 'placard' which is located in the family house: the wall-closet where the ancestor's archives are stored (*Les G*, 193). Thus the novel indicates a double point of departure for

---

34 See Thomas Klinkert, *Bewahren und Löschen. Zur Proust-Rezeption bei Samuel Beckett, Claude Simon und Thomas Bernhard*, Tübingen, Narr, 1996, pp. 169–242.

its writing. Foregrounding its origins in the family archives, it inscribes itself simultaneously in the context of cinematography, like a text insert appearing in the course of a film.

Thus *Les Géorgiques*, often considered as a *summa* of Simon's fiction and as a guide to its characteristic features, also points to a close interplay between technology and writing. For a retrospective view of his earlier novels, it might therefore be illuminating to choose a mediological perspective, regarding them not only as autoreferential mirror rooms, as intertextual echo chambers or as virtual art galleries, but also as written artefacts haunted by the competing artefacts of the technical age. Viewed from such a perspective, it could perhaps be shown that Simon's protagonists and narrators learned almost as much in railway waggons or on cinema seats as they learned in museums and libraries.

9

One Step Further: Claude Simon's
Photographies 1937–1970

Mireille Calle-Gruber

[C]ette connaissance fragmentaire, incomplète, faite d'une addition de brèves images, elles-mêmes incomplètement appréhendées par la vision, de paroles, elles-mêmes mal saisies, de sensations, elles-mêmes mal définies, et tout cela vague, plein de trous, de vides, auxquels l'imagination et une approximative logique s'efforçaient de remédier par une suite de hasardeuses déductions [...] (*Le Vent*, p.10)

Si, bien sûr, photographier, c'est fixer au moyen d'une image quelque chose qui s'est produit à un certain endroit et à un certain moment, cette image en soi a sa propre existence, indépendante de toute fonction mémorisante ou de conservation. (*Photographies 1937–1970*)

Published in 1992 and presenting prints of photographs taken between 1937 and 1970, Claude Simon's book *Photographies 1937–1970* is itself a kind of retrospective.[1] Moreover, the themes of *Photographies* are related to those which can be found in the novels of the period, particularly *Le Vent*, *La Route des Flandres* and *Histoire*. This essay will demonstrate that Simon's methods as a photographer offer a retrospective understanding of his art as a novelist and, in particular, of his treatment of the themes of reminiscence and the acquisition of memories. Retrospection is one of the fundamental procedures of his work. *Album d'un amateur* (1988), the second collection of photographs published by Simon,[2] like the folio he recently assembled for the review *Du*,[3] are splendid examples of this theme, as are the novels, *Les Géorgiques*, *L'Acacia* and, in particular, *Le Jardin des Plantes*, a

---

1 Claude Simon, *Photographies 1937–1970,* Paris, Maeght, 1992. Hereafter referred to as *Photographies*.
2 Claude Simon, *Album d'un amateur,* Remagen-Rolandseck, Verlag Rommerskirchen, 1988.
3 'Claude Simon. Bilder des Erzählens', *Du, Die Zeitschrift der Kultur,* Januar 1999, Heft Nr. 691.

masterly retrospective of his *oeuvre* by the author himself. In the preface to *Photographies*, Simon insists less on the commemorative power of photography than on its capacity to present concrete reality: 'seule, à ma connaissance du moins, la photographie peut saisir et garder une trace de ce qui n'avait encore jamais été et ne sera plus jamais'.[4]

The pages which follow will analyse the way in which the writer works with the photographs and the *gaps between them*, in order to build the structure of a book that makes sense by putting the viewer's observational powers to work. The importance of the notion of construction is revealed in a 'diptych' which figures in *Photographies* (pp. 86–87): the left panel is composed of a photograph of a wall made up of alternate rows of pebbles and bricks (*Page d'écriture*), while to the right we see a wall of undressed stone (*Mur à Salses*). In Simon's aesthetic, making a wall and making a book flow from the same need: that of finding an order, of matching elements, of organising a sequence, of giving them direction and of rendering them readable. These are the main concerns of the writer/photographer who unleashes, through his images of the external world, a complex dynamics of perception and understanding (i.e. putting both physical sensibility and intelligence to work). In short, his work, whether it is carried out at his desk or in the darkroom, consists of a reworking of memories.

> [S]i je peux enrichir ou parfaire un texte en y insérant ici ou là un mot, une phrase ou même un paragraphe entier, je ne dispose pour corriger mes brouillons photographiques que du choix entre les gradations de divers papiers plus ou moins contrastés et de la possibilité d'y retrancher, jamais d'y ajouter. Pas plus en photographiant qu'en écrivant je n'ai le don de spontanéité, de sorte que, me méfiant de moi-même, il m'arrive le plus souvent (parfois aussi faute de disposer d'un téléobjectif) de cadrer mon 'sujet' très largement, sachant qu'au calme de la chambre noire, sans hâte et en toute tranquillité, je pourrai toujours supprimer ce qui me semble inutile, risque de disperser l'attention ou de déséquilibrer la composition.[5]

Through this search for balance within the composition, a search requiring tireless reformulation on the page, Claude Simon avoids the tautological trap of representation, the illusion of the photographer/ novelist, in Stendhal's phrase, 'promenant un miroir le long de la route'. Here, the mirror has been replaced by an eye that is invested with keen powers of observation, an eye that does not limit itself to

4 Claude Simon, 'Préface', *Photographies 1937–1970*, unpaginated.
5 'Préface', *Photographies 1937–1970*, unpaginated.

recording its observations, but that scrutinises them by means of the composition and the compositional process. This eye strives to see more clearly and, in so doing, brings the blind spot into play, forcing us to see the mechanisms of capture and relinquishment that inform it. In Simon, there is no knowledge without doubt; like Orion, we feel our way slowly and tentatively, one step at a time. To know is to try, modestly and using all one's strength, to go *one step further*.

Simon the photographer and Simon the writer have a common watchword: 'strive', i.e. strive to describe, to reconstruct ('tentative de restitution' are the opening words of the subtitle of *Le Vent* whose protagonist Montès tries to capture the world armed with that 'third eye' – his camera – which pulsates permanently on his abdomen). *Photographies* seeks to show time passing rather than time past (the photographic souvenir). It is not just a matter of taking a photograph, but of reconstructing the taking of it, of fixing the passage of time and its synapses, the transitions of the being-in-time. That is why these photographs are not still-lifes, but rather are full of the life that gives rhythm to this book; here the image is not transformed into some object or character, rendered inanimate as soon as transfixed; rather it displays the phenomenon of its appearance on the page. This photographic volume allows us to glimpse the existence of something that has no being other than these fleeting appearances, no logic other than the logic of the images.

This is what is at issue in the novels. In *Le Vent*, for example, the use of certain techniques – the syntactic modulations which the parentheses and interpolations produce in Simon's sentence – signal the volatility of life's phenomena:

cette histoire (ou du moins ce qu'il en savait, lui, ou du moins ce qu'il en imaginait, n'ayant eu des événements qui s'étaient déroulés depuis sept mois, comme chacun, comme leurs propres héros, leurs propres acteurs, que cette connaissance fragmentaire, incomplète, faite d'une addition de brèves images, elles-mêmes incomplètement appréhendées par la vision, de paroles, elles-mêmes mal saisies, de sensations, elles-mêmes mal définies, et tout cela vague, plein de trous, de vides, auxquels l'imagination et une approximative logique s'efforçaient de remédier par une suite de hasardeuses déductions – hasardeuses mais non pas forcément fausses, car *ou tout n'est que hasard et alors les mille et une versions, les mille et un visages d'une histoire sont aussi ou plutôt sont, constituent cette histoire, puisque telle elle est, fut, reste dans la conscience de ceux qui la vécurent, la souffrirent, l'endurèrent, s'en amusèrent,* ou bien la réalité est douée d'une vie propre, superbe, indépendante de nos perceptions et par conséquent de notre connaissance et surtout de notre appétit de logique – et alors essayer de la trouver, de la découvrir, de la débusquer, peut-être est-ce aussi vain, aussi décevant que ces jeux d'enfants, ces poupées gigognes d'Europe Centrale emboîtées les unes dans les autres, chacune contenant, révélant une plus petite, jusqu'à quelque chose d'infime, de minuscule, insignifiant: rien du tout; et maintenant, maintenant que tout est fini, tenter de rapporter, de reconstituer ce qui s'est passé, c'est un peu comme si on essayait de recoller les débris dispersés, incomplets d'un miroir, s'efforçant maladroitement de les réajuster, n'obtenant qu'un résultat incohérent, dérisoire, idiot, où peut-être seul notre esprit, ou plutôt notre orgueil, nous enjoint sous peine de folie et en dépit de toute évidence de trouver à tout prix une suite logique de causes et d'effets là où tout ce que la raison parvient à voir, c'est cette errance, nous-mêmes ballottés de droite et de gauche, comme un bouchon à la dérive, sans direction, sans vue, essayant seulement de surnager et souffrant, et mourant pour finir, et c'est tout...). (V, 10, my italics)

A rapid survey of *Photographies* reveals the part played by art and chance, suggesting the 'one thousand and one versions, the thousand and one faces' of reality. Analysis of the photographs inevitably raises questions about the place of the photographer-subject, especially since at no point in this book does Simon turn the camera on himself. He takes no self-portraits, presents no image of himself. It is as if a subject at work can only be revealed in writing or photography by means of a detour through the portrayal of others rather than directly in a frozen image of what once was. I shall return to this question of the photographer-subject and self-portraits at the end of the essay.

Visions of time passing: one step further

I shall begin my survey with the analysis of two photographs on facing pages (pp. 34–35), entitled *Jeux* and *Plus tard*, which show two streets in a working-class district. The photograph on the left offers a view of an alleyway, with washing hanging at the windows and a dilapidated wall in the background; children are playing, jostling and laughing. The photograph on the right presents the same view, the same washing hanging at the windows, but more sombre light and decrease in contrast testify to the advancing day. The scene has emptied, but against the background of the dilapidated wall an old woman's silhouette, black and stooped, is passing by. Behind her, there remains a solitary child, one of those who appear in the picture on the left, identifiable by her pinafore, sandals and ankle socks. She is leaning against the wall, motionless and expressionless. Although the

prints are identical in size, the framing is not the same: a slight shift to the right in the second photograph allows us to decipher the figure 4 inscribed over a door scarcely visible in the preceding photo, because clipped by the frame. The photograph of the children is entitled *Jeux*; the one with the old woman has the caption *Plus tard*. The titles say it all, with the greatest economy – by means of words, but also by means of the iconic arrangement. Together they denote the passing of time, which on a cosmic scale regulates the planets (hence the changes in the light), and on the human scale regulates the ages of human beings as they pass from childhood to old age and death (hence the juxta-position of the little girl and the old woman). This temporal dimen-sion is all the more striking for being captured in the period of photographic time that has elapsed between snapshots: in the blink of an eye the infinite cycle is suddenly glimpsed.

What the three words of the captions underline, by sending the eye back to the image, is the revelation of what is not seen, or rather, what is only revealed after the photographs have been seen together and then after another interval during which they have been scrutinised. In other words, Simon makes us see things that can only be seen through differentiation, at the periphery of vision, between percep-tion and the time it takes for the eyelid to flutter, the shutter to click, the page to turn. It must be remembered that in order to see, it is necessary to stop seeing, to blink. Considered in this light, *Plus tard* can be seen to refer not only to the moment of the second snapshot, but also to the moments captured in this picture-book project: the impression on film in the space of an instant of passing time and also the recording of the memories in the book that reproduces them. Herein lies the force of the tension. Time makes its impression in layers – cosmic, human, mechanical, organic, perceptual – which it compresses with surprising force. In the blink of an eye, in a flash, the wheel of life turns; between two static scenes, the planets revolve. Here, time takes a short cut from one moment to another, from beginning to end, from life to death (childhood to old age), from day to night (the white dress of the little girl, the black dress of the old woman), from plural to singular (group of children, solitary woman). From one moment to another, we see the anarchic dance of the childhood game and the single-minded gait of the old woman as she goes *one step further*. This juxtaposition of scenes is also emblematic of the half-seen exchange of looks on two faces confronting each other across a page: to the reader's left, moving to his/her right, is the little girl; to the reader's right, the old woman making her way to the street on the left, retracing her steps.

What we have here are a number of short cuts, in time, in space, in life. Moreover, as we shall see, the only possible measure of life, that is to say both of the present and of presence is, as far as human eyes are concerned, the short cut. Life as a perceived phenomenon is always in the present, the shortest moment. Life and sight are fragmented and ephemeral and, for this fragmentation to become visible and readable, photographic montage is required: the various sequences of images of *Photographies*, which establish an alternating rhythm of continuity and disruption. It matters little whether the interval between photographs is a second, an hour, years: it is as if the law of proximity and approximation structures the flow of images. This law accommodates the random; indeed, as we compare *Jeux* and *Plus tard*, it is the slight accident in the play of symmetries that moves us most. As a result of the non-identical framing of the photographs, the reader's eye has to hesitate as it moves from left to right between the spaces photographed: in this case it is the number 4 that the shift in perspective reveals. Though apparently insignificant, this shift highlights the recording of the event – time passing as an event – and offers a means of interpreting it. This event includes the photographer who has changed position. Moreover, this shift highlights the role of chance in alerting the viewer to the passage of time and to the signs of the intangible, the effects of which are only perceptible in infinitesimal changes.

Thus, *Photographies* can be seen to bring a multitude of discrete things together in conjunctions that are at once fortuitous and precisely labelled. Here, the photographic technique acts as a filter through which the world passes. Everything in the photographs connects to the world; everything is ordered according to correspondences that surprise the viewer, by framing that conceals and reveals, alerting the eye to what is happening at the edges of the image, out of the visual field, bringing the visual into play by means of the blank page which acts as a kind of paradigm. For, as *Photographies* shows, the present can only be recorded as a now that has already passed, a now that can only be grasped by the indication of its absence. Even as he represents the frail tenacity of existence, Simon suggests – through the meticulous placing of the image on the page, the careful regulation of the flow of the photographs within the book and the calculated contrapuntal play between the captions – the inescapable approach of annihilation. These images are 'about' going one step further, going beyond the limits a step at a time; they are 'about' the passing of time, which leaves memories in its wake and continues on its way.

This is also the sense, it seems to me, of the photograph on the front cover, of which an enlarged version appears on page 19: the silhouette of the figure in *Homme marchant dans une ville* equally symbolises that one step further. This is an image of someone walking within time, within that photographic time that leaves its traces on film. When the print is enlarged, it reveals a sign on the angle of the wall on the right in front of the moving silhouette. The sign reads 'Dépôt central de journaux et publications'. Here, chance has brought together in the blink of an eye the photo and the graphic, time in motion and time frozen; the words of the foreground sign draw attention to the key principles that govern the distribution of images in the book. The activities of depositing, storing up, chronicling and rendering legible are precisely what this book does. As far as *Photographies* is concerned, these words have the following meanings: 'deposit' means both the process of recording data and the data which are left on the page; 'store up' refers to the assembling of images in a sequence; the notion of 'chronicling' which is implicit in the reference to newspapers highlights the fact that the visible must be closely scrutinised if we are to see the invisible that lies within it; the idea of 'rendering legible' which is also suggested by the reference to newspapers draws attention to the fact that, if the photograph is to become a space to be read, its meaning must be reflected in the caption. The order in which these photographs are presented and the words that form the caption function rather like a magic lantern through which the subject or subjects pass. Neither still nor 'living', they come alive, in stages, in the mind's eye of the viewer-reader; the functioning of the camera produces a progression, which gives them a sort of jerky motion – progression by one step at a time – and brings them to life in the blink of an eye. It is this sort of cine-graphic (de)composition which is described in *L'Acacia*:

> Comme si lui aussi non pas se mouvait mais passait successivement d'une attitude fixe à une autre attitude fixe décomposant le mouvement, l'officier assis à côté du chauffeur bondit de son siège et va ouvrir la porte arrière à côté de laquelle il s'immobilise au garde-à-vous. [...] l'automobile aussitôt remplacée par une semblable, chacune l'une après l'autre brusquement tirée sur la gauche comme ces images que l'opérateur des lanternes magiques fait se succéder horizontalement, emportés (voitures, oiseaux, aigrettes et plumets), et effacés. (*A*, 314-15)

Thus, the art of photography reveals its main constituent – time at work – and that passing of time is suggested by the scarcely perceptible 'balance between forms and voids', between the images, between the image and its captions, between a series of images and their captions.

In this respect, the photograph entitled *Vent* (p. 101) is exemplary. Though the photograph focuses on a scene of rural repose – a horse unharnessed from the plough, a parked moped, a man sitting on the ground between a thicket of trees on the left and a row of reeds on the right – the title draws our attention to something else. For it is in naming the intangible – the wind – that the photographer discloses to the reader-viewer, who until then had not noticed this element, the horizontal angle of the reeds, an angle that can only be explained by the impact of a gust of wind sweeping across the landscape at precisely the moment when the photograph was taken. The naming of the element in the caption prompts us to see, to make the wind 'appear' in the photograph, manifesting itself in the effect that it has on the landscape. In short, the subject of this photograph owes its visibility to the life breathed into it by the word that names it, and that word puts on record the exposure time. That this photograph was taken within the space of a breath is suggested by the word that forms the caption, the very absence of the article evoking the expulsion of air from the lungs: *pneuma*, breath, wind.

Photographs taken, then reworked in writing

Far from remaining at the stage of snapshots, Claude Simon's photographs are recomposed in writing and show a consciousness at work or, more precisely, put to the test. Interpretation and scrutiny of the images release them from their referential contexts and site them anew, giving birth to new meanings. The captions create disturbances that set the images apart from what they represent and create tension on the page.

The caption goes beyond naming, often re-naming and/or adding names: it underlines the pictorial; it multiplies meanings. The compositional plurality elicited by these associations turns photography into an artistic exercise rather than a means of recording events; thus the panoramic view over the roofs of a town becomes *Habitat de sédentaires* (pp. 78–79) when contrasted with the preceding images of travelling people and their caravans arranged as a triptych: *Nomades I* (p. 72), *Nomades II* (p. 73), *Nomades III* (p. 74). The statue of Christ lying on its side is called *Homme au front ensanglanté* (p. 81), and this echoes the photograph on the facing page of a human form, a cripple, stretched out with his crutch propped beside him, entitled *Homme endormi* (p. 80), a correspondence that confers on both images the same degree of reality. At the same time, in the space between these two photos and because of the echo of one title in the other, we suddenly become aware both of a confusion of registers – the artificial with the real, the divine with the trivial – and of the biblical resonance (the son of God *fait homme*, who died on the cross to redeem the sins of the world). The photographic caption, in referring elliptically to the quotation, motivates and justifies both the consequent inversion in the hierarchy of representations and the new meanings opened up by the simultaneous effects of metonymy and metaphor.

Sometimes it is by way of synecdoche that new paths are opened – a thanksgiving plaque is entitled *Miracles* (p. 125); women's underwear and aprons drying on a line become *Enveloppes de femmes* (p. 97) – thus suggesting that to take a photograph is to engage in a relationship involving exchange, taking one thing for another, an object for an image, a geographical location for the space on the page. In short, mistaking becomes the work's guiding principle. But it is also by the reverse process that semantic displacement happens: for example, by giving the title *Tramway* (p. 76), a title derived from the object's original function, to what was in fact a tram and is now a makeshift house. Having changed destinations, come off the rails, stuck fast on blocks in waste ground, the tramcar has become home to a group of travellers (a man and child are standing on their doorstep). Or rather, this is neither house nor tram, but something in between: the margin of liberty and, no doubt, the only possible home for travelling folk. It is also a fine symbol for Simon's photographic method, which works between iconic reproduction and the written word, in a space and time that offer room for creative manoeuvre.

Sometimes it is through metaphor that the images proceed: for example, the crosses in the cemetery, hung and, as it were, winged with swirling open-work crowns of pearls, suggesting the title *Tombe d'un papillon* (p. 114). Elsewhere, the realistic effect of the snapshot is undermined by an equivalence: the photo presents itself as painting and designates its own motifs: *Femme et fleurs* (p. 134), *Modèle et chevalet* (p. 135) and, in the style of Picasso, *Peintre et modèle* (pp. 132–33). Through associations such as these, the admirable nudes and intimate scenes – *Femme à sa toilette* (p. 64) and *De l'autre côté de la fenêtre* (pp. 30–31) – flaunt their hybrid status between photograph and painting. In short, the photograph, having captured the real, declares itself as true to life as... a painting. Caravans appear as *Hommage à Van Gogh* (p. 77); the legs of tailors' dummies at the flea market become *Hommage à Piero della Francesca* (p. 122). As for life itself, if it is not quite fiction, it often comes close to legend. To be more precise, captions evoke the legendary: *La Sainte Famille* (pp. 68–69), a group portrait of a (travelling?) family – father, mother and three infants in arms – sums up the sacrosanct tribal spirit of these travellers of the open road. *Madone* (p. 67) is the title given to the image of a travelling woman and her naked child. The result of this interchange between what lies within the frame and what lies outside is to encourage reverse readings: the de-consecration of accepted values and the consecration of everyday life.

More often than not, there is discrepancy between text and photo in Simon's book; a threshold is crossed, a step taken beyond the bounds imposed by sight or by framed and codified reality. To give something a title is to flout the conventions of representation and to re-christen the world. Thus the round-bellied travelling woman leading a child by the hand is called *Maternité* (p. 41), or another with a guitar is *Musique* (p. 75). Generally speaking, names magnify, make for abrupt leaps from banality to hyperbole, from moment to eternity. The words of the caption function, in effect, like the enlarger of the photographer's dark room.

Yet this heightening of vision and significance is not simply abstract symbolism. Herein lies the strength of these photographs: they illustrate a process of symbolisation, while never letting us forget the compositional process by which visual elements are assembled step by step. For example, the triptych *Méditerranée* (pp. 91–93) shows a couple mending fishing nets on the jetty of a port; the distended shadow of nets hung up over a jetty to dry; the prow of a fishing boat decorated with holy figures, beached on the shingle. Through a series of words and images, these three photos allow us to see and understand the Mediterranean – a sea surrounded by land – by seeing, on land, evidence of the work of the sea.

Further on, two photographs with the same title on facing pages, *Espagne* (pp. 128–29), complete this reworking of images and their meanings. On the left are two carts in motion, one behind the other, their foreshortened shadows lying on a flat white road that stretches as far as the eye can see. On the right, a corpulent shepherd with a broad-brimmed hat and a large crook watches his sheep against a background of parched landscape and drystone dykes (p. 129). These are the choice photographs of a collector, and their titles reveal them as precisely that. But they also reveal the inordinate power of photography to make a world out of a stretch of wall, a section of the horizon, a slice of life. Nothing becomes everything; photography captures the surface of things, but also the essential.

States of existence, mysteries of being

It is now time to make some more general remarks, based on what happens in *Photographies*. First of all, Simon's photography comprises scenes of time passing which are also scenes of splitting; their space offers vision and division. In the course of a sequence of pages, a particular representation or title may weaken or reinforce another; alternatively, the caption may influence our viewing/reading, the framework of a photograph constantly 'shifting', never stabilising, as thresholds are crossed and jumps are made. The effect is that Simon's photographs present themselves as simultaneously here and yet, marginally, elsewhere; here and now (placed within the book), but displaced (in another time, either slightly earlier or slightly later); perpetually oscillating between what is 'represented' and 'what it might be or might mean'; between what depends on the photographic impression (what has been seen) and what depends on reflective vision, on the mind's eye. In short, this is an unusual method: photography through the eyes and work of the photographer-subject.

Second, this division also gives rise to the difference between an image of reality (to which all photographic activity is supposedly wedded) and the reality of the image which only the work of the photographer captures. For this 'capture' can only take place in the effort to release the photographic image from the reality from which it so obviously seems to derive, and thus to recognise its possibilities for revelation.

As a result, we see more and more of the photographer as subject, because he is exercising his powers, in search not of the superficial appearance of things, but of the world in all its relationships, in search of the unperceived presence of the world and of the unknown:

> Si, sur bien des points, on peut établir un parallèle entre les différents arts et la photographie, celle-ci possède cependant un assez étrange pouvoir dont ont certainement parlé d'autres que moi mais qui lui est tellement spécifique qu'il ne cesse de m'émerveiller: c'est celui de fixer, de mémoriser ce que notre mémoire elle-même est incapable de retenir, c'est-à-dire l'image de quelque chose qui n'a lieu, n'a existé, que dans une fraction intime du temps.[6]

It follows then that the principal concern of the photographer/writer will be to restore to the present all the moments recorded on film or on paper, to make them perceptible, in other words, as fully informed with meaning as possible, in a network of multiple meanings. To be more precise, this is not a question of reconstructing a fleeting present of transient things and beings, but of making them present to the reader/viewer, of presenting these moments of the past, these fragments of memory without hiding that they are out of date or that they are the debris (the ruins) of a vanished world. The themes of Simon's book gravitate in this direction: the images are of agricultural life and rural scenes, travelling people on the margins of town life, small-scale craftsmen, religious ceremonies and folk customs. *Photographies* stages the preservation of memory as an act of remembering.

Photography is threaded together from the traces retained by the fixative and a forgetting that never quite forgets. And the play of black and white which Simon handles with such great care is closely linked to the sense of the intangible that coexists in his work with the most sharply defined images: he carefully grades the half-tones, brings out

6 'Préface', *Photographies 1937–1970*, unpaginated.

the various shades of grey, to the extent that the grain of the print becomes visible, becomes light, like a transitory nimbus, or the softening effect of camera shake. We see, for example, the head of an ox in the foreground picked up in the death sentence pronounced in the caption below (*À abattre*, p. 47) or again the gable of a house which serves as a background to *Procession* (p. 27) and which, dilapidated and overexposed, has the fluidity of gauze undulating in the breeze or, finally, forming a halo round the well-defined features of a young travelling girl, the play of shadows and reflected light which scatters her hair in the wind (*Fête*, pp. 70–71).

The strange nostalgic beauty that emanates from these photographs derives from a generalised 'désistance':[7] it is as if these beings, these objects are in the process of withdrawing at the very moment they seem to offer themselves to view. Here is the winking of light as it strikes the sensitive surface of the film, the pulsing of time itself. Simon's practice announces exactly what it is and does at the very moment it shows what has been seen: that is, the emergence of a world whose elements are brought to the surface by means of appropriate techniques. For this is the nature of photography: it is an art of emergence, of bringing things to the surface, of unfolding the fine films of being. It is like the *Enveloppes de femmes* that Simon renders insubstantial by means of transparent blacks, whites and greys. The most 'poignant'[8] thing about *Photographies* is this emergence of the world into the world, this coming into the light, the attainment of fragile existence in the darkroom and in the laboratory of the book.

It is also possible to read this book of photographs like an altarpiece: scene by scene, individual tableau by tableau, this journey through life gradually forms a sequence. The book unfolds along an axis that moves from the anonymous *Homme marchant dans une rue*, *Homme à bicyclette* (p. 21), *Femme poussant une bicyclette* (pp. 22–23), to photographs of groups, of everyday events and seasonal landscapes, then to named people – *Jacques Prévert* (p. 136), *Alain Robbe-Grillet (L'Ecole du regard)* (p. 138), *Daniel Boulanger* (p. 139) – and finally to someone who has just a first name (*Réa*, p. 141), the face of a woman set in the surroundings of a room, a light room which closes the work. In other words, the work is organised in a trajectory from anonymous to intimate, highlighted by the movement from distant or middle-ground

---

7 I have borrowed the term from Jacques Derrida. See *De l'esprit*, Paris, Galilée, 1987.
8 'Poignant' in the Barthesian sense of *'punctum'*. See Roland Barthes, *La Chambre claire*, Gallimard/Seuil, 1980.

shots to the close-ups of portraits which make up the last part of the book. Such a progression heightens the paradox of photography as an art: the emergence of being in its various states of existence which is, in a sense, the quest for an interiority which can only be grasped on the surface. In the words of Michel Deguy:

> Une vue, c'est toujours 'comme' une vue, ou quasi-vue: sur ce qui n'est pas visible et qui n'a que le visible pour paraître (ou que le paraître pour être). Le sensible (à la vue, à l'oeil nu) est le milieu du transport, de la traduction: là où se transpose ce qui n'est pas visible. La métaphore est ce qui apporte originellement à visibilité la figure de ce qui n'en est pas.[9]

Photographies makes things visible, brings to light the face of that which is always unseen in the seen, unseen by the naked eye. Claude Simon, who never succumbs to the realist illusion, thus reminds us that, in fact, the photographer's eye is not naked, that it requires the assistance of crystals, enlargers, captions to enable meaning – meaning made from the sensual and from other meanings – to crystallise. Photography is another form of existence for the places and beings caught on film. In his photography, Simon never forgets to be... photographic: there is always something to be seen. He invites the reader, not to instant seeing and understanding, but to an apprenticeship which is symbolised, once again, by the photo of the wall. The title *Page d'écriture* is a metaphor for the schoolboy's first scribbled attempts at writing.

The photographs of graffiti also suggest the process of learning to read. The captions give them the same status as the protagonists of other photos: *Chat* (p. 48), *Portrait* (p. 49), *Pisseur* (p. 52), *Homme en érection* (p. 53), *Enfant sautant à la corde* (p. 58), *Personnages aux grands pieds* (p. 59). Simon uses these walls (which are far removed from the monumental *Rempart* (p. 88) or *Forteresse côtière* (p. 89)) to instruct us how to read lines, sketches, scratches, representations worn out rather than ready for use, the obsolescent incisiveness of graffiti whose raw, lapidary, playful meanings are a form of thinking before thought. How well this is expressed, without need of further commentary, in the wonderful *Lucie et le désir* (pp. 50–51) where the title is limited to quoting the graffiti itself. He teaches us to read these transient writings. In this respect, graffiti, these momentary gestures, are the equivalents of the snapshot in photography.

9 Michel Deguy, 'Le Grand Dire', in *Du sublime*, ouvrage collectif, Paris, Belin, 1988, p. 16.

As for the photographer/writer, subject of both writing and image, he is on the side of the *Plante grimpante* (p. 113), the title he gives to the photograph of a statue. This is an astonishing title in that it diverts attention from this reproduction of a gothic Virgin to the roots of the creeper smothering it, and the leaves that surround it. Hence the subject who sees and writes is on the side of life, in favour not only of sprouting and growth, but also of the loss of the petrified memory that they efface.

This highlights the paradox of the photographer-subject who needs to see life through art to refine his sensibility but whom that very mediation condemns to misunderstanding and dispossession. Thus he is destined, tirelessly, to go one step further: a subject at work, moving forward but, in doing so, distancing himself from himself; continually redefining, recreating himself.

Here the practice of photography intersects with questions raised by one approach to autobiography, where the issue is less a question of capturing an image of the self in the world than of fixing the acts by which this 'capture' is effected, of fixing these phenomenological acts which, while constructing the self, deconstruct, undermine its unity. The photographer or photo-autobiographer is less a living subject than a subject on the *qui-vive*. Poised between loss and preservation, he keeps watch.

I began by saying that there are no self-portraits in *Photographies*. But the recent collection of photos in *Du* contains one which corresponds to what *Photographies* leads one to expect: *Selbstporträt 1997* (pp. 72–73) in which the shadow or double of the photographer is projected on to the carefully assembled walls of the fort at Salses.[10] The photographer is not photographed, but photographing himself photographing himself, saying farewell to the hope of seeing (something), but continuing to exercise his sight. This distinction matters: the task of the photographer is to make images (make them so they can be seen) and not to be an image (fossilised). *Selbstporträt 1997* lets us see the subject in the process of in(ter)vention. Thus, in taking himself taking a photograph, he turns himself into a new *Page d'écriture*.

Translated by David Fowler

10 This photograph is reproduced on the front cover of this book.

10

Truth, Verbiage and *Ecriture* in *Le Jardin des Plantes*

Jean H. Duffy

The role of the references to Poussin's painting in the work of Claude Simon is a familiar topic in the critical corpus. Stuart Sykes, Celia Britton and Michel Bertrand have provided penetrating commentaries on the role of Poussin's *Landscape with Blind Orion* in Simon's fiction and aesthetics,[1] while Jean Rousset, Françoise van Rossum-Guyon, Mária Minich Brewer and Else Jongeneel have all offered subtle interpretations of the role of the description of *The Victory of Joshua over the Amorites* in *La Bataille de Pharsale*.[2] My own publications on the topic have focused on the formal and thematic similarities between Simon's *oeuvre* and that of Poussin and Cézanne and the metafictional and generative functions of the description of certain paintings.[3] The publication of *Le Jardin des Plantes* in 1997 established a new intriguing link in the Simon–Poussin chain and, of course, posed new interpretative problems. Among other references to Poussin, this novel incorporates a substantial description of his early *Plague at Ashdod* (JP, 106–07).[4] On the most obvious level of interpretation, the description

1 Stuart Sykes, *Les Romans de Claude Simon*, Paris, Minuit, 1979, pp. 158–59; Celia Britton, *Claude Simon: Writing the Visible*, Cambridge, Cambridge University Press, 1987, pp. 56–59; Michel Bertrand, *Langue romanesque et parole scripturale: Essai sur Claude Simon*, Paris, Presses Universitaires de France, 1987, pp. 177–80.

2 Jean Rousset, *Passages: échanges et transpositions*, Paris, Corti, 1990; Françoise van Rossum-Guyon, 'Ut pictura poesis. Une lecture de *La Bataille de Pharsale*', *Degrés*, vol. 1, no. 3, 1973, K1–K15; Mária Minich Brewer, 'An Energetics of Reading: The Intertextual in Claude Simon', *Romanic Review*, vol. 73, no. 4, 1982, pp. 489–504; Else Jongeneel, 'Movement into space': la belligérence de l'image dans *La Bataille de Pharsale* de Claude Simon', *Revue Romane*, vol. 26, no. 1, 1991, pp. 78–100.

3 Jean H. Duffy, *Reading Between the Lines: Claude Simon and the Visual Arts*, Liverpool, Liverpool University Press, 1998, pp. 197–247; 'Inscription et Description, Image et Ecriture: Poussin vu à travers les romans de Simon', *Revue des Lettres Modernes, Série Claude Simon, 3: Lectures de 'Histoire'*, 2000, ed. Ralph Sarkonak, pp. 163–89.

4 See Brigitte Ferrato-Combe's commentary on the similarities between the *Plague at Ashdod* and the descriptions of the Poussin wash in *Le Palace* and *Histoire*. Ferrato-

of *The Plague* contributes to the development of several themes that Simon shares with Baroque art and literature, most notably, order and disorder, the body and the senses, and death, decay and morbidity. While the tracking of these familiar themes in a new text offers the *Simonien* the undeniable pleasure of recognition, this article will focus principally on the contribution that the description of Poussin's painting makes to the development and foregrounding of a number of other issues, which are perhaps less striking on an initial reading of the passage, but which constitute important thematic strands running through *Le Jardin des Plantes*. Thus, the first section of my analysis will suggest, through an examination of the parallels between the subject of Poussin's painting and a number of other sections of the text, that the description of *The Plague at Ashdod* is part of a much more general meditation upon faith, the history of religion and the revisability of 'divine truth'. The second section will argue that the relationship between some of the figure groups in the painting not only reflects the communicative gulf between S. and several of the other characters in the novel, but also draws attention to the contrast that is implicitly established, through these social encounters, between various types of functional discourse and *écriture*. The third and final section will examine one of the main principles of Simon's own *écriture* – the priority that he gives to the internal aesthetic coherence of the text – and will analyse some of the ways in which it is achieved in practice in *Le Jardin des Plantes*. While this last section inevitably takes us down certain well-worn paths, the analysis of the ways in which the passage devoted to *The Plague* is formally integrated into the text will throw into relief some of the more distinctive motifs of *Le Jardin des Plantes*.

Ephemeral truth(s)

The Plague at Ashdod depicts the events recounted in *I Samuel* 5:1–6.[5] Following the theft of the Ark of the Covenant from the Israelites by the Philistines, the statue of Dagon, the Philistine god of fertility, next to which the Ark had been placed, was mysteriously broken and the

---

Combe argues that these descriptions refer to the work listed as number 196 in Friedlaender's *catalogue raisonné* and entitled *La Peste d'Ashdod* (*Ecrire en peintre: Claude Simon et la peinture*, Grenoble, ELLUG, 1998), pp. 74–76.

5 See Oskar Bätschmann, *Nicolas Poussin: Dialectics of Painting*, London, Reaktion, 1990, p. 119.

inhabitants of the town were infected with plague. The biblical episode and Poussin's pictorial version of it illustrate the punishment meted out to those who practise idolatry and polytheism and the triumph of the one true God over the multiple gods of the Philistines. Although the story illustrated by the painting is not recounted in *Le Jardin des Plantes*, the numerous references in the text to religious art and architecture and especially to damaged artworks and buildings establish a thematic context that confers a representative status on Poussin's version of the biblical narrative. As I shall demonstrate in this section, the description of the *Plague at Ashdod* is just one of many references to religious artworks and architecture that serve at one and the same time to highlight man's propensity for belief and to illustrate the many diverse forms that that belief takes. The description of *The Plague at Ashdod*, like the numerous references to other forms of religious representation, to religious buildings and to the various religious practices experienced or witnessed by S., testifies to the range and diversity of the creeds – both living and defunct – that have figured in the history of human civilisation, while the broken statue of Dagon is just one of many references to damaged effigies and buildings that suggest the inevitably limited lifespan of any belief system.

The evidence for man's propensity for faith is seen in all cultures and all periods of history. S.'s own vivid memories of the rituals imposed by his strict Catholic education (*JP*, 137, 189–94, 224, 249 51) combine with the images that he has retained from his travels to illustrate the diversity of some of the modern world's main 'living' religions and the variety of their practices, attire and symbols: the Muslim worshippers whom he observes heading for prayer every day and those whom he watches praying at Kennedy airport (*JP*, 134), the line of rabbis seen in a coach in New York (*JP*, 135) and the sacred cow which he encounters in a narrow street in India (*JP*, 131). Moreover, man's age-old predilection for idols, monuments and magnificent religious edifices is everywhere apparent in the temples and churches that S. has visited in various parts of the globe and in the highly diverse representations of different deities that he has encountered in the course of his life and travels.

However, if these effigies and buildings illustrate the human desire to transcend the contingent and the transient, their poor state of conservation in many cases testifies to the ephemerality of the symbols fabricated by man and, indeed, of the belief systems that engendered them. The vast cathedrals, temples and mosques that man has erected to honour his chosen god or gods, to accommodate the hordes of the faithful or to receive his own mortal remains are subject to physical degradation and to ideological demotion. Numerous pages of *Le Jardin des Plantes* testify to nature's power to appropriate man's constructions and man's own tendency to depose the gods he has created. The temple complexes at Medinet-Abou (*JP*, 362–363), Luxor (*JP*, 31–33) and Al Karnak (*JP*, 19) have been eroded and fissured by time and the harsh weather conditions of the desert; the colossi at Medinet-Abou stand 'insolites et solitaires' like 'les gardiens de quelque inexistante énigme' (*JP*, 363) and serve now to provide shade for the peasants working in the bean and tobacco fields. The mosque that S. visits in Cairo may still be a compulsory stage in the tourist's itinerary, but the dripping walls and damp carpets are evidence of the inroads already made by the elements (*JP*, 134–35). In St Petersburg, the rise of a new belief system that, although secular, turned out to be as dogmatic as the religions it repressed has driven the faithful out of St Isaac's Cathedral and brought about its transformation into a rarely visited museum (*JP*, 285–86).

The effigies created by man to represent his gods are subject to the same processes of decay and demotion as the buildings erected to house them. Wind, sand, extreme temperature swings and the passage of time have mutilated the statues of the Temple of Medinet-Abou and all but effaced its intricate bas-reliefs (*JP*, 362–63). The little armless and boot-shaped god represented on a column in the temple of Al Karnak is clearly a god of fertility, but he belongs to a long-defunct culture and the modern visitor not only cannot identify him with any precision, but has to rely on dubious translations for the elucidation of the symbolism: 'quel dieu à la haute coiffure ovale terminée en escargot [...] son membre raidi horizontal fertilisant de son sperme une salade (tradition ou mauvaise traduction?: en fait plante à haute tige feuillue)' (*JP*, 19). On the Egyptian postage stamp described on page 31, the Great Sphinx of Giza may have undergone a facelift, but its original function as a prominent symbol within a complex culture has been lost, and it has assumed a much more banal metonymic function as an emblem of Egypt. In S.'s memories of his school art classes, the Classical gods of Greece and Rome have been demoted to the status of insipid models to be copied by unimpressed pupils (*JP*, 194–95), while his visit to Las Vegas reveals a further degradation in the crass copies of antique statues that decorate the esplanade in front of Caesar's Palace (*JP*, 303).

In the twentieth century, the god of Christianity has had to cede territory to the competing deities of communism and consumerism. In Civil War Spain, Lenin and Stalin temporarily ousted the suffering Christs of Spanish religious art (*JP*, 29–30),[6] while S.'s visit to Austin, Texas reveals a new twist in the chequered history of man's invention of deities: here it is oil that has usurped the place of the gods of the past, the new god assuming material form in the shape of the first petrol pump, which has been erected as a monument in the middle of the public park (*JP*, 301). However, it is perhaps S's musings on the uncertain fate of an anonymous classicising statue, which he vaguely remembers having seen in a public garden, that offer the most explicit commentary on the finite lifespan of the godhead and its dependence upon the whims of taste, convenience or ideology: 'Je ne me rappelais plus la statue [...] fantôme [...] renié repoussé maintenant sur le côté pour dégager la vue en attendant d'être jeté au rebut remplacé par l'effigie de quelqu'une des nouvelles divinités' (*JP*, 29–30). The 'turn-over' of deities may vary from age to age and culture to culture, but if some survive longer than others, the countless damaged, debased and recycled effigies that litter the Earth point to the inevitable decay of all things, even those 'truths' that were once considered to be absolute, eternal and inviolable.

If these numerous references to idols, churches and religious practices serve to suggest the historical and geographical relativity of the godheads in which man invests his faith, they are not, however, I would argue, to be read as evidence of cynicism on Simon's part or as an attack on religion. While Simon has consistently rejected the notion of a transcendent, metaphysical belief system and while he has described himself as 'naturellement athé',[7] he remains fascinated by the art and architecture by which man has expressed his faith and which he has used to confer meaning on his world. The various faiths invented by man may have turned out to be perishable, but the surviving vestiges of those faiths testify to lives that, in rendering concrete their aspirations, have left their mark on the world and upon the cultural baggage of those who have followed:

> Après tout, les ruines sont des manifestations de la vie dans ce qu'elle a de plus robuste, et tout passé est une addition de ruines auxquelles le temps,

---

6 Compare *Album d'un amateur*, Remagen-Rolandseck, Rommerskirchen, 1988, p. 42.
7 A. Bourin, 'Techniciens du roman: Claude Simon', *Les Nouvelles littéraires*, 29 décembre 1960, p. 4.

les mutilations, confèrent une majesté durable que l'édifice ainsi ennobli n'avait pas à l'état neuf. Nous sommes tous constitués de ruines: celles des civilisations passées, celles des événements de notre vie dont il ne subsiste dans notre mémoire que des fragments.[8]

The divine 'truth' asserted by *The Plague at Ashdod* may fail to convince either S. or Simon, but the scene depicted in Poussin's painting offers a résumé of the history of human belief as it is represented in *Le Jardin des Plantes*. In *Le Jardin des Plantes*, the history of religion is seen as a succession of 'truths' whose currency value is limited in both time and space and whose definition is contingent upon prevailing political and ideological circumstances. Nowhere is the relativity of 'truth' more apparent than in the manuscripts of Erasmus's *Colloquia* which S. views in the library of the University of Salamanca. This manuscript bears the physical evidence of the schisms which divided the Roman Catholic Church during the Reformation and Counter-Reformation, the thick black ink of the censor that obliterates sometimes extensive passages of Erasmus's text highlighting the Church's uneasy relationship with humanism and man's predilection for adapting the 'truths' of the past to accommodate changes in church politics. If the story of the deposal and shattering of the statue of Dagon and the plague inflicted upon the Philistines has long since lost its credibility and ideological force, the multiple correspondences which Simon establishes between the broken effigy of Poussin's work and the other damaged, decaying and demoted religious artworks and edifices make it a representative relic of the civilisations that, although long since defunct, continue to inform our collective memory and, consequently, our identity.

Culture, ideology and verbiage

The function of the description of *The Plague at Ashdod* is not, however, restricted to its status as a résumé of Simon's idiosyncratic history of religious belief. In his scrutiny of *The Plague*, S.'s attention gradually shifts from the central foreground scene of death and tumult to take in other elements of the composition, his eye pausing first on two figures who seem to be leaving the scene, and then on the small figures standing on the balcony in the middle distance. As he focuses successively on these details, S. animates the scene in his

8 *Album d'un amateur*, p. 18.

mind's eye.[9] According to this imaginary animation, the departing figures tire of the 'palabres' of the crowd assembled in front of the temple and walk away, while the figures on the balcony look on, as passive observers. It is my contention here that the animation of the painting and the interpretation of the body language and positioning of these two sets of figures act as an oblique commentary on S.'s status as an outsider and on his impatience with certain types of discourse and certain attitudes to language: notably, political rhetoric, Ricardolian theory, free associative discourse and utilitarian conceptions of language which invest it with the power to convey a message or to give access to 'the truth'. As readers of Simon's interviews will recognise, S.'s marginality and his attitudes to utilitarian concepts of language mirror the sentiments expressed by the author in his public statements and his sense of ideological marginality within his own country and culture:

> Je suis rejeté presque à l'unanimité dans mon propre pays où, pour reprendre une expression de mon ami le philosophe Kostas Axelos, n'étant *'ni chrétien, ni communiste, ni existentialiste, ni surréaliste'*, je suis en quelque sorte en situation de *'personne déplacée'* [...] En tout état de cause, je reste, comme vous le voyez, un marginal et, après tout, peut-être n'ai-je pas ma place parmi ceux que vous cherchez à réunir.[10]

If S. cannot be identified with Simon – this is a novel, not autobiography – it is clear that he is, nevertheless, a kind of fictional *alter ego* whose contact with other literary and artistic figures and whose attendance at various literary events allow Simon to suggest obliquely – through a series of corresponding and contrasting speeches, dialogues and debates – the limitations of language and, simultaneously, to highlight the aesthetic principles according to which all his novels have been composed. By virtue of the body of parallels that link the description of the *Plague at Ashdod* with many of the other scenes of *Le*

---

9 Ferrato-Combe offers an interesting insight into the role of the balcony figures and the animation of the scene in *Le Jardin des Plantes*: 'Ce tableau intéresse particulièrement Claude Simon qui l'avait choisi pour un projet cinématographique en collaboration avec le musée du Louvre (notamment en raison de la présence de petits personnages d'observateurs, de témoins qui se trouvent au premier étage du palais représenté sur la droite du tableau – comme il s'en trouve d'ailleurs, à un emplacement identique, dans l'*Enlèvement des Sabines*. La caméra aurait adopté le point de vue de ces personnages, nouvelles incarnations du "voyeur" souvent présent dans ses descriptions' (*Ecrire en peintre: Claude Simon et la peinture*, p. 76).

10 Claude Simon, 'L'Art, "la lutte contre l'obscurantisme"', *Le Monde*, 5 décembre 1986, p. 13.

Nicholas Poussin, *The Plague at Ashdod*, c. 1630, Louvre, Paris © RMN, Paris

Jardin des Plantes, the departing couple and the balcony figures of
Poussin's painting take on a representative status, offering S./ Simon
visual correlatives of his own sense of marginality and his unwilling-
ness to engage in 'palabres'.

   Although *Le Jardin des Plantes* consists primarily of descriptions, it is
punctuated by a series of dialogues in which little or no communication takes place. The impediments to communication vary according to the context and the personalities, histories and status of the
participants. Effective communication is hampered by a variety of
factors, including ideological incompatibility, innate reticence, dis-
trust, linguistic shortcomings and cultural and social inequalities. In
the sections devoted to Josef Brodsky's trial, the judge and the accused
are separated by an unbridgeable ideological gulf, which makes the
poet's direct, but uncompromisingly laconic answers unacceptable to
his interrogator (*JP*, 101–02, 105–06, 110–11). In Civil War Spain, the
prevailing atmosphere of suspicion and insecurity and the dubious
allegiances of some of the participants discourage loose talk and curb
candour. At the drunken, nocturnal debate on 'Freud, Marx, Jésus,
Strindberg' that takes place during a visit to Scandinavia, fatigue and

lack of interest in the sweeping, directionless discussion make S. adopt once again the role of the silent onlooker (*JP*, 121–24), while his poor English impairs his ability to defend himself against or even respond to the verbal attacks of an unidentified female companion who sees him off at the airport (*JP*, 142, 144, 149, 153). Even the extracts from Proust's *A la recherche du temps perdu* illustrate some of the pitfalls that beset social intercourse. These extracts, which are scattered through the second section of the novel, offer a range of examples of communicative problems. The marquise de Cambremer and 'le premier président' are not on speaking terms (*JP*, 200). The efforts of the toothless 'marquise douairière' to contribute to discussions on art and music are rendered grotesque by the excessive saliva which she produces (*JP*, 173). Finally, the account of the rather embarrassing ride in the lift with Albertine and the lift attendant highlights the impediments which sex and class pose in the way of communication.

If the foregoing examples clearly indicate a thematic pattern highlighting the complexities and pitfalls of human intercourse, it is, nevertheless, in the sections devoted to his visit to the Soviet Union, the Cerisy colloquium on the *nouveau roman*, the informal *première* of Picasso's *Désir attrapé par la queue* and the interview with the journalist that S.'s status as a cultural outsider is most clearly signalled. It is also in these sections and in the description of an evening spent in Calcutta with Antoine V. and Roger C. that Simon's own views on the communicative limitations and aesthetic potential of language are most fully, if indirectly, developed.

S.'s impatience with political rhetoric is established in the first section of the novel, which is punctuated by textual sections based upon Simon's visit to Russia and Kirghistan in October 1986 as a member of a party of international VIPs who had been invited to the Soviet Union in order to participate in a forum on world peace.[11] Neither the forum nor the various official engagements cut any ice with S. who quickly recognises his own status as a dissident outsider. To S., the speech made by the Soviet leader at a reception held for the VIPs is a crude and self-contradictory propaganda exercise. Its references to openness and humanist values are designed to impress his Western audience, but are undermined not only by the evidence of the state's repressive history and inhumanity, but also by the vestiges of totalitarian mentality that are unconsciously revealed in the

---

11 See Simon, 'L'Art, "la lutte contre l'obscurantisme"', p. 13.

intractable severity of the speaker's facial expressions and in the pro-
hibitionist riders with which he qualifies his declarations of freedom
(*JP*,18). Of the guests, S. is, apparently, the only one to show any resistance to the General Secretary's address. The two 'Harlem Brothers'
suspend their double act long enough to show their respect (*JP*, 18).
The 'Second mari de la plus belle femme du monde' (*JP*, 18) seems to
be equally impressed by their host's stirring words. By contrast, S.,
irritated, tired and tight-lipped, musters just enough civility to make
the bland, formulaic compliments that his interpreter and her superior
evidently want to hear (*JP*, 51, 322).

If the formality of the official audience with the Soviet head of state
provides S. with a convenient camouflage for his personal sentiments
and if he manages to keep his tongue in check during that audience,
the forum and, in particular, the formulation and negotiation of the
concluding joint statement force him out into the open. Like the
couple who walk away from the earnest discussions of the central
figures in the *Plague at Ashdod*, Simon's weariness of the 'verbeuses et
vides interventions' is translated into physical terms when he gets up
and walks out of the final banquet (*JP*, 327). For S. the forum is an
ordeal in which he is subjected to five days of 'verbiage' and 'idioties'
and he dismisses the joint statement that emerges from the debate as a
'bafouillis' consisting of 'salmigondis' and 'âneries'. Alone among the
guests, he refuses to sign the statement, resolutely resisting the efforts
of the interpreters and one of the other participants to cajole, persuade
and, finally, shame him into signing. If he initially derives amusement
from baiting the interpreter, his mock indignation turns into fury as
soon as 'le diplomate hispanique' (*JP*, 327) applies pressure on him.
His signature is simply not negotiable (*JP*, 102–04, 136). However, S.'s
refusal is not born of bloody-mindedness. Too much is at stake for him
to subscribe to a document that has its origin in a conception of
language that he believes to be fundamentally flawed and that draws
upon the hackneyed imagery of a bankrupt political ideology: 'Bon
Dieu!: "les moissons futures"! Vous croyez que je vais signer quelque
chose comme ça?' (*JP*, 136). Revision of the document is pointless,
because he contests the validity of the principle on which the forum is
founded: i.e. the belief that language can be manipulated to convey a
message that will change the world. If his acceptance of the role of
'brebis galeuse, mouton noir' (*JP*, 18) causes some temporary embar-
rassment and animosity, it is, ultimately, a small price to pay for the
preservation of personal and artistic integrity.

The extract from the 1971 Cerisy colloquium on the *nouveau roman* which figures on pages 355–58 offers another instance of 'palabres' and further evidence of S.'s marginality. Here, S. finds himself in conflict with a viewpoint that is very different from that formulated in the Soviet forum, but that is no less dogmatic.[12] This section repeats *verbatim* the contributions of Jean Ricardou, Alain Robbe-Grillet, Françoise van Rossum-Guyon and Léon Roudiez to a discussion about the status of the 'referents' that Simon had supplied for exhibition at Cerisy. The extract is prefaced by a brief commentary on the stir caused by Simon's exhibits and by a summary of the ideological questions that they had raised. Both the preface and the extract highlight one thing: Simon's problematic status as a *nouveau romancier*. The digest of questions on pages 355–56 shows that Simon's provision of documentary material for the exhibition accompanying the colloquium had been interpreted as a challenge to the fundamental principles of the group and, consequently, as a threat to its ideological cohesion.

In fact, as the directly quoted exchanges show, the group was never as cohesive as its self-appointed spokesman Jean Ricardou liked to think. The extract, which is taken from the debate following Ricardou's opening paper, 'Le Nouveau Roman existe-t-il?',[13] shows telling differences in the reactions of the participants to Simon's fiction. The rather tortuous reasoning of J.R. and of the anonymous 'intervenant' and J.R.'s rather cavalier attitude to concrete evidence – 'S'agissant de théorie, les lettres d'un officier de cavalerie, je dois avouer qu'elles m'importent assez peu' (*JP*, 356) – show the determination of the anti-referentialist camp to accommodate Simon's fiction to fit its own highly theorised critical framework. By contrast, the response of the anonymous 'participante' is based upon intuition and textual evidence rather than upon the imposition of a predetermined ideological framework, and shows a willingness to acknowledge the referential dimension of Simon's fiction (*JP*, 356). R.-G.'s position is rather more equivocal: he is keen to toe the theoretical line and seems willing to recognise J.R.'s status as ideological spokesman, but his reiteration of the issues raised by S.'s banknotes shows that he cannot quite bring himself to be as nonchalant as J.R. about the concrete evidence supplied by S.

12 *Nouveau Roman, hier, aujourd'hui*, ed. Jean Ricardou, 2 vols, Paris, Union Générale d'Editions, 1972, vol. I, pp. 29–31, 33.
13 *Nouveau Roman, hier, aujourd'hui*, vol. I, pp. 9–20.

Veteran *nouveau roman* critics will read this extract with rueful amusement, recognising in it the early signs of the theoretical stranglehold which Ricardou was going to maintain on debate on the *nouveau roman* in the decade which followed. For *Simoniens*, the isolation of this particular set of exchanges highlights the feature of Simon's work – its referential dimension – which was to constitute the fundamental stumbling block to Ricardou's attempt to 'assimilate' it within his dogmatically formalist definition of the *nouveau roman*, while the summary of hitherto unrecorded discussion that precedes the extract reveals that, even in 1971, Simon was regarded, by at least some of the colloquium participants, as an interloper within the group.

S.'s isolation at the Soviet forum and his rank-breaking exhibition of referents at Cerisy were, however, not the first signs of his status as a cultural outcast. These occasions simply reinforce the feelings of dissociation provoked by his much earlier encounter with the literary intelligentsia of Montparnasse during the war. S. is a reluctant member of the audience that assembles for the first reading of *Le Désir attrapé par la queue*, the play that Picasso wrote in 1941, which was performed in Michel Leiris's apartment in 1944 with Camus as the producer and Sartre and Simone de Beauvoir reading some of the parts.[14] From the moment he arrives, S. is uneasy in the circle in which he finds himself: the other members of the audience all seem to belong to Montparnasse's affluent and fashionable artistic bohemia, 'une sorte de société secrète' (*JP*, 340) whose elegance makes him feel like a 'rustaud' and whose urbane chatter forces him to take refuge in the nearest corner (*JP*, 339). The play, supposedly a symbolic evocation of the deprivations of the Occupation, consists, by and large, of unintelligible tirades, insults, onomatopoeic exclamations, expletives and shouting that, in contrast with Picasso's ground-breaking painting and sculpture, hark back to the spirit and style of Jarry and Apollinaire. S.'s dominant impression is that of a deafening and senseless hubbub. Here, as at the Soviet forum and like the departing couple in the *Plague at Ashdod*, he signals his alienation by distancing himself physically from the proceedings. His physical withdrawal into a corner of the room is followed by distraction from the play by the sight of a column of German soldiers which he glimpses through the windows of the apartment (*JP*, 344) and, then, by mental withdrawal into his memories of a war that, despite the symbolism of the play,

14 *Le Désir attrapé par la queue,* Paris, Réunion des musées nationaux, Gallimard, Spadem and Maya, 1989.

seems to have made relatively little impact on the lives of the assembled company. The account of the *soirée* closes with a passage that can be read as a variation on the *Vanitas* motif: as S.'s awareness of the sights and sounds of his immediate surroundings gives way to grim memory images revived by the sight of the column of soldiers heading for the Front, the vanity of the antics and words of this exclusive clique are thrown into relief. Nor is it coincidental that the most vivid of these images – his two brief but haunting encounters with a unit of African soldiers – are associated with silence, the eloquent silence of men who sense the horror ahead, who know they are doomed and who recognise the pointlessness of words.

S.'s recollections of the Second World War are, of course, the principal topic of conversation in his interview with the journalist. Of the various sections which suggest S.'s impatience with certain types of discourse, the account of the interview stands out from the rest by virtue of the number and length of the textual segments devoted to it. Just as he endeavoured to be a courteous guest in the USSR, so, on his home ground, S. tries to be a hospitable host and a patient interviewee. His efforts to answer the, at times, obtuse and frequently repetitive questions with which the journalist bombards him are earnest. Nevertheless, the interview is a fiasco. The journalist fails to elicit the answers which he is seeking and his insistent line of questioning not only makes S. restless, but effectively inhibits his contributions. Even the hardware of his profession – the tape recorder which he switches on before S. has had time to give his permission – further obstructs the progress of the interview, the various mechanical operations involved in its use not only discouraging spontaneity, but actually cutting short S.'s attempts to reply and interfering with his train of thought.

There is a clear mismatch between the journalist's interviewing tactics and the interviewee's attitude to biographical data. The interviewer comes to his task with a ready-made taxonomy of emotional and psychological reactions by which he clearly intends to classify S.'s experience. Many of the questions he asks are evidently designed to corroborate his own preconceptions rather than to elicit real responses; when the responses that S. furnishes fail to fit his predetermined categories of emotional response, the journalist is reluctant to accept the answers that his subject gives him, returning again and again to the same questions in the hope, perhaps, that a second or third attempt might secure the 'acceptable' reply. He seems to believe that, if his questions are precise enough, he will be able to obtain from S. an orderly, objective and comprehensible account of his war experience. It is, however, clear from an early stage in the interview that the journalist's objectives are unachievable for a number of reasons. First, the sheer plethora of the data that the senses have to accommodate at any one moment, the fact that certain information is only available in retrospect and the gaps in S.'s recollections (*JP*, 279) make orderly reconstruction impossible. Second, it is, as S. points out, impossible to give an objective account of any event (*JP*, 273). Third, the journalist cannot hope to reconstruct or understand what S. himself still cannot explain (*JP*, 270) or even recall with precision (*JP*, 83). Moreover, the journalist's youth and limited life-experience preclude understanding of the experience that his subject tries to describe to him (*JP*, 76, 96, 97). Finally, words are by their very nature loaded with connotations and associations that vary from generation to generation (*JP*, 76) and from individual to individual (*JP*, 301, 302) and which make the direct communication of experience impossible.

S. recognises the pointlessness of the exercise almost as soon as it starts – 'Je savais que je perdais mon temps, que c'était comme si je lui parlais dans une langue inconnue' (*JP*, 83) – but toils on, noting, nevertheless, the tell-tale changes in his interviewer's expression and voice that make it clear that he is not living up to expectations. Not only does the journalist's tape recorder make him uneasy, but the discrepancy between his own voice and the voice recorded on the tape (*JP*, 82–83) actually seems to illustrate his belief that all retrospective testimony will be at best a distortion. In spite of the disapproval (*JP*, 77, 299), irritation (*JP*, 100, 299), scepticism (*JP*, 299) and condescension (*JP*, 288–89) that he can read on the journalist's face, S. remains courteous throughout the interview, but his attention is constantly being diverted from the business in hand and from his own account of the past by the details of his immediate surroundings and by the sensory impressions of the present: the light hitting the lenses of his interviewer's glasses (*JP*, 83, 95), the interviewer's anxious glances at his multi-dial watch (*JP*, 269), the sounds of the traffic (*JP*, 97, 270), the melting of the ice-cubes in the glasses (*JP*, 273).

The various interruptions caused by the tape-changes afford him some respite and it is in these moments that the parallelism between S. and the secondary figures of Poussin's painting is most apparent. Like the couple who turn and walk away from the central group of *The Plague at Ashdod*, S. almost invariably gets up during these interruptions and wanders away from the journalist and his tape recorder.

Moreover, the position he adopts at these times – he goes over to the window to look out onto the square below – has a parallel in the figures observing the scene from a balcony overlooking the square in front of the temple. Like the figures who walk away from the tumult in the foreground of *The Plague at Ashdod*, S. has no insights to offer on the dramatic events that he has witnessed; like the figures on the balcony, he is an observer rather than a participant in the world around him.[15] It is no accident, surely, that the scenario for the film which concludes the novel includes two lengthy shots of a window, one of which is devoted to the description of the window, the balcony and the view beyond, the second of which follows the movement of a figure as he approaches the window, opens it, looks out and finally closes it and sits down to resume typing the manuscript on his desk. These frames can be read as a cinematographic continuation of S.'s imaginary animation of *The Plague at Ashdod*. They take up the action where Poussin leaves off, the observer withdrawing from the balcony, shutting out the noise and bustle of the outside world and returning to the description of what he has seen.

Ecriture

As the preceding analysis has demonstrated, cultural dialogue in *Le Jardin des Plantes* is beset by problems and tends by and large simply to highlight S.'s marginality. However, the novel does include one very important, if discreet, exception to this pattern. The account of the reading of Picasso's play has a contrasting pendant in the description some 230 pages earlier of the 'vive discussion' that takes place in a Calcutta hotel between Antoine V. and Roger C. and that revolves around the metre and verse patterns of Racinian drama. Although S. does not actively participate in the debate and although he is alert to the incongruity of the recitation of lengthy extracts from *Andromaque*, *Athalie*, *Bajazet*, *Phèdre* and *Iphigénie* in a vast, virtually deserted and semi-dark hotel dining-room in post-colonial India, he, nevertheless, listens to attentively to the debate and is able, years on, to recall precisely the image used by Antoine V. to describe the principles of the alexandrine:

15 S.'s status as observer is highlighted elsewhere in the text in the numerous references to various types of windows and the descriptions of what S. sees through them (pp. 26, 52, 56, 129, 136–37, 145, 151, 153, 221, 225, 264–65, 298, 313, 314). Compare the numerous writer-characters who appear in Simon's fiction and who tend to work at a desk in front of a window.

V. essayant de lui expliquer qu'il en était là du langage comme de ces jardins, ces parcs aux allées taillées en forme de murailles, d'entablements, langue et nature également soumises à la même royale volonté d'ordre, de mesure et de mathématiques (*JP*, 104)

The account of the scene concludes with a passage that, by virtue of its references to the ghostly presences conjured up in the tirades recited by V. and C., is very similar to the conclusion of the account of the Picasso reading. However, the informal 'performance' in Calcutta is distinguished from the reading in Montparnasse by the expertise of the performers and by the quality of their script. In contrast with the amorphousness of Picasso's play, Racine's drama is characterised above all by the discipline of its form and, whereas the disorderly reading of *Le Désir attrapé par la queue* simply alienated S. and forced him to retreat into his memories, V.'s and C.'s recitation of extracts from Racine combines with the associations of the eerie decor and the tropical storm that breaks as they declaim their lines to conjure up in his imagination the spectres of Racine's heroes and heroines (*JP*, 105)

The key to the interpretation of this contrast between the two theatrical sections of *Le Jardin des Plantes* lies, of course, in the horticultural comparison that V. uses to describe Racine's language. Not only does this comment act as a formal link with the text's most prominent *mise en abyme* – the descriptions of the Jardin des Plantes – and with the numerous descriptions of other gardens,[16] but like these descriptions, it can also be read as an oblique commentary on Simon's own conception of the writing process, which, like gardening, consists in large part of imposing order upon disorder.[17] Whereas the extravagant and unrestrained invective of *Le Désir attrapé par la queue* fails to 'passer la rampe', the controlled cadence of Racine's speeches invests them with a communicative power that allows them, even in an informal 'performance,' in the most unlikely setting, to conjure up the characters of his drama and the nuances of their emotions.

Moreover, there is also a strong parallel between the evocative power of Racine's drama and the effect that *The Plague at Ashdod* has upon S. Just as the Racinian extracts conjure up the ghostly presences of Iphigénie, Phèdre and Pyrrhus, so, as we have seen, *The Plague at Ashdod* is animated in S.'s imagination, its tightly controlled play and interplay of movement, gesture and expression generating in his

---

16 See pages 29, 31, 53–55, 62, 222, 223, 234, 256, 296, 301.
17 M. Alphant, 'Simon l'invité', *Libération*, 10 décembre 1985, p. 29.

mind's eye the stages of an unfolding drama. Simon's admiration for both Racine and Poussin is based upon their common ability to create aesthetically coherent works of art out of the turbulent subject-matter with which they both worked. In *Le Jardin des Plantes*, the 'content' is highly diverse and often 'turbulent', consisting as it does of a plethora of disparate images based upon Simon's own memories of childhood, the Spanish Civil War, the Second World War, his extensive travels and a motley assortment of fictional and documentary intertexts. These heterogenous images and intertexts are presented without regard for chronology or narrative logic in discrete textual segments of varying length. However, even a relatively superficial reading of the novel reveals that each segment of text is linked to a number of other apparently very different segments by means of a network of thematic and situational parallels, serial motifs and linguistic echoes. The exploration of this extensive and highly intricate network merits a separate full-length analysis of the novel. Nevertheless, even a brief and selective analysis of the contribution made by the description of *The Plague at Ashdod* to the establishment of cross-textual links will offer some insight into the novel's formal substructure and will also demonstrate the role played by the serial motif in the development of some of the text's most prominent thematic strands.

The description of Poussin's *Plague at Ashdod* is only one of a series of references to the painter. These references include the extracts from *A la recherche du temps perdu* recounting the conversation between Marcel and Mme de Cambremer, the account of S.'s rather disappointing tour of the Hermitage (*JP*, 287), the analogy with Poussin's 'ruines antiques' that figures in the description of the devastated streets of Berlin (*JP*, 163) and the references to Picasso's debt and tribute to Poussin's work (*JP*, 228, 229). In addition to their formal role as cross-textual motifs, the references to Poussin serve a range of thematic functions. The comparison with Poussin's 'ruines antiques' that springs to S.'s mind as he watches a young woman walk along a ruined street in Berlin (*JP*, 163) illustrates one of the most prominent themes of Simon's *oeuvre*: the inseparability of perception and cultural baggage. Here, the data received by S.'s senses stimulate a cultural memory that is so strong that, twenty years on, S.'s recollection of the 'lived' scene automatically and involuntarily calls to mind the painted scene. The section describing S.'s trip to the Hermitage and his cursory viewing of Poussin's *Tancred and Hermione* acts as a pendant to the extracts from Josef Brodsky's trial. The museum guide's evident irritation, her lack of interest in the Poussin and her dogmatic and distortive readings of other paintings in the collection are based upon the same blinkered, utilitarian approach to art that underlies the Soviet judge's obtuse questions and the ultimate condemnation of Brodsky to five years in a Soviet labour camp. Mme de Cambremer's prejudices may be less dangerous, but the inclusion of her conversation with the narrator regarding the relative merits of Poussin and the Impressionists not only provides Simon with a comic variation on the motif of problematic or abortive communication, but also allows him to highlight indirectly the theme of artistic ancestry that runs through the text. The reference in the extract from *A la recherche* to Degas's admiration for the Poussins at Chantilly and in the Louvre and the two references to Picasso's reworking of Poussinesque motifs serve at once to highlight Poussin's status in the history of art, and to complement and reinforce the lineage theme, which is developed through the tributes which Simon makes, in the form of epigraphs, intertextual extracts and biographical anecdotes, to the authors whom he considers to be his own literary ancestors: in particular, Dostoievski, Proust, Conrad and Faulkner.

Biographical coincidence provides a convenient link between Poussin and one of Simon's own contemporary artistic heroes, Gastone Novelli. At the time of S.'s visit to Rome, Novelli's studio was situated in the Via del Babbuino, the street in which Poussin was living when he painted *The Plague at Ashdod* (*JP*, 107, 117). However, the rather conspicuous recurrence in the text of the street name points to a similarity between the two painters that extends beyond coincidence and that reinforces one of the text's central themes: the relationship between biography and art. As I have demonstrated elsewhere,[18] the links between Novelli's life and art offer Simon the means by which to illustrate his own conception of the relationship between life and work, the paintings that Novelli produced after the war reflecting indirectly his response to the atrocities he had witnessed during the war and the period he spent living with a South American Indian tribe. *The Plague at Ashdod* also has its origins in Poussin's own life-experience and in contemporary history, in the mysterious illness which struck him down in 1628–30 and in the plague which hit Milan in 1630:

---

18   See Jean H. Duffy, 'Artistic Biographies and Aesthetic Coherence in Claude Simon's *Jardin des Plantes*', *Forum for Modern Language Studies*, 1999, vol. 35, no. 2, pp. 175–92.

Poussin vient d'être gravement malade; la peste a ravagé Milan en 1629. Le choix du récit biblique n'est donc pas gratuit: il reprend à l'actualité la plus atroce mais touche aussi personnellement le peintre.[19]

If there is a clear parallel between the narrative content of Poussin's painting and his own recent experience and between Novelli's paintings and the primitive language that he had learned among the South American tribespeople, in both cases the aesthetic coherence of their works depends not upon biography or anecdote, but upon the establishment of chromatic and formal echoes across the composition. The two artists are linked by the fact that they have each, in their own ways, attempted to establish order amidst the disorder out of which their work was born. In Novelli, the repetition of forms and letters and the establishment of geometric grids covering the entire composition create cohesive surface patterns, while in Poussin's *Plague*, the various elements of the scene are held together by the *reprise* of colours in different areas of the canvas, the regularly aligned and framing structures of the antique cityscape and the rhythms and counter-rhythms established by the gestures and postures of the figures. Although the description of the painting in *Le Jardin des Plantes* makes no reference to its technique, Simon's admiration for Poussin is, I would argue, in large part based upon the formal coherence of his compositions.

In addition to the explicit references to Poussin which figure in the novel and to the biographical and aesthetic parallels which link the references to Poussin and Novelli, the textual segment devoted to *The Plague at Ashdod* is related to many of the other sections of *Le Jardin des Plantes* by the occurrence in the description of the painting of a number of individual lexical items that form the basis of some of the text's numerous serial motifs. Here, as elsewhere in Simon, a high proportion of the 'single-word' motifs relate to sensory perception and natural phenomena. The colours of the figures' robes in *The Plague* – 'ocre, lilas, bronze, jonquille, olive, safran' – reappear in numerous other scenes in the novel, while the analogy with the striped garments of two of the figures and the 'couvertures qu'on voit dans les bazars orientaux' is linked to the 'Oriental' motif which runs through the text[20] and to the various descriptions of the bazaars, souks, markets

---

19 Jacques Thuillier, *Nicolas Poussin*, Paris, Fayard, 1988, p. 105. See also Alain Mérot, *Poussin*, Paris, Hazan, 1990, p. 57.
20 See pp. 12, 16, 44, 68, 105, 134.

and emporia that S. visits in the course of his travels.[21] The sunset motif provides a link between several of the novel's intertexts,[22] the many nightfalls and twilit skies which S. has viewed in different parts of the globe[23] and some of the most vividly remembered moments of his life: childhood memories of the Jura (*JP*, 74), the announcement of the death of his mother (*JP*, 226), his observation, from his sickbed, of the fading of the light on the wall outside his window (*JP*, 86), the long shadows projected by the setting sun during army exercises (*JP*, 110), the 'rayons du soleil déclinant' on the afternoon of the ambush in which he was almost killed (*JP*, 81) and the late-afternoon light glimpsed during his transportation to the prison camp (*JP*, 147). The lowering oppressiveness of the dying light – 'la suffocante lumière du jour finissant' – also connects this passage with the numerous references to suffocation and breathlessness that are scattered throughout the text and that include the descriptions of S.'s TB (*JP*, 85, 129, 312–13), his difficulties in breathing during his flight from the enemy after the ambush in which he was almost killed (*JP*, 96, 154) and after his escape from the POW camp (*JP*, 152), the oppressive and airless heat of India (*JP*, 125), the breathless shouting of an angry officer (*JP*, 43), the panting of the members of an imaginary geological expedition (*JP*, 66), the suffocating scent of incense during the masses he attended as a child (*JP*, 176) and the oppressive smells of flowers and candle wax in the 'chapelle ardente' which had been improvised to receive his mother's coffin (*JP*, 233–34).

Finally, the theme of physical vulnerability which is, of course, not only one of the dominant themes of Baroque art but also of Simon's fiction, figures prominently in both *The Plague at Ashdod* and *Le Jardin des Plantes*. Poussin's *Plague* is a work which foregrounds the body and its ultimate fate: the scavenging rats, the grey skin-tones of the dead and the figures who shield their noses and mouths in reaction to the 'l'air nauséabond' (*JP*, 107) all draw attention to the perishable nature of all organic matter. Given the typically Baroque nature of Poussin's subject and the recurrence in Simon's other work of many of the

---

21 For example, the souk leading to the Wailing Wall in Jerusalem (p. 44), the indoor market in Calcutta (pp. 131–32), the bazaar in Cairo (p. 134), and the fish market in Istanbul (pp. 182–83).

22 See, in particular, the intertextual material relating to Rommel (p. 131), Proust (pp. 162, 164), Dostoievski (p. 253) and Trotsky (pp. 91–92).

23 Berlin, pp. 17, 163; Chicago, p. 56; USSR, pp. 69, 91; India, pp. 132–33; Istanbul, p. 182; New York, p. 265.

central themes and conceits of Baroque art, it is not surprising that several of the text's serial motifs relate to corporal morbidity and putrefaction. The description of the putrefying bodies of the dead and the stench they emit is echoed in numerous other references to corpses and putrefaction,[24] while the rats of Poussin's painting not only figure in a network of references to rats and rat-like people that link several of the intertextual extracts and summaries,[25] but are also elements in a more extensive set of references to the various species of scavenger encountered in the text, including various types of human and animal scavengers observed by S. during the war (*JP*, 152, 262) and on his travels (*JP*, 15, 89).

Analysis of the various thematic and formal functions of the section relating to Poussin's *Plague at Ashdod* highlights both the continuity of Simon's work and some of the distinctive features of *Le Jardin des Plantes*. The role of *The Plague at Ashdod* as generative source for a number of cross-textual echoes comes as no surprise to the reader who is familiar with Simon's earlier fiction and with his textual exploitation of the visual arts. The subject of the painting and, in particular, its representation of disorder, death and decay offer Simon the opportunity for the development of new variations on old themes. In addition to these broad thematic parallels, the description of *The Plague at Ashdod* also serves to highlight some of the more distinctive themes of *Le Jardin des Plantes*. Thus, as we saw in the first section, the Old Testament story depicted by Poussin provides Simon with an example by which to illustrate his 'history' of religion and faith. While it is true that Simon's earlier fiction provides considerable evidence both of his atheism and his fascination for religious iconography, it is in *Le Jardin des Plantes* that one finds his most sustained meditation upon religion, the in-built obsolescence of the religious 'truths' which man is apparently compelled to invent and the extraordinary variety of the symbols, effigies, buildings and rituals by which he expresses his faith(s). However, it is the detail of the painting rather than its central action that strikes the most personal chord in Simon, the relationship between the figure groups of Poussin's composition offering him a visual equivalent of his own relationship with certain types of cultural discourse. In particular, the positioning of the figures on the canvas allows him to suggest obliquely the distance that he has consistently

24 See pp. 71, 73–74, 87, 101, 132–33, 134, 150, 159, 167, 240, 252, 277.
25 See the intertextual material relating to Proust (p. 142), Churchill (pp. 168, 181) and Rommel (p. 351).

maintained between himself and contemporary ideological trends and cliques, *including* the *nouveau roman*. The parallels that he develops between the figures who are walking away from the focal dramatic scene and the behaviour and attitude of his fictional *alter ego*, S., translate into fictional terms not only his own feeling of marginality, but also his reluctance to engage in debate on the social function of art and his impatience with the referentialist/anti-referentialist critical lobbies.[26] *Le Jardin des Plantes* can, on one level, I would argue, be read as a response to some of the questions which Simon's work has repeatedly raised in the minds of critics and interviewers over many years, notably, questions concerning the relationship between life and art, the nature of his association with the *nouveau roman*, and the extent of his debt to other writers including those cited or paraphrased in this novel. That his response to these questions should be relayed indirectly via the parallels and cross-textual echoes of a fictional work is a logical conclusion of his own views on both the limitations and the potential of language and is consistent with his own description of himself as a self-taught writer whose literary knowledge does not go beyond an amateur level.[27] Unlike the various 'professionals' whom S. encounters and who seem intent upon converting, brainwashing or pigeonholing him, the only message which Simon has to offer here is that art can have no message. Moreover, if the easy loquacity of these self-appointed authorities on literature exhibits their pleasure in talk for talk's sake, the internal coherence of Simon's text testifies rather to his attentiveness to the associative properties of language and to the painstaking labour on the linguistic medium that *writing* demands of him:

> Mes romans sont, je ne crains pas de le dire, très laborieusement fabriqués. Mais oui: leur *fabrication* me demande beaucoup de *labeur*![28]

26 It is significant that the only reference in the novel to S.'s public statements on literature and art is made in a very short segment that notes the delivery of a speech (pp. 301–02) at the University of Bologna. This fictional incident is, of course, based upon an address that Simon made on the occasion of the conferral of an honorary degree and in which he articulates many of the views on language that are implicit in *Le Jardin des Plantes*. See Claude Simon, 'Problèmes que posent le roman et l'écriture', *Francofonia*, no. 18, Spring 1990, pp. 3–10.
27 See Claude Simon's untitled address to the colloquium on the New Novel, New York, University, October 1982, in Lois Oppenheim (ed.), *Three Decades of the French New Novel*, Urbana, IL, University of Illinois Press, 1986, p. 71.
28 J.-P. Goux and A. Poirson, 'Un homme traversé par le travail: entretien avec Claude Simon', *La Nouvelle Critique*, vol. 105, 1977, p. 34. See also page 33.

Bibliography

Works by Claude Simon

Books

Le Tricheur, Paris, Sagittaire, 1945.
La Corde raide, Paris, Sagittaire, 1947.
Gulliver, Paris, Calmann-Lévy, 1952.
Le Sacre du printemps, Paris, Calmann-Lévy, 1954.
Le Vent, Paris, Minuit, 1957.
L'Herbe, Paris, Minuit, 1958.
La Route des Flandres, Paris, Minuit, 1960.
Le Palace, Paris, Minuit, 1962.
Femmes, Paris, Maeght, 1966.
Histoire, Paris, Minuit, 1967.
La Bataille de Pharsale, Paris, Minuit, 1969.
Orion aveugle, Geneva, Skira, 1970.
Les Corps conducteurs, Paris, Minuit, 1971.
Triptyque, Paris, Minuit, 1973.
Leçon de choses, Paris, Minuit, 1975.
Les Géorgiques, Paris, Minuit, 1981.
La Chevelure de Bérénice, Paris, Minuit, 1983.
Discours de Stockholm, Paris, Minuit, 1986.
L'Invitation, Paris, Minuit, 1987.
Album d'un amateur, Remagen-Rolandseck, Rommerskirschen, 1988.
L'Acacia, Paris, Minuit, 1989.
Photographies, *1937–1970*, Paris, Maeght, 1992.
Jean Dubuffet and Claude Simon, *Correspondance*, *1970–1984*, Paris, L'Echoppe, 1994.
Le Jardin des Plantes, Minuit, 1997.
Le Tramway, Minuit, 2001.

Short texts

'Babel', *Les Lettres nouvelles*, no. 31, 1955, pp. 391–413.
'Le Cheval', *Les Lettres nouvelles*, no. 57, 1958, pp.169–89, and no. 58, 1958, pp. 379–94.

'Le Candidat', *Arts*, 26 novembre–2 décembre 1958, p. 3.

'Cendre', *Revue de Paris*, mars 1959, pp. 79–82.

'Mot à mot', *Les Lettres nouvelles*, 8 avril 1959, pp. 6–10.

'La Poursuite', *Tel Quel*, no. 1, 1960, pp. 49–60.

'Matériaux de construction', *Les Lettres nouvelles*, no. 9, décembre 1960, pp. 112–123.

'Comme du sang délayé', *Les Lettres françaises*, 1–7 décembre 1960, pp. 1, 5.

'Sous le kimono', *Les Lettres françaises*, 19–25 janvier 1961, p. 5.

'Funérailles d'un révolutionnaire assassiné', *Médiations*, no. 4, 1961, pp. 11–24.

'Inventaire', *Les Lettres nouvelles*, no. 22, février 1962, pp. 50–58.

'L'Attentat', *La Nouvelle Revue française*, vol. 19, no. 111, 1962, pp. 431–52.

'Des roches striées vert pâle parsemées de points noirs', *Les Lettres nouvelles*, juin–août 1964, pp. 53–68.

'La Statue', *Mercure de France*, vol. 352, no. 1213, 1964, pp. 393–409.

'Correspondance', *Tel Quel*, no. 16, 1964, pp. 18–32.

'Propriétés des rectangles', *Tel Quel*, no. 44, 1971, pp. 3–16.

'Deux personnages', *Art Press*, février 1973, pp. 14–15.

'Essai de mise en ordre de notes prises au cours d'un voyage en Zeeland (1962) et complétées', *Minuit*, no. 3, mars 1973, pp. 1–18.

'Progression dans un paysage enneigé', *Etudes littéraires*, vol. 9, no. 1, 1976, pp. 217–21.

'Le Général', *Art Press*, été 1977.

'Le Régicide', *La Nouvelle Critique*, juin–juillet 1977, pp. 45–46.

'Les Géorgiques', *La Nouvelle Revue française*, vol. 52, no. 308, 1978, pp. 1–27.

'Parenthèse', *Revue de la Bibliothèque Nationale*, printemps 1985, pp. 3–7.

'Fragment', in A. B. Duncan (ed.), *Claude Simon: New Directions*, Edinburgh, Scottish Academic Press, 1985, pp. 2–11.

'Note sur le plan de montage de *La Route des Flandres*'; 'Plan de montage de *La Route des Flandres*' and (with M. Calle) 'Transcription du "plan de montage"', in M. Calle (ed.), *Claude Simon: chemins de la mémoire*, Sainte–Foy, Le Griffon d'aigle, 1993, pp. 185–200.

'Les jardins publics (extrait)' in M. Calle-Gruber (ed.), *Les Sites de l'écriture: Colloque Claude Simon*, Paris, Nizet, 1995, pp. 25–37.

'Lecture publique d'une pièce de théâtre. Fragment d'un texte', *L'Infini*, no. 56, hiver 1996, pp. 3–10.

'Polygone', *Cahiers de la Bibliothèque Jacques Doucet*, no. 1, 1997, pp. 11–15.

Interviews and other public statements

Ajame P., 'Leurs projets? dans un mois? dans un an?', *Les Nouvelles Littéraires*, no. 1743, 26 janvier 1961, p. 2.

Alphant, M., 'Claude Simon: La Route du Nobel', *Libération*, 10 décembre 1985, pp. 27–28.

Alphant, M., 'Simon L'Invité', *Libération*, 6 janvier 1988, pp. 28–29.

Alphant, M., *Océaniques: les hommes-livres*, entretien filmé avec Claude Simon, La Sept / INA, 1988 (directed by Roland Allar).

Alphant, M., 'Et à quoi bon inventer?', *Libération*, 31 août 1989, pp. 24–25.

Apeldoorn, J. van, and C. Grivel, 'Entretien avec Jo van Apeldoorn et Charles

Grivel, 17 avril 1979', in C. Grivel (ed.), *Écriture de la religion. Écriture du roman*, Lille, Presses Universitaires de Lille, 1979, pp. 87–107.

Armel, A., 'Claude Simon: le passé recomposé', *Magazine littéraire*, no. 275, mars 1990, pp. 96–103.

Aubarède, G. de, 'Claude Simon. Instantané', *Les Nouvelles littéraires*, no. 1567, 7 novembre 1957, p. 7.

Bauret, G., 'Claude Simon: écriture en noir et blanc', *Photographies magazine*, no. 4777, 1992, pp. 33–35.

Berger, Y. and C. Simon, 'Deux écrivains répondent à Jean-Paul Sartre', *L'Express*, 28 mai 1964, pp. 30–33.

Bertin, C., 'Claude Simon: un écrivain qui ne veut être qu'un écrivain', *Arts-loisirs*, no. 82, 19–25 avril 1967, pp. 14–16.

Birn, R. and K. Gould, 'Simon on Simon. An Interview with the Artist', in R. Birn and K. Gould (eds), *Orion Blinded: Essays on Claude Simon*, Lewisburg, PA, Bucknell University Press, 1981, pp. 285–88.

Biro-Thierback, K., 'Claude Simon sur les sentiers de la création', *La Gazette littéraire*, 27 juin 1970.

Bourdet, D., 'Images de Paris: Claude Simon', *Revue de Paris*, vol. 68, no. 1, 1961, pp. 136–41.

Bourin, A., 'Techniciens du roman: Claude Simon', *Les Nouvelles littéraires*, no. 1739, 29 décembre 1960, p. 4.

Bourin, A., 'Cinq romanciers jugent le roman', *Les Nouvelles Littéraires*, no. 1764, 22 juin 1961, p. 7 and no. 1765, 29 juin 1961, p. 8.

Calle, M., 'L'Inlassable Réa/encrage du vécu', in M. Calle (ed.), *Claude Simon: Chemins de la mémoire*, Sainte-Foy, Griffon d'aigle, 1993, pp. 3–25.

Calle-Gruber, M., 'Claude Simon, dans l'arc du livre il y a toute la corde', *Nuit blanche*, no. 74, printemps 1999, pp. 55–58.

Casanova, N., 'Entretien', *Le Quotidien de Paris*, 30 septembre 1975.

Casanova, N., 'L'Inspiration ça n'existe pas', *Le Quotidien de Paris*, 18 octobre 1985, p. 24.

Casanova, P., 'Entretien: Claude Simon. Choses vues', *Art Press*, no. 174, novembre 1992 , pp. 30–33.

Chalon, J, 'Réponses à une enquête: "Les débuts obscurs d'écrivains célèbres"', *Le Figaro*, 11 mars 1972, pp. 13–14.

Chapsal, M., 'Entretien avec Claude Simon', *L'Express*, 10 novembre 1960, reprinted in Madeleine Chapsal (ed.), *Les Écrivains en personne*, Paris, U.G.E., 1973, pp. 163–71.

Chapsal, M., 'Le Jeune Roman', *L'Express*, no. 506, 12 janvier 1961, pp. 31–33.

Chapsal, M., 'Entretien: Claude Simon parle', *L'Express*, 5 avril 1962, pp. 32–33.

Chapsal, M., 'Entretien avec Claude Simon: "Il n'y a pas d'art réaliste"', *Quinzaine littéraire*, no. 41, 15–17 décembre 1967, pp. 4–5.

Clavel, A., 'Claude Simon: "La guerre est toujours là"', *L'Evénement*, 31 août–6 septembre 1989, pp. 86–87.

Descargues, P., 'Claude Simon publie un nouveau roman: *Histoire*', *Tribune de Lausanne*, 9 avril 1967, p. 7.

Dällenbach, L., 'Attaques et stimuli', in Lucien Dällenbach, *Claude Simon*, Paris, Éditions du Seuil, 1988, pp. 170–81.

Descaves, P., 'Réalités du roman', *La Table Ronde*, no. 157, janvier 1961, pp. 163–172.

Dörr, G., 'Biographie oder Bildersprache? Claude Simon über sein neuestes Werk: *Les Corps conducteurs*', *Die Neueren Sprachen*, Heft 5, 1972, pp. 294–96.

Duncan, A. B., 'Interview with Claude Simon', in A. B. Duncan (ed.), *Claude Simon: New Directions*, Edinburgh, Scottish Academic Press, 1985, pp. 12–18.

Duranteau, J., 'Claude Simon, "Le roman se fait, je le fais, et il me fait"', *Les Lettres françaises*, no. 1178, 13–19 avril 1967, pp. 3–4.

Duverlie, C., 'Pour un "Comment j'ai écrit certains de mes livres" de Claude Simon', *Romance Notes*, vol. 14, no. 2, 1972, pp. 217–21.

Duverlie, C., 'Interview with Claude Simon', *Substance*, vol. 8, 1974, pp. 3–20.

Duverlie, C., 'The Crossing of the Image', *Diacritics*, vol. 8, no. 4, 1977, pp. 47–58.

Duverlie, C., 'The Novel as Textual Wandering', *Contemporary Literature*, vol. 28, no. 1, 1987, pp. 1–13.

Eribon, D., 'Entretien. Fragments de Claude Simon', *Libération*, 29–30 août 1981, p. 21.

Eribon, D., 'Claude Simon sur la route de Stockholm', *Le Nouvel Observateur*, 6 décembre 1985, pp. 72–73.

Eyle, A., 'Claude Simon: The Art of Fiction', *Paris Review*, 1992, no. 122, pp. 116–36.

Gaudemar, A. de, '"Je me suis trouvé dans l'œil du cyclone"', *Libération*, 18 septembre 1997, p. III (http://www.liberation.fr/livres/97sept/simon1809.html).

Garzarolli, F. R., 'Pas de crise du roman français', *Tribune de Lausanne*, 7 juin 1970, pp. 25–27.

Gallaz, C., 'Claude Simon: la guerre, la terre, l'écriture et la menuiserie', *Le Matin Tribune*, 22 novembre 1981.

Goux, J. P., and A. Poirson, 'Claude Simon: pour en finir avec l'équivoque du réalisme', *L'Humanité*, 20 mai 1977.

Goux, J. P., and A. Poirson, 'Un homme traversé par le travail: entretien avec Claude Simon', *La Nouvelle Critique*, vol. 105, juin–juillet 1977, pp. 32–46.

Haroche, C., 'Claude Simon, romancier', *L'Humanité*, no. 11560, 26 octobre 1981, p. 15.

Janvier, L., 'Réponses de Claude Simon à quelques questions écrites de Ludovic Janvier', *Entretiens*, no. 31, 1972, pp. 15–29.

Jardin, C., 'L'Ancien du nouveau roman', *Le Figaro*, 28 novembre 1967, p. 14.

Joguet, M., 'Dialogue avec Claude Simon: "Le poids des mots"', *Le Figaro littéraire*, 3 avril 1976, pp. 13–14.

Josipovici, G., 'Claude Simon: Behind Enemy Lines', *The Independent*, no. 826, 18 September 1989, p. 21.

Juin, H., 'Les Secrets d'un romancier: Claude Simon s'explique', *Les Lettres françaises*, no. 844, 12 octobre 1960, p. 5.

Knapp, B., 'Interview avec Claude Simon', *Kentucky Romance Quarterly*, no. 2, 1970, pp. 179–90.

Lamy, J.-C., 'Je ne crois pas écrire des choses compliquées', *France Soir*, 26 septembre 1989.

Lebrun, J.-C., 'L'Atelier de l'artiste', *Révolution*, no. 500, 27 septembre 1989, pp. 37–40.

Lebrun, J.-C., 'Parvenir peu à peu à écrire difficilement', *L'Humanité*, 13 mars 1998 (http://www.humanite.presse.fr/journal/archives.html).

Le Clec'h, G., 'Claude Simon, prix de la nouvelle vague: "Je ne suis pas un homme-orchestre"', *Témoignage chrétien*, 16 décembre 1960, pp. 19–20.

Le Clec'h, G., 'Claude Simon a découvert à cinquante-quatre ans le plaisir d'écrire', *Le Figaro littéraire*, 4–10 décembre 1967, pp. 22–23.

Le Clec'h, G., 'Claude Simon: le jeu de la chose et du mot', *Les Nouvelles littéraires*, 8 avril 1971, p. 6.

Lévy, B.-H., '... peuvent et doivent s'arrêter parfois d'écrire...', in B.-H. Lévy, *Les Aventures de la liberté: Une histoire subjective des intellectuels*, Paris, Grasset, 1991, pp. 12–21.

Mallet, F., 'Quatre entretiens avec Claude Simon: un monde nécessaire à certains', *Les Cahiers littéraires de l'ORTF*, no. 16, 9–12 mai 1971, pp. 9–10.

Michel, C., and R. Robert, 'Entretien avec Claude Simon', *Scherzo*, no. 3, avril–juin 1998, pp. 5–11.

Montrémy, J.-M. de, 'Je travaille comme un peintre', *La Croix*, 19 octobre 1985.

Neefs J., and A. Grésillon, 'Le Présent de l'écriture', *Genesis: manuscrits, recherche, invention*, no. 13, 1999, pp. 115–21.

Nuridsany, P., 'Claude Simon: une maturité rayonnante', *Le Figaro*, 4 septembre 1981, p. 16.

Osemwegie Elaho, R., *Entretiens avec le Nouveau Roman*, Sherbrooke (Québec), Editions Naaman, 1985, pp. 53–63.

Parot, J., 'Claude Simon part en guerre contre la signification', *Les Lettres françaises*, no. 859, 19–25 janvier 1961, p. 5.

Paulhan, C., 'Claude Simon: "J'ai essayé la peinture, la révolution, puis l'écriture"', *Les Nouvelles littéraires*, no. 2922, 15–21 mars 1984, pp. 42–45.

Piatier, J., 'Claude Simon ouvre *Les Géorgiques*', *Le Monde*, 4 septembre 1981, pp. 11, 13.

Poirson, A., 'Avec Claude Simon sur des sables mouvants', *Révolution*, vol. 99, 22–28 janvier 1982, pp. 34–39.

Pugh, A. C., 'Interview with Claude Simon: Autobiography, the Novel, Politics', *The Review of Contemporary Fiction*, vol. 5, no. 1, 1985, pp. 4–13.

Rieben, P. A., 'Claude Simon à Lausanne: compte rendu d'une conférence de Claude Simon', *Études de Lettres*, vol. 4, no. 1, janvier–mars 1971, pp. 57–58.

Rollin, A., 'L'Autre Jour, j'ai passé tout un après-midi sur six lignes', in A. Rollin (ed.), *Ils écrivent où ? quand ? comment ?*, Paris, Mazarine, 1986, pp. 323–28.

Sainte-Phalle, T. de, 'Claude Simon, franc-tireur de la révolution romanesque', *Le Figaro littéraire*, 6 avril 1967, p. 7.

Sarraute, C., 'Avec *La Route des Flandres* Claude Simon affirme sa manière', *Le Monde*, 8 octobre 1960, p. 9.

Senlis, J., 'Nous avons choisi Claude Simon', *Clarté*, décembre 1960, pp. 27–28.

Simon C., 'Réponse à une enquête: "Qu'est-ce que l'avant-garde en 1958?"', *Les Lettres françaises*, no. 719, 24–30 avril 1958, pp. 1, 5.

Simon, C., 'Un bloc indivisible', *Les Lettres françaises*, no. 740, 4–10 décembre 1958, p. 5.

Simon, C., 'Réponse à une enquête: "Pensez-vous avoir un don d'écrivain?"', *Tel Quel*, printemps 1960, pp. 38–43.

Simon, C., 'Réponse à une enquête', *Premier Plan*, no. 18, octobre 1961, pp. 32–33.

Simon, C., 'Je ne peux parler que de moi', *Les Nouvelles littéraires*, no. 1809, 3 mai 1962, p. 2.

Simon, C., 'Gastone Novelli and the Problem of Language', in *Gastone Novelli, Paintings*, Exhibition Catalogue, New York, The Alan Gallery, 1962, unpaginated.

Simon, C., 'Réponses à une enquête sur la critique', *Tel Quel*, no. 14, été 1963, p. 84.

Simon, C., 'Débat. Le romancier et la politique: "Et si les écrivains jouaient le rôle de la presse du coeur?" demande Claude Simon', *L'Express*, 25 juillet 1963, pp. 25–26.

Simon, C., 'Pour qui donc écrit Sartre?', *L'Express*, 28 mai 1964, pp. 32–33.

Simon, C., 'Pour Monique Wittig', *L'Express*, 30 novembre 1964, pp. 69–71.

Simon, C., 'Lettre ouverte à l'Union des Etudiants Communistes', *L'Express*, 7–13 décembre 1964, pp. 80–81.

Simon, C., 'Réponse à une enquête: "Pourquoi Céline?" Huit écrivains répondent', *Arts*, 13 décembre 1965, pp. 12–13.

Simon. C., 'La Littérature est une fin en soi', *Témoignage chrétien*, 24 mars 1966, p. 15.

Simon, C., 'Réponse à une enquête: "Film et roman: problèmes du récit"', *Cahiers du Cinéma*, no. 185, décembre 1966, pp. 103–04.

Simon, C., 'Contre un roman utilitaire', *Le Monde hebdomadaire*, 6–12 avril 1967, pp. 10–12.

Simon, C., 'Je ne suis pas un mandarin', *Le Monde*, no. 6932, 26 avril 1967, p. 4.

Simon, C, 'Les Ecrivains français prennent leur distance', *Le Monde*, 8 mai 1967, p. 5.

Simon, C., '*Problèmes du nouveau roman*: trois avis autorisés', *Les Lettres françaises*, no. 1203, 11–17 octobre 1967, p. 3.

Simon, C., 'Réponse à un questionnaire: "Le roman par les romanciers"', *Europe*, octobre 1968, p. 230.

Simon, C., 'La Fiction mot à mot', in *Nouveau Roman: hier aujourd'hui*, 2 vols, vol. 2, Paris, U.G.E., 1972, pp. 73–116.

Simon, C., 'Rendre la perception confuse, multiple et simultanée du monde', *Le Monde des livres*, 26 avril, 1967, p. v.

Simon, C., 'Littérature: tradition et révolution', *Quinzaine littéraire*, no. 27, 1–15 mai 1967, pp. 12–13.

Simon, C., *et al.*, 'L'Opinion des nouveaux romanciers', *Quinzaine littéraire*, no. 121, 1–15 juillet 1971, p. 9. (On J. Ricardou, *Pour un théorie du nouveau roman*.)

Simon, C., 'Réponse à une enquête sur la femme en tant qu'écrivain', *La Quinzaine littéraire*, 1–31 août 1974, pp. 29–30.

Simon, C., 'Claude Simon à la question', in J. Ricardou (ed.), *Colloque de Cerisy: Claude Simon*, Paris, U.G.E., 1975, pp. 403–31.

Simon, C., 'Entretien', in N. Botherel, F. Dugast et J. Thoraval, *Les Nouveaux romanciers*, Paris, Bordas, 1976, p. 95.

Simon, C., 'Lieu', *L'Humanité*, 9 décembre 1977, p. 2.

Simon, C., Tribute to Gaëton Picon in *L'Oeil double de Gaëton Picon*, Paris, Centre Georges Pompidou, 1979, p. 48.

Simon, C, 'Roman, description et action', in P. Hallberg (ed.), *The Feeling for Nature and the Landscape of Man*, Proceedings of the 45th Nobel Symposium, Gothenberg, 1981, pp. 78–93.

Simon, C., 'Correspondance avec Jacques Henric', *Art Press*, no. 53, nov. 1981, p. 47.

Simon, C., 'Tenez vous un journal intime?', *Le Monde*, 20 août 1982.

Simon, C., 'La Voie royale du roman', *Le Nouvel Observateur*, no. 900, 6 février 1982, p. 74.

Simon, C., 'Reflections on the Novel: Claude Simon's Address to the Colloquium on the New Novel, New York University, 1982', *The Review of Contemporary Fiction*, vol. 5, no. 1, 1985, pp. 14–23.

Simon, C., *et al.*, 'Hugo et moi', *La Quinzaine Littéraire*, no. 448, 1–15 octobre 1985, pp. 6–8.

Simon, C., 'Le Métier de romancier', *Le Monde*, 19 oct. 1985, p. 13.

Simon, C., 'About Literary Creation', *Foreign Literatures*, vol. 1, 1986, pp. 77–78.

Simon, C., 'Laissez la culture tranquille', *Le Nouvel Observateur*, 24–30 janvier 1986, pp. 13–14.

Simon, C., Untitled Paper, in L. Oppenheim (ed.), *Three Decades of the French New Novel*, Urbana, IL, University of Illinois Press,1986, pp. 71–86.

Simon, C., 'La Lutte contre l'obscurantisme', *Le Monde*, 5 décembre 1986, p. 13.

Simon, C., 'Problèmes que posent le roman et l'écriture', *Francofonia*, vol. 10, no. 18, Spring 1990, pp. 3–10.

Simon, C., '"Roman et mémoire", extrait d'une conférence inédite', *Revue des sciences humaines*, no. 220, 1990–4, pp. 191–92.

Simon, C., 'La Déroute des Flandres', *Le Figaro*, 13 juillet 1990, pp. 10–11.

Simon, C., 'Passions et polémique à propos du texte de Claude Simon: la réponse de Claude Simon', *Le Figaro*, 27 juillet 1990, p. 5.

Simon, C., 'Entretien: choses vues', *Art Press*, no. 174, November 1992, pp. 30–33.

Simon, C., 'Allocution aux étudiants de Queen's University', in Mireille Calle-Gruber (ed.), *Les Sites de l'écriture. Colloque Claude Simon*, Paris, Nizet, 1995, pp. 16–21.

Simon, C., 'Cher Kenzaburô Ôe', *Le Monde*, 21 septembre 1995, p. 1.

Simon, C., 'Réponse à une enquête: "Pour quel temps écrit-on?"', *La Quinzaine littéraire*, no. 777, 1 août 1998, p. 30.

Sollers, P., 'La Sensation, c'est primordial', *Le Monde*, 19 septembre 1997, pp. I–II.

Vial, C., 'Claude Simon en apprentissage', *Le Monde*, 22 janvier 1988, p. 11.

Villelaur, A., 'Le Roman est en train de réfléchir sur lui-même', *Les Lettres françaises*, no. 764, 12–18 mars, 1959, pp. 1, 4–5.

Secondary Works

Books wholly or partly devoted to Simon

Alexandre, D., *Claude Simon*, Paris, Editions Marval, 1991.

Alexandre, D., *Le Magma et l'horizon. Essai sur 'La Route des Flandres' de Claude Simon*, Paris, Klincksieck, 1997.

Alexandre, D., *et al.*, *'La Route des Flandres': ouvrage collectif*, Paris, Ellipses, 1997.

Améry, J., *Claude Simon: Bilder des Erzählens*, Zürich, TA-Media AG, 1999.

Andrès, B., *Profils du personnage chez Claude Simon*, Paris, Minuit, 1992.

Apeldoorn, J. van, *Pratiques de la description*, Amsterdam, Rodopi, 1982.

Bertrand, M., *Langue romanesque et parole scripturale: Essai sur Claude Simon*, Paris, Presses Universitaires de France, 1987.

Birn, R., and K. Gould (eds), *Orion Blinded: Essays on Claude Simon*, Lewisburg, PA, Bucknell University Press, 1981.

Brewer, M. M., *Claude Simon: Narrativities without Narrative*, Lincoln, NE, and London, University of Nebraska Press, 1995.

Britton, C., *Claude Simon: Writing the Visible*, Cambridge, Cambridge University Press, 1987.

Britton, C. (ed.), *Claude Simon*, Harlow, Longman, 1993.

Burden, R., *John Fowles, John Hawkes, Claude Simon, Problems of Self and Form in the Post-Modernist Novel: A Comparative Study*, Wurzburg, Königshausen and Neumann, 1980.

Calle, M. (ed.), *Claude Simon: chemins de la mémoire*, Sainte-Foy, Le Griffon d'argile, 1993.

Calle-Gruber, M. (ed.), *Les Sites de l'écriture: Colloque Claude Simon*, Paris, Nizet, 1995.

Carroll, D., *The Subject in Question: The Languages of Theory and the Strategies of Fiction*, Chicago, Chicago University Press, 1982.

Clément-Perrier, A., *Claude Simon: la fabrique du jardin*, Paris, Nathan, 1998.

Cresciucci, A. (ed.), *Claude Simon: 'La Route des Flandres'*, Paris, Klincksieck, 1997.

Dällenbach, L., *Claude Simon*, Paris, Seuil, 1988.

Duffy, J., *Reading Between the Lines: Claude Simon and the Visual Arts*, Liverpool, Liverpool, University Press, 1998.

Dugast-Portes, F., and M. Touret, *Lectures de 'La Route des Flandres'*, Rennes, Presses Universitaires de Rennes, 1997.

Dummer, B., *Von der Narration zur Deskription: generative Textkonstitution bei Jean Ricardou, Claude Simon und Philippe Sollers*, Amsterdam, B. R. Gruner, 1988.

Duncan, A. B. (ed.), *Claude Simon: New Directions*, Edinburgh, Scottish Academic Press, 1985.

Duncan, A., *Claude Simon: Adventures in Words*, Manchester and New York, Manchester University Press, 1994 (2nd, expanded edition, forthcoming 2002).

Evans, M. J., *Claude Simon and the Transgressions of Modern Art*, Basingstoke, Macmillan, 1987.

Ferrato-Combe, B., *Ecrire en peintre: Claude Simon et la peinture*, Grenoble, ELLUG, 1998.

Fletcher, J., *Claude Simon and Fiction Now*, London, Calder and Boyers, 1975.

Genin, C., *L'Echeveau de la mémoire: 'La Route des Flandres' de Claude Simon*, Paris, Champion, 1997.

Genin, C., *L'Expérience du lecteur dans les romans de Claude Simon: lecture studieuse et lecture poignante*, Paris, Champion, 1997.

Gocel, V., *'Histoire' de Claude Simon: écriture et vision du monde*, Leuven, Peeters 1997.

Gould, K., *Claude Simon's Mythic Muse*, Columbia, SC, French Literature Publications, 1979.

Guermès, S., *L'Echo du dedans: essai sur 'La Route des Flandres' de Claude Simon*, Paris, Klincksieck, 1997.

Hollenbeck, J., *Eléments baroques dans les romans de Claude Simon*, Paris, Pensée Universelle, 1982.

Hennermann-Bellina, E., *Wandel und Kontinuität in Claude Simons Prosa. Am Beispiel der Romane 'Histoire', 'La Bataille de Pharsale', 'Les Corps conducteurs' und 'Triptyque'*, Frankfurt and New York, Peter Lang, 1993.

Janssens, P., *Claude Simon: faire l'histoire*, Villeneuve d'Ascq, Presses Universitaires du Septentrion (Objet), 1998.

Janvier, L., *Une parole exigeante*, Paris, Minuit, 1964.

Jimenez-Fajardo, S., *Claude Simon*, Boston, Twayne, 1975.

Kadish, D. Y., *Practices of the New Novel in Claude Simon's 'L'Herbe' and 'La Route des Flandres'*, Fredericton, N.B., York Press, 1979.

Kirpalani, M.-C., *Approches de 'La Route des Flandres', roman de Claude Simon*, New Dehli, Vignette Arts, 1981.

Klinkert, T., *Bewahren und Löschen. Zur Proust-Rezeption bei Samuel Beckett, Claude Simon und Thomas Bernhard*, Tübingen, G. Narr, 1996.

Kuhnle, T. R., *Chronos und Thanatos. Zum Existentialismus des 'nouveau romancier' Claude Simon*, Tübingen, Nicmeyer, 1995.

Laurichesse, J.-Y., *La Bataille des odeurs: l'espace olfactif des romans de Claude Simon*, Paris, L'Harmattan, 1998.

Lehmann, G., *Des mots et des choses ou Claude Simon se penche sur l'écriture*, Odense, Romansk Institut, 1977.

Lindahl, M., *La Conception du temps dans deux romans de Claude Simon*, Uppsala, Uppsala University, 1991.

Longuet, P., *Lire Claude Simon: la polyphonie du monde*, Paris, Editions de Minuit, 1995.

Longuet, P., *Claude Simon*, Paris, Ministère des Affaires étrangères – ADPF, 1998.

Loubère, J. A. E., *The Novels of Claude Simon*, Ithaca, NY, Cornell University Press, 1975.

Mecke, J., *Roman-Zeit. Zeitformung und Dekonstruktion des französischen Romans der Gegenwart*, Tübingen, G. Narr, 1990.

Mougin, P., *Lecture de 'L'Acacia' de Claude Simon: l'imaginaire biographique*, Archives des lettres modernes, no. 267, Paris, Minard, 1997.

Mougin, P., *L'Effet d'image: essai sur Claude Simon*, Paris, L'Harmattan, 1997.

Neumann, G., *Echos et correspondances dans 'Triptyque' et 'Leçon de choses' de Claude Simon*, Lausanne, L'Age de l'homme, 1983.

Nitsch, W., *Sprache und Gewalt bei Claude Simon: Interpretationen zu seinem Romanwerk der sechziger Jahre*, Tübingen, G. Narr, 1992.

Orr, M., *Claude Simon: the Intertextual Dimension*, Glasgow, University of Glasgow French and German Publications, 1993.

Phalèse, Hubert de, *Code de 'La Route des Flandres': examen du roman de Claude Simon*, Paris, Nizet, 1997.

Piégay-Gros, N., *Claude Simon: 'Les Géorgiques'*, Paris, Presses Universitaires de France, 1996.

Pugh, A. C., *Simon: 'Histoire'*, London, Grant and Cutler, 1982.

Raccanello, M., and G. Benelli, *Introduzione al romanzo di Claude Simon*, Trieste, Edizione del Tornasole, 1993.

Rannoux, C., *L'Ecriture du labyrinthe: 'La Route des Flandres' de Claude Simon*, Orléans, Paradigme, 1997.

Reitsma-La Brujeere, C., *Passé et présent dans 'Les Géorgiques' de Claude Simon: étude intertextuelle et narratologique d'une reconstruction de l'Histoire*, Amsterdam, Rodopi, 1992.

Ricardou, J. (ed.), *Claude Simon: Colloque de Cerisy*, Union Générale d'Editions, 1975; reprinted as *Lire Claude Simon*, Paris, Les Impressions Nouvelles, 1986.

Rossum-Guyon, F. van, *Le Coeur critique: Butor, Simon, Kristeva, Cixous*, Amsterdam, Rodopi, 1997.

Roubichou, G., *Lecture de 'L'Herbe' de Claude Simon*, Lausanne, L'Age d'homme, 1976.

Sarkonak, R., *Claude Simon: les carrefours du texte*, Toronto, Paratexte, 1986.

Sarkonak, R., *Understanding Claude Simon*, Columbia, SC, South Carolina University Press, 1990.

Sarkonak, R., *Les Trajets de l'écriture: Claude Simon*, Toronto, Paratexte, 1994.

Schmidt, D., *Schreiben nach dem Krieg. Studien zur Poetik Claude Simons*, Heidelberg, Carl Winter, 1997.

Schoentjes, P., *Claude Simon par correspondance: 'Les Géorgiques' et le regard des livres*, Geneva, Droz, 1995.

Starobinski, J., G. Raillard, L. Dällenbach and R. Dragonetti, *Sur Claude Simon*, Paris, Minuit, 1987.

Storrs, N., *Liquid*: *A Source of Meaning and Structure in Claude Simon's 'La Bataille de Pharsale'*, New York, Lang, 1983.

Sykes, S., *Les Romans de Claude Simon*, Paris, Minuit, 1979.

Szöllösi-Brenig, V., *Die 'Ermordung' des Existentialismus oder das letzte Engagement: künstlerische Selbstfindung im Frühwerk von Claude Simon zwischen Sartre und Merleau-Ponty*, Tübingen, G. Narr, 1995.

Thierry, F., *Claude Simon: une expérience du temps*, Paris, SEDES, 1997.

Thouillot, M., *Les Guerres de Claude Simon*, Rennes, Presses Universitaires de Rennes, 1998.

Tost Planet, M. A., *Claude Simon: Novelas espanolas de la guerra y la revolucion*, Barcelona, Ediciones Peninsula, 1989.

Ventresque, R., *Claude Simon: A partir de 'La Route des Flandres', tours et détours d'une écriture*, Montpellier, Université Paul Valéry, 1997.

Viart, D., *Une mémoire inquiète: 'La Route des Flandres' de Claude Simon*, Paris, Presses Universitaires de France, 1997.

Wasmuth, A., *Subjektivität, Wahrnehmung und Zeitlichkeit als poetologische Aspekte bei Claude Simon: Untersuchungen zu den Romanen 'Le Vent', 'L'Herbe' und 'La Route des Flandres'*, Hamburg, Romanisches Seminar der Universität Hamburg, 1979.

Wehle, W., *Französischer Roman der Gegenwart. Erzählstruktur und Wirklichkeit im Nouveau Roman*, Berlin, Erich Schmidt, 1972.

Wilhelm, K., *Der Nouveau Roman. Ein Experiment der französischen Gegenwartsliteratur*, Berlin, Stolz, 1969.

Zeltner-Neukomm, G., *Die eigenmächtige Sprache. Zur Poetik des Nouveau Roman*, Olten und Freiburg, Walter, 1965.
Zeltner, G., *Im Augenblick der Gegenwart*, Frankfurt am Main, Fischer, 1974.

Special numbers of periodicals on Simon

Cahiers de l'Université de Perpignan, vol. 1, *Claude Simon*, ed. M. Roelens, Perpignan, Presses Universitaires de Perpignan, 1986.
Cahiers de l'Université de Perpignan, vol. 30, *'Le Jardin des Plantes' de Claude Simon, Actes du colloque de Perpignan*, ed. J. Laurichesse, Perpignan, Presses Universitaires de Perpignan, 2000.
Critique, 'La Terre et la guerre dans l'œuvre de Claude Simon', vol. 37, no. 414, novembre 1981.
Critique, nos. 584–585, janvier–février 1996.
Corbières, no. 38, http://perso.cybercable.fr/naintern/labyrinthe/framesimon.html
Du, no. 691, January 1999, pp. 24–93.
Entretiens, no. 31, 1972.
Esprit Créateur, vol. 27, no. 4, 1987, ed. Mária M. Brewer.
Etudes Littéraires, vol. 9, no. 1, avril 1976, ed. Jean-Pierre Vidal.
La Licorne, no. 35, 1995.
Littératures contemporaines, no. 3, 1997.
Littératures, juin 1999.
Modern Language Notes, vol. 103, no. 4, September 1988.
Op. Cit., Revue de littérature française et comparée, vol. 9, novembre 1997.
Review of Contemporary Fiction, vol 5, no. 1, Spring 1985.
Revue des lettres modernes, Série Claude Simon 1: À la recherche du référent perdu, 1994, ed. Ralph Sarkonak.
Revue des lettres modernes, Série Claude Simon 2: L'Écriture du féminin/masculin, 1997, ed. Ralph Sarkonak.
Revue des lettres modernes, Série Claude Simon 3: Lectures de 'Histoire', 2000, ed. Ralph Sarkonak.
Revue des sciences humaines, no. 220, 1990–4, ed. Guy Neumann.
Scherzo, 3, avril–juin 1998, pp. 3–29.

Publications devoted to Le Jardin des Plantes

Alexandre, D., 'L'Enregistrement du *Jardin des Plantes*', *Littératures*, vol. 40, Spring 1999, pp. 5–18.
Alexandre, D., 'Le Renard du jardin: remarques sur l'insertion du personnage historique dans le récit simonien', *Cahiers de l'Université de Perpignan*, vol. 30, *'Le Jardin des Plantes' de Claude Simon, Actes du colloque de Perpignan*, Perpignan, Presses Universitaires de Perpignan, 2000, pp. 67–88.
Bernard, M., '*Le Jardin des Plantes* ou l'hypotypose de la Place Monge', http://perso.cybercable.fr/naintern/labyrinthe/framesimon.html
Blanc, A.-L., 'Le "Jardin zoologique" du *Jardin des Plantes*: visite guidée', *Littératures*, vol. 40, Spring 1999, pp. 47–57.
Calle-Gruber, M., 'Claude Simon, un jardin de la mémoire où cultiver l'art d'écrire', *Nuit Blanche*, no. 74, printemps 1999, pp. 58–60.

Calle-Gruber, M., 'Une harmonie contre tendue: des principes de l'arc et de la lyre appliqués à l'écriture du roman chez Claude Simon', *Cahiers de l'Université de Perpignan*, vol. 30, *'Le Jardin des Plantes' de Claude Simon, Actes du colloque de Perpignan*, Perpignan, Presses Universitaires de Perpignan, 2000, pp. 39–56.

Clément-Perrier, A., 'Le Jeu des couleurs dans *Le Jardin des Plantes*', *Littératures*, Spring 1999, pp. 31–46.

Darnat, S., 'L'Epiphanie du blanc', *Littératures*, vol. 40, Spring 1999, pp. 19–30.

Dilettato, J.-M., and P. Longuet, 'Les Feuilles au fond du bassin: sur *Le Jardin des Plantes* de Claude Simon', *L'Infini*, no. 65, 1999.

Duffy, J. H., '"Ce n'est pas une allégorie. C'est une feuille tout simplement": Text, Intertext and Biography in Claude Simon's *Jardin des Plantes*', *Romanic Review*, vol. 89, no. 4, 1998, pp. 583–609.

Duffy, J. H., 'Artistic Biographies and Aesthetic Coherence in Claude Simon's *Jardin des Plantes*', *Forum for Modern Language Studies*, vol. 35, no. 2, 1999, pp. 175–92.

Ferrato-Combe, B., 'Simon et Novelli: l'image de la lettre', *Cahiers de l'Université de Perpignan*, vol. 30, *'Le Jardin des Plantes' de Claude Simon, Actes du colloque de Perpignan*, Perpignan, Presses Universitaires de Perpignan, 2000, pp. 103–18.

Labbe, M., 'Paysages perdus dans *Le Jardin des Plantes* de Claude Simon', *Courrier du Centre International d'Etudes Poétiques*, vol. 217, January–March 1998, pp. 21–37.

Laurichesse, J.-Y., 'Aux quatre coins du monde: *Le Jardin des Plantes* comme album d'un voyageur', *Cahiers de l'Université de Perpignan*, vol. 30, *'Le Jardin des Plantes' de Claude Simon, Actes du colloque de Perpignan*, Perpignan, Presses Universitaires de Perpignan, 2000, pp. 119–36.

Longuet, P., 'Échos et palimpseste. Sur *Le Jardin des Plantes* de Claude Simon', *Cahiers de l'Université de Perpignan*, vol. 30, *'Le Jardin des Plantes' de Claude Simon, Actes du colloque de Perpignan*, Perpignan, Presses Universitaires de Perpignan, 2000, pp. 25–38.

Miguet-Ollagnier, M., '*Le Jardin des Plantes* à l'ombre de Marcel Proust', *Bulletin d'informations proustiennes*, vol. 29, 1998, pp. 129–40.

Mougin, P., 'Du *Tricheur* au *Jardin des Plantes*: la figure de la mère défunte', *Cahiers de l'Université de Perpignan*, vol. 30, *'Le Jardin des Plantes' de Claude Simon, Actes du colloque de Perpignan*, Perpignan, Presses Universitaires de Perpignan, 2000, pp. 89–102.

Roelens, M., 'Figures de la "gouaille" et de la raillerie dans *Le Jardin des Plantes*', *Cahiers de l'Université de Perpignan*, vol. 30, *'Le Jardin des Plantes' de Claude Simon, Actes du colloque de Perpignan*, Perpignan, Presses Universitaires de Perpignan, 2000, pp. 57–66.

Sarkonak, R., 'Les Quatre Saisons au *Jardin des Plantes*', *Revue des lettres modernes, Série Claude Simon 3: Lectures de 'Histoire'*, 2000, ed. Ralph Sarkonak, pp. 191–214.

Serca, I., '*Le Jardin des Plantes*: une "composition en damier"', *Littératures*, vol. 40, Spring 1999, pp. 59–77.

Viart , D., 'Portrait de l'artiste en écrivain. *Le Jardin des Plantes* de Claude Simon', *Cahiers de l'Université de Perpignan*, vol. 30, *'Le Jardin des Plantes' de Claude*

Simon, Actes du colloque de Perpignan, Perpignan, Presses Universitaires de Perpignan, 2000, pp. 9–24.

Viart, D., 'Remembrances et remembrements: cultiver les friches de la mémoire. *Le Jardin des Plantes*', *Scherzo,* no. 3, 1998, pp. 23–28.

Articles, essays and chapters on Simon

Alexandre, D., 'Cartes postales d'Amérique: le cliché dans les romans de M. Butor, C. Simon et la peinture américaine des années 1960', *Polysèmes*, *Arts et Littérature*, vol. 1, 1989, pp. 119–48.

Alexandre, D., 'La Figure de Christophe Colomb dans *Les Corps conducteurs* de Claude Simon', in J. Houriez (ed.), *Christophe Colomb et la découverte de l'Amérique: mythe et histoire*, Paris, Belles Lettres, 1994, pp. 103–22.

Alexandre, D., 'Claude Simon and Jean Dubuffet: terroirs d'origine', *Dalhousie French Studies*, vol. 31, 1995, pp. 39–64.

Andrès, B., 'Simon et Balzac: "patiemment, sans plaisir"', in S. Vachon (ed.), *Balzac: une poétique du roman*, Presses Universitaires de Vincennes, 1996, pp. 435–45.

Andrews, M., 'Formalist Dogmatisms, Derridean Questioning, and the Return of Affect: Towards a Distributed Reading of *Triptyque*', *L'Esprit créateur*, vol. 27, no. 4, 1987, pp. 37–47.

Andrews, M. W., 'Narrative Discontinuity and the Warring Image: the Role of the Spanish Civil War in the Novels of Claude Simon', in F. Brown (ed.), *Rewriting the Good Fight: Critical Essays on the Literature of the Spanish Civil War*, East Lansing, MI, Michigan State University Press, 1989, pp. 147–60.

Apeldoorn, J. van, 'Claude Simon: mots, animaux et la face cachée des choses', *Cahiers de recherches interuniversitaires néerlandaises: l'homme et l'animal*, vol. 19, 1988, pp. 72–82.

Apeldoorn, J. van, 'Écriture et compassion: sur *L'Acacia* de Claude Simon', in Suzan Van Djik and Christa Stevens (eds), *Enjeux de la communication romanesque: hommage à Françoise van Rossum-Guyon*, Amsterdam, Atlanta, Rodopi, 1994, pp. 185–95.

Arseth, A., 'Myth and Metanarration in the Modern Novel: Remarks on Faulkner's *Absalom, Absalom!* and Claude Simon's *La Route des Flandres*', in *Actes du IXème congrès de l'association internationale de littérature comparée*, Innsbruck, Innsbruck University Press, 1981, pp. 341–45.

Bajomée, D., 'Blessure du temps: mythe et idéologie dans *Le Palace* de Claude Simon', *Cahiers internationaux de symbolisme*, 1981, vols 42–44, pp. 29–40.

Baron. A.-M., '*La Route des Flandres* de Claude Simon, roman filmique', *L'Ecole des lettres*, vol. 7, 1998, pp. 99–110.

Bell, M., '*La Route des Flandres*', in M. Bell, *Aphorism in the Francophone Novel of the XXth century*, Montreal, London, Queen's University Press, 1997, pp. 79–92 and 136–40.

Benoit-Morinière, C., 'La Logique de l'histoire dans *Histoire* de Claude Simon', *Queste*, vol. 4, 1988, pp. 99–106.

Berger, Y., 'L'Enfer, le temps', *Nouvelle Revue française*, vol. 97, 1961, pp. 95–109.

Bertrand, M., 'Le Roman du bâtard utopiste: *Le Vent* de Claude Simon', *Roman 20–50*, vol. 23, juin 1997, pp. 149–61.

Bessière, J., 'Hybrides romanesques, interdiscursivité et intelligibilité com-
mune – Claude Simon, Italo Calvino, Botho Strauss', in Jean Bessière (ed.),
Hybrides romanesques, Fiction (1960–1985), Paris, P.U.F., 1988, pp. 127–43.

Birn, R., 'Proust, Claude Simon and the Art of the Novel', *Papers on Language
and Literature*, vol. 13, 1977, pp. 68–186.

Birn, R., 'From Sign to Saga: Dynamic Description in Two Texts by Claude
Simon', *Australian Journal of French Studies*, vol. 21, no. 2, 1984, pp. 148–60.

Bischof, M., 'L'Incipit de *L'Acacia* de Claude Simon', *Versants*, no. 27, 1995, pp.
115–30.

Bishop, M., 'Tournier, Simon, Hyvrad and Cixous', in D. Bevan (ed.), *Literature
and spirituality*, Amsterdam, Rodopi, 1992, pp. 121–32.

Blades, M. W., 'Claude Simon's Theory of Perception and Reality in *L'Acacia*',
Language Quarterly, vol. 29, nos 3–4, 1991, pp. 32–43.

Blanc, A.-L., 'Une image de l'Espagne dans *Histoire* de Claude Simon: étude
d'une ekphrasis', *Littératures*, vol. 32, printemps 1995, pp. 177–89.

Bon, F., 'Claude Simon: fantastique et tragédie', *Critique*, no. 511, 1989, pp. 980–96.

Borgomano, M, 'Fins de siècles dans l'univers romanesque de Claude Simon:
L'Acacia', in Alexandre Ablamovicz (ed.), *Le Romanesque français d'une fin de
siècle à l'autre*, Katowice, Wydawnictwo Universytetu Slaskiego, 1998, pp.
188–97.

Borreil, J, 'Claude Simon: le légendaire comme métaphore', *Cahiers de Paris
VIII*, no. 2, 1989, pp. 61–86.

Borrel, J., and J. Richard, 'Fragments from Claude Simon's Legendary: Images
of Northern Catalonia', *Catalonia Review*, vol. 2, June 1989, pp. 159–73.

Borrut, M., '*Le Sacre du printemps* et les origines de l'Espagne romanesque chez
Claude Simon', *Revue de littérature comparée*, vol. 71, no. 3, 1997, pp. 323–
39.

Bourque, G., 'La Parabole: analyse végétale de *L'Herbe*', *Etudes Littéraires*, vol. 9
no. 1, avril 1976, pp. 161–87.

Brandt, J., 'History and Art in Claude Simon's *Histoire*', *Romanic Review*, vol. 73,
no. 3, 1982, pp. 373–84.

Branko, F., '*La Route des Flandres*. Outline of an Analysis', *Neophilologus*, vol.
65, no. 1, 1981, pp. 42–49.

Brewer, M. M., 'An Energetics of Reading: The Intertextual in Claude Simon',
Romanic Review, vol. 73, no. 4, 1982, pp. 489–504.

Brewer, M. M., 'Recasting Oedipus: Narrative and the Discourse of Myth in
Claude Simon', *Stanford French Review*, vol. 9, no. 3, 1985, pp. 415–34.

Brewer, M. M., 'Narrative Fission: Event, History and Writing in *Les
Géorgiques*', in *Michigan Romance Studies*, vol. 6, 1986, pp. 27–39.

Britton, C., 'Voices, Absence and Presence in the Novels of Claude Simon',
French Studies, vol. 36, 1982, pp. 445–54.

Britton, C., 'The Imagery Origins of the Text', *Degré Second*, vol. 5, 1981, pp.
115–30.

Britton, C., 'Diversity of Discourse in Claude Simon's *Les Géorgiques*', *French
Studies*, vol. 38, 1984, pp. 423–42.

Britton, C., 'Visual effects by Claude Simon', *Paragraph*, vol. 10, October 1987,
pp. 45–64.

Brosman, C. S., 'Man's Animal Condition in *La Route des Flandres*', *Symposium*, vol. 29, 1975, pp. 57–68.

Brosman, C. S., 'Reading Behind the Lines: the Interpretation of War', *Sewanee Review*, vol. 100, no. 11, 1992, pp. 69–97.

Boucheron, S., 'La Ponctuation dans le texte: parenthèses, sujets et linéarité dans l'incipit du *Palace* de Claude Simon', *Recherches linguistiques de Vincennes*, no. 28, 1999, pp. 33–39.

Budini, P., 'Le Réel et l'écriture dans *L'Invitation* de Claude Simon', *Francofonia: Studi e Ricerche sulle Letterature di Lingua Francese*, vol. 17, 1989, pp. 3–20.

Burke, R. E., 'Sixth Movement: Painterly Jigsaw Puzzles: Claude Simon and *Triptyque*', in R. E. Burke, *The Games of Poetics. Ludic Criticism and Post-Modern Fiction*, New York, Berlin, Peter Lang, 1994, pp. 153–72.

Bustarret, C., 'La "Main écrivant" au miroir du manuscrit', in P. Joret and A. Remael (eds), *Language and Beyond: Actuality and Virtuality in the Relations between Word, Image and Sound*, Amsterdam, Rodopi, 1998, pp 431–47.

Butlin, N. H., 'Sens et textualité dans *Leçon de choses* de Claude Simon', *Initiales*, vol. 8, 1988, pp. 44–51.

Buuren, M. van, 'L'Essence des choses: étude de la description dans l'oeuvre de Claude Simon', *Poétique*, no. 43, 1980, pp. 324–33.

Calas, F., and G. Guillemin, 'L'Echeveau débridé de *La Route de Flandres* de Simon', *Information grammaticale*, vol. 76, janvier 1998, pp. 46–49.

Cali, A., 'Problèmes de la fragmentation textuelle à partir de "Propriétés des rectangles" de Simon', in A. Cali, *Pratiques de lecture et d'écriture*, Paris, Nizet, 1980, pp. 63–105.

Calle-Gruber, M., 'Roman, idylle, épistolaire: les déplacements du genre littéraire dans *Les Géorgiques* de Claude Simon', in C. Lagel (ed), *Les Genres insérés dans le roman*, Lyon, Centre d'Etudes des Interactions Culturelles de L'Université Jean Moulin-Lyon III, 1994, pp. 75–84.

Calle-Gruber, M, 'Sur les brisées du roman', *Micromégas*, vol. 8, no. 1, 1981, pp. 108–13.

Calle-Gruber, M., 'Claude Simon: le temps, l'écriture', *Littérature*, vol. 83, 1991, pp. 31–42.

Calle Gruber, M., 'Les Corps ouvrables: à propos de *Femmes* de Joan Miró et Claude Simon', *New Novel Review*, vol. 3, no. 2, 1996, pp. 39–50.

Caminade, P., 'Simon, lyrisme, musique du texte, érotisme et pornographie', *Sud*, vol. 27, 1978, pp. 113–18.

Carroll, D., 'Diachrony and Synchrony in *Histoire*', *Modern Language Notes*, vol. 92, no. 4, 1977, pp. 797–824.

Carroll, D., 'For Example: Psychoanalysis and Fiction or the Conflict of Génération(s)', *Sub-stance*, vol. 21, 1978, pp. 49–76.

Castro-Segovia, J., 'Mythe et réalité de l'Amérique latine dans *Les Corps conducteurs*', *Marche Romane*, vol. 21, 1971, pp. 93–96.

Chapier, H., 'Claude Simon: *La Route des Flandres*', *Synthèses*, vol. 174, 1960, pp. 121–24.

Claudon, F., '*Histoire* et la représentation de l'histoire chez Claude Simon', *Beiträge zur Romanischen Philologie*, vol. 26, no. 2, 1987, pp. 253–58.

Clemmen, Y., 'Claude Simon's *L'Acacia*, the Text-Album: Photography and Narrative Construction', *Romance Notes*, vol. 33, no. 2, 1992, pp. 125–32.

Clemmen, Y., 'Claude Simon: Painting and Photography, the Need to Construct and the Desire to See', *Romance Languages Annual*, vol. 4, 1992, pp. 29–32.

Clément-Perrier, A., 'Etude de mains. Petite esquisse d'un motif simonien', *Poétique*, vol. 105, 1996, pp. 23–40.

Cloonan, W., 'Memory and the Collapse of Culture: Claude Simon's *La Route des Flandres*', *Symposium*, vol. 51, no. 3, spring 1997, pp. 146–57.

Cobley, E. M., 'Absence and Supplementarity in *Absalom! Absalom!* and *La Route des Flandres*', *Revue de Littérature comparée*, vol. 62, 1988, pp. 23–44.

Daddesio, T. C., 'History and Formalism in the Writing of Claude Simon', *Romance Languages Annual*, vol. 1, 1989, pp. 239–43.

Daddesio, T. C., 'Is Claude Simon a Post-Modern Writer?', *Romance Languages Annual*, vol. 2, 1990, pp. 77–81.

Dällenbach, L., 'A l'origine de *La Recherche* ou "la raie du jour"', in S. Bertho (ed.), *Proust contemporain*, Amsterdam, Rodopi, 1994, pp. 51–59.

Dällenbach, L., 'Dans le noir: Claude Simon et la genèse de *La Route des Flandres*', in L. Hay (ed.), *Genèses du roman contemporain: incipit et entrée en écriture*, Paris, Editions du C.N.R.S., 1993, pp. 105–20.

Dällenbach, L., 'La Lecture comme suture', in L. Dällenbach and J. Ricardou (eds), *Problèmes actuels de la lecture*, Paris, Clancier-Guénaud, 1982, pp. 35–47.

Dällenbach, L., 'Simon ou le travail du texte comme bricolage analogique', in B. Didier and J. Neefs (eds), *Penser, classer, écrire: de Pascal à Perec*, Paris, Presses Universitaires de Vincennes, 1990, pp. 137–48.

Daprini, P., 'Claude Simon, History, and "l'innommable réalité"', in D. Bevan (ed.), *Literature and War*, Amsterdam, Rodopi, 1990, pp. 167–78.

Dauge, A., 'George Orwell, "O", Claude Simon: triptyque d'une réécriture', *Archipel*, vol. 8, 1994, pp. 67–87.

Deborne-Bonnefoy, M., 'Volumes, Feuillets, Planches', *Communications*, vol. 19, 1972, pp. 19–24.

Déga, J.-L., 'Balzac et *Les Géorgiques* de Claude Simon', *Revue du Tarn*, no. 174, 1999, pp. 357–68.

Desvaux, A. P., 'L'Art de la description: démystification du réalisme', *Anuario de Filología*, vol. 8, 1982, pp. 329–35.

Duffy, J. H., 'Art as Defamiliarisation in the Theory and Practice of Claude Simon', *Romance Studies*, no. 2, Summer 1983, pp. 108–23.

Duffy, J. H., '*Les Géorgiques* by Claude Simon: a Work of Synthesis and Renewal', *Australian Journal of French Studies*, vol. 21, no. 2, 1984, pp. 161–79.

Duffy, J. H., 'Suggestion versus Information in Claude Simon and Roland Barthes', *French Forum*, vol. 9, no. 3, 1984, pp. 328–42.

Duffy, J. H., 'Meaning and Subversion in Claude Simon's *Le Vent*: Some Structural Considerations', *French Studies Bulletin*, no. 15, 1985, pp. 8–10.

Duffy, J. H., 'M(i)sreading Claude Simon: a Partial Analysis', *Forum for Modern Language Studies*, vol. 23, no. 3, 1987, pp. 228–40.

Duffy, J. H., 'The Psychological Indicator as Point of Reference in the Novels of Claude Simon: a Typological Study of Subversive Strategies', *Degré Second*, vol. 12, November 1989, pp. 87–99.

Duffy, J. H., 'Antithesis in Simon's *Le Vent*: Authorial Red Herrings versus Readerly Strategies', *The Modern Language Review*, vol. 83, no. 3, 1988, pp. 571–85.

Duffy, J. H., 'Claude Simon, Merleau-Ponty and Perception', *French Studies*, vol. 46, no. 1, 1992, pp. 33–52.

Duffy, J. H., 'Claude Simon, Merleau-Ponty and Spatial Articulation', *Romance Studies*, no. 20, 1992, pp. 59–73.

Duffy, J. H., 'Claude Simon and Paul Cézanne: a Comparative Study', *Degré Second*, vol. 13, 1992, pp. 35–50.

Duffy, J. H. 'Claude Simon and Jean Dubuffet: "Voyageurs égarés"', *French Forum*, vol. 19, no. 1, 1994, pp. 95–116.

Duffy, J. H., 'Claude Simon: *Photographies*: a Formal and Thematic Study', *Nottingham French Studies*, vol. 33, no. 2, 1994, pp. 65–77.

Duffy, J. H., 'Conflicts of Genre in Claude Simon's *L'Herbe*', *Romance Studies*, no. 24, 1994, pp. 85–99.

Duffy, J. H., 'Claude Simon's *L'Acacia:* History as Anonymity, the Name as Word', *Modern Language Review*, vol. 90, no. 1, 1995, pp. 29–40.

Duffy, J. H., 'Claude Simon, Joan Miró et l'Interimage', in E. Le Calvez and M.-C. Canova-Green (eds), *Texte(s) et Intertexte(s)*, Amsterdam, Rodopi, 1997, pp. 113–39.

Duffy, J. H., 'Cultural Autobiography and *Bricolage*: Claude Simon and Robert Rauschenberg', *Word and Image*, vol. 13, 1997, pp. 92–101.

Dugastes-Portes, F., 'le spectre de l'ascendance: fonction tragifiante du personnage de l'ancêtre au fil de l'oeuvre de Claude Simon', *Revue des sciences humaines*, no. 215, 1989, pp. 200–20.

Dugast-Pòrtes, F., 'Claude Simon et l'Histoire', *Romanistische Zeitschrift für Literaturgeschichte* , vol. 14, nos. 1–2, 1990, pp. 179–89.

Dugast-Portes, F., 'Vestiges et fragments: l'antiquité selon Claude Simon', in *Au miroir de la culture antique. Mélanges offerts au Président René Marache*, Rennes, Presses Universitaires de Rennes, 1992, pp. 113–34.

Duncan, A., 'Claude Simon and William Faulkner', *Forum for Modern Language Studies*, vol. 9, no. 3, 1973, pp. 235–52.

Duncan, A., 'La Description dans *Leçon de choses* de Claude Simon', *Littérature*, vol. 10, 1980, pp. 95–105.

Duncan, A., 'Claude Simon's *Les Géorgiques*: an Intertextual Adventure', *Romance Studies*, no. 2, 1983, pp. 90–107.

Duncan, A., 'Le Nouveau Roman jurassien', *Le Jura français*, vol. 58, 1991, pp. 7–11.

Duncan, A., 'Enfance et jeunesse de nouveaux romanciers', in P. Lejeune and C. Leroy (eds), *Le Tournant d'une vie*, Paris, Université Paris X (*Cahiers du RITM*, 10), 1995, pp. 117–28.

Duncan, A., 'La Famille arboisienne dans l'oeuvre de Claude Simon', in *Claude Simon: Prix Nobel de littérature. Retour à Arbois. Mai 1996*, Arbois, Pasteur Patrimoine Arbois, 1998, pp. 19–32.

Dupuy Sullivan, F., 'Recherche pour une textualité dans *Histoire* de Claude Simon', *Romanic Review*, vol. 79, 2, 1988, pp. 354–65.

Duverlie. C., 'Sur deux oeuvres récentes de Claude Simon', *Die Neueren Sprachen*, Heft 9, September 1972, pp. 543–49.

Duverlie, C., '"Amor Interruptus": The Question of Eroticism, or Eroticism in Question in the Works of Claude Simon', *Sub-stance*, vol. 8, 1974, pp. 21–33.

Ellison, D. R., 'Narrative Levelling and Performative Pathos in Claude Simon's *Les Géorgiques*', *French Forum*, vol. 12, no. 3, 1987, pp. 303–21, reprinted in D. R. Ellison, *Of Words and the World: Referential Anxiety in Contemporary French Fiction*, Princeton, NJ, Princeton University Press, 1993, pp. 55–68.

Engler, W., 'Die Aufkundigung der Mimesisvereinbarung im Roman von Claude Simon: Notizen zu *La Route des Flandres*', *Zeitschrift für französische Sprache und Literatur*, vol. 105, no. 2, 1995, pp. 137–55.

Essaouri, M., 'Les Ecrivains modernes et la peinture ou le refus du discours critique: l'exemple de Claude Simon', *Cahiers internationaux des études françaises*, mai 1985, pp. 229–41.

Evans, M. J., 'Two Uses of Intertextuality: References to Impressionist Painting and *Madame Bovary* in Claude Simon's *Leçon de choses*', *Nottingham French Studies*, vol. 19, no. 1, 1980, pp. 33–45.

Evans, M. J., 'Intertextual Triptych: Reading across *La Bataille de Pharsale, La Jalousie* and *A la recherche du temps perdu*', *Modern Language Review*, vol. 76, no. 4, 1981, pp. 839–47.

Ferrato-Combe, B., 'Fragments de journaux dans les roman de Simon', *Recherches et travaux*, vol. 48, 1995, pp. 152–63.

Ferrato-Combe, B., 'Claude Simon et Jean Dubuffet', *Recherches et travaux*, vol. 52, 1997, pp. 217–29.

Ferrato-Combe, B., 'Fiction et discours sur l'art: l'exemple de *La Bataille de Pharsale* de Claude Simon', *Dix-Neuf-Vingt: revue de littérature moderne*, vol. 3, 1997, pp. 115–37.

Ferrato-Combe, B., 'Perec, Simon et le Condottiere', *Cabinet d'amateur: Revue d'études perecquiennes*, nos. 7–8, 1998, pp. 99–106.

Fitch, B. T., 'Participe présent et procédés narratifs chez Claude Simon', *Revue des lettres modernes*, nos. 94–99, 1964, pp. 199–216.

Fitch, B. T., 'When the Fictive Referent is Itself a Work of Art: Simon's *Histoire*', in B. T. Fitch (ed.), *Reflections in the Mind's Eye: Reference and its Problematization in Twentieth-Century French Fiction*, Toronto, University of Toronto Press, 1991, pp. 153–79.

Fletcher, J., 'A Translator's Second Thoughts: The First Page of *The Georgics*', *Franco-British Studies*, vol. 10, autumn 1990, pp. 107–15.

Fletcher, J., 'Metamorphoses of the Text', *Franco-British Studies: Journal of the British Institute in Paris*, vol. 1, spring 1986, pp. 13–25.

Fraisse, L., 'La Lentille convexe de Claude Simon', *Poétique*, no. 117, 1999, pp. 27–46.

Gaudin, C., 'Niveaux de lisibilité dans *Leçon de choses* de Claude Simon', *Romanic Review*, vol. 48, 1977, pp. 175–96.

Gay-Crosier, R., '*Orion aveugle*, ou les configurations du serpent: la palette du verbe', *French Forum*, vol. 2, no. 2, 1977, pp. 168–73.

Gay-Crosier, R., 'De l'intertextualité à la métatextualité: *Les Géorgiques*', in R. Theis and H. T. Siepe (eds), *Le Plaisir de l'intertexte: Formes et fonctions de l'intertextualité*, Frankfurt, Peter Lang, 1986, pp. 317–44.

Gay-Crosier, R., 'Claude Simon et le surréalisme', *Romance Notes*, vol. 31, no. 3, 1991, pp. 171–86.

Gay-Crosier, R., 'Points de rencontre et points de choc, désir transformateur et violence génératrice: Claude Simon et l'acte de lecture', in J. Frolich (ed.), *Actes du Colloque international d'Oslo, 7–10 septembre 1994: Le Roman*, vol. 2, Oslo, University of Oslo, 1995, pp. 307–20.

Genin, C., 'La Fenêtre ouverte: parcours d'un "livre d'images": *Orion aveugle* de Claude Simon', *Littérales*, vol. 3, 1988, pp. 77–100.

Gibert, B., 'Fin de partie dans *Les Géorgiques* de Claude Simon', *Poétique*, no. 105, 1996, pp. 41–53.

Gilbert, J., 'Langage et histoire chez Claude Simon: d'*Orion aveugle* aux *Corps conducteurs*', in G. Falconer and H. Mitterand (eds), *La Lecture sociocritique du texte romanesque*, Toronto, Samuel Stevens, Hakkert and Co., 1975, pp. 115–25.

Gille, P., 'Génération et corruption dans *La Route des Flandres* de Claude Simon', *Studi Francesi*, vol. 33, no. 2, 1989, pp. 296–302.

Gleize, J., 'Comme si c'était une fiction: sur un dispositif analogique dans *L'Acacia* de Claude Simon', *Michigan Romance Studies*, vol. 13, 1993, pp. 81–102.

Gleize, J., 'La Détaille et le détail: sur *L'Acacia* de Claude Simon', in L. Louvel (ed.), *La Licorne, Hors Série: Le Détail*, Poitiers, Université de Poitiers, 1999, pp. 205–16.

Gosselin, C. H., 'Voices of the Past in Claude Simon's *La Bataille de Pharsale*', *New York Literary Forum*, vol. 2, 1978, pp. 23–33.

Gould, K. L., 'Mythologizing in the Nouveau Roman: Claude Simon's Archetypal City', in P. Crant (ed.), *Mythology in French Literature*, Columbia, SC, University of South Carolina, College of Humanities and Social Sciences. Department of Foreign Languages and Literatures, 1976, pp. 118–28.

Gregorio, L. A., 'Prométhée et la croix: mythe et métatexte dans *Les Corps conducteurs*', *Romance Notes*, vol. 23, no. 1, 1982, pp. 3–9.

Grodek, E., 'Hypertextualisation de Claude Simon: tentative de restitution d'une oeuvre', http://www.chass.utoronto.ca/french/foire2000/colloque/grodek.htm

Gruber, E., 'L'Enigme du cinquième cheval: reflexions sur l'esthétique philosophique dans *La Route des Flandres*', *New Novel Review*, vol. 3, no. 1, 1995, pp. 37–48.

Guichardet, J., 'Barcelone malade de la guerre dans *Le Palace* de Claude Simon', in M. Milner (ed.), *Littérature et Pathologie*, Saint-Denis, Presses Universitaires de Vincennes, 1989, pp. 167–78.

Guicharnaud, J., 'Remembrance of Things Passing: Claude Simon', *Yale French Studies*, no. 24, 1959, pp. 101–08.

Harper, L., 'Spatial Composition and Formal Harmonies in Claude Simon's *Histoire*', *Modern Language Studies*, vol. 9, 1978–79, pp. 73–83.

Hesbois, L., 'Qui dit ça? Identification des voix narratives dans *L'Herbe* de Claude Simon', *Revue du Pacifique*, vol. 2, 1976, pp. 144–59.

Higgins, L. A., 'Language, the Uncanny, and the Shapes of History in Claude Simon's *The Flanders Road*', *Studies in Twentieth Century Literature*, vol. 10, no. 1, 1985, pp. 117–40.

Higgins, L. A., 'Problems of Plotting: *La Route des Flandres*', in L. A. Higgins, *New Novel, New Wave, New Politics. Fiction and the Representation of History in Postwar France*, Lincoln, NE, and London, University of Nebraska Press, 1996, pp. 55–82.

Houppermans, S., 'L'Etranger dans l'œuvre de Claude Simon', in D. de Ruyter-Tongnotti (ed.), *L'Etranger dans la littérature française*, Groningen, University of Groningen Press, 1989, pp. 122–49, reprinted in J. Cauville and M. Zupancic (eds), *Réécriture des mythes. L'Utopie au féminin*, Amsterdam, Rodopi, 1997, pp. 316–41.

Howard, R., 'Divination by Ashes: an Introduction to Claude Simon', *The Georgia Review*, vol. 49, no. 1, Spring 1995, pp. 141–65.

Husseini, F., 'Architecture romanesque dans *Leçon de choses* de Claude Simon', *Phares-Manarât*, vol. 13, 1994, pp. 80–104.

Hutcheon, L., 'Modes et formes du narcissisme littéraire', *Poétique*, no. 29, 1977, pp. 90–106.

Janssens, P., 'Une restitution par la peinture: Claude Simon', in P. Joret and A. Remael (eds), *Language and Beyond: Actuality and Virtuality in the Relations between Word, Image and Sound*, Amsterdam, Rodopi, 1988, pp. 415–29.

Janvier, L., 'Vertige et parole dans l'œuvre de Claude Simon', in L. Janvier, *Une parole exigeante: le nouveau roman*, Paris, Editions de Minuit, 1964, pp. 89–110.

Jean, R., 'Commencements romanesques', in M. Mansuy (ed.), *Positions et oppositions sur le roman contemporain*, Paris, Klincksieck, 1971, pp. 129–36.

Jenny, L., 'La Stratégie de la forme', *Poétique*, no. 27, 1976, pp. 257–81.

Jimenez-Fajardo, S., 'A Descriptive Approach to Claude Simon's Novel *Leçon de choses*', in R. D. Pope (ed.), *The Analysis of Literary Texts. Current Trends in Methodology*, Ypsilanti Mi, Bilingual Press, 1980, pp. 298–313.

Jimenez-Fajardo, S., 'Generative Representations in the Post-Modern Fiction of Claude Simon', *Cincinnati Romance Review*, no. 1, 1982, pp. 19–27.

Jongeneel, E., 'Buveurs de thé avec peintre et modèle', in Y. Went-Daoust (ed.), *Description – écriture – peinture*, Groningen, University Press of Groningen, 1987, pp. 101–18.

Jongeneel, E., '"Movement into space": la belligérance de l'image dans *La Bataille de Pharsale* de Claude Simon', *Revue Romane*, vol. 26, no. 1, 1991, pp. 78–100.

Jongeneel, E., '"Un de ces tableaux impressionnistes": l'image comme fixatif de l'histoire dans *L'Herbe* de Claude Simon', in S. Dijk and K. Stevens (eds), *Enjeux de la communication romanesque*, Amsterdam, Rodopi, 1994, pp. 257–69.

Jost, F., 'Les Aventures du lecteur', *Poétique*, no. 29, 1977, pp. 77–89.

Kadish, D. Y., 'From the Narration of Crime to the Crime of Narration: Claude Simon's *Le Palace*', *The International Fiction Review*, vol. 4, 1977, pp. 128–36.

Kadish, D. Y., 'Claude Simon and the French Revolution', in G. Prince (ed.), *Alternatives*, Lexington, KY, French Forum, 1993, pp. 121–32.

Kelly, L. H., 'Claude Simon's *La Route des Flandres*: An Experiment in "Cubist" Fiction', in D. W. Tappan and W. A. Mould (eds), *French Studies in Honor of Philip A. Wadsworth*, Birmingham, AL, Summa, 1985, pp. 111–21.

Kim, J.-S, 'Le Descriptif de Claude Simon et l'excroissance textuelle', *Etudes de langue et littérature françaises*, vol. 36, no. 1, 1998, pp. 385–92.

Konieczna, E., 'La Mise en abyme dans *La Bataille de Pharsale* de Claude Simon', *Kwartalnik Neofilologiczny*, vol. 32, no. 4, 1985, pp. 463–70.

Kreiter, J. A., 'Perceptions et réflexions dans *La Route des Flandres*: signes et sémantique', *Romanic Review* , vol. 77, no. 4, 1981, pp. 489–94.

Kronegger, M., 'The Impact of Speech-Act Theory and Phenomenology on Proust and Claude Simon', in M. Herzfeld (ed.), *Semiotics 1980*, New York, Plenum, 1982, pp. 275–79.

Krysinski, W., 'Le "Paralittéraire" et le "littéraire" dans le texte romanesque moderne: fonctionnement de la citation et de l'objet chez John Dos Passos et Claude Simon', *Carrefours de signes: essais sur le roman moderne*, The Hague, Mouton, 1981, pp. 295–309.

Labriolle, J. de, 'De Faulkner à Claude Simon', *Revue de littérature comparée*, vol. 53, 1979, pp. 358–88.

Lanceraux, D., 'Modalités de la narration dans *La Route des Flandres* de Claude Simon', *Poétique*, vol. 14, 1973, pp. 235–49.

Lanceraux, D., 'Modalités de la narration dans *Le Palace* de Claude Simon', *Littérature*, no. 16, décembre 1974, pp. 3–8.

Lefère, R., 'Claude Simon et Marcel Proust', *Studi Francesi*, vol. 34, no. 1, 1990, pp. 91–100.

Lefère, R., 'Claude Simon: description de procès et travail de l'aspect', *Lettres Romanes*, vol. 48, nos. 3–4, 1994, pp. 309–15.

Léonard, D. R., 'Simon's *L'Herbe*: Beyond Sound and Fury', *French-American Review*, vol. 1, no. 1, 1976, pp. 13–30.

Léonard, M., 'Photographie et littérature: Zola, Breton, Simon: Hommage à Roland Barthes', *Etudes françaises*, vol. 18, no. 3, 1983, pp. 93–108.

Lesage, L., 'Claude Simon et l'Ecclésiaste', *Revue des lettres modernes*, vol. 94–99, 1964, pp. 217–33.

Levitt, M. P., 'Disillusionment and Epiphany: the Novels of Claude Simon', *Critique, Studies in Modern Fiction*, vol. 12, 1970, pp. 43–71.

Longuet, P., 'La Chair des femmes dans *La Route des Flandres*', *Littératures*, no. 37, 1997, pp. 169–80.

Lopes, J. M., 'Lectures d'images visuelles et descriptions de cartes postales dans *Histoire* de Claude Simon', *Dalhousie French Studies*, vol. 22, 1992, pp. 85–96.

Loubère, J. A. E., '*Le Palace*: a Paradigm of Otherness', *Symposium*, vol. 27, 1973, pp. 46–63.

Loubère, J. A. E., 'Views through the Screen: In-Site in Claude Simon', *Yale French Studies*, no. 57, 1979, pp. 36–47.

Magny, O. de, 'Claude Simon: *Le Vent*', *Les Lettres nouvelles*, no. 2, 1957, pp. 784–86.

Makward, C., 'Claude Simon: Earth, Death and Eros', *Sub-stance*, vol. 8, 1974, pp. 35–43.

Mercier, V, 'Claude Simon. Order and Disorder, Memory and Desire', in V. Mercier, *The French New Novel from Queneau to Pinget*, New York, Farrar, Straus and Giroux, 1971, pp. 266–314.

Miguet, M., 'Lecture mythique des *Géorgiques* de Claude Simon', in G. Freyburger (ed.), *De Virgile à Jacob Blade: Hommage à Mme Andrée Thill, Bulletin de la faculté de lettres de Mulhouse*, no. 15, 1987, pp. 273–84.

Miraglia, A.-M., 'La Route des Flandres: défi aux voix narratives', Studi Francesi, vol. 34, no. 2, 1990, pp. 236–47.

Mortier, R., 'Discontinu et rupture dans La Bataille de Pharsale', Degrés, vol. 1, 1973, pp. 1–6.

Mougin, P., 'Mondes lexicaux et univers sémantiques: le logiciel ALCESTE au service de l'étude de l'imaginaire simonien, à partir du traitement de La Route des Flandres', Literary and Linguistic Computing: Journal of the Association for Literary and Linguistic Computing, vol. 10, no. 1, 1995, pp. 59–68.

Neef, J., 'Les Formes du temps dans Les Géorgiques de Claude Simon', Littérature, vol. 68, 1987, pp. 119–28.

Neumann, G., 'Claude Simon et Michelet: exemple d'intertextualité génératrice dans Les Géorgiques', Australian Journal of French Studies, vol. 24, no.1, 1987, pp. 83–99.

Neumann, G., 'Claude Simon: La Chevelure de Bérénice, ou le texte au travail', French Review, vol. 65, no. 4, 1992, pp. 557–66.

O'Donnell, T. D., 'Claude Simon's Leçon de choses: Myth and Ritual Displaced', International Fiction Review, vol. 5, no. 2, 1978, pp. 134–42.

Oppenheim, L., 'Narrating Hi(s)story: a Brief Commentary on Claude Simon's L'Invitation', New Novel Review, vol. 2, no. 2, 1995, pp. 18–29.

Orr, M., 'Lytton Strachey, Literary Embellishment or Functional Intertext in Claude Simon's Les Géorgiques?', French Studies Bulletin, vol. 26, 1988, pp. 14–17.

Orr, M., 'Mot à Mot: Translation as (Inter)Textual Generator in Five Novels by Claude Simon', New Comparison, vol. 8, 1989, pp. 66–74.

Orr, M., 'Intertextual Bridging: Across the Genre Divide in Claude Simon's Les Géorgiques', Forum for Modern Language Studies, vol. 26, no. 3, 1990, pp. 231–39.

Park, R., 'L'Expression métaphorique du complexe de castration dans La Bataille de Pharsale de Claude Simon', in J. Le Galliot (ed.), Psychanalyse et langages littéraires, Paris, Nathan, 1977, pp. 68–70.

Park, R., 'Pour une nouvelle lecture de La Bataille de Pharsale de Claude Simon', Revue des lettres modernes, nos 605–610, 1981, pp. 153–72.

Passias, K., 'Meaning in Structure and the Structure of Meaning in La Modification and La Route des Flandres', Studies in Twentieth Century Literature, vol. 9, no. 2, 1985, pp. 323–51.

Pellegrin, J., 'Du mouvement et de l'immobilité de Reixach', Revue d'Esthétique, vol. 25, 1972, pp. 335–49.

Perramond, M. M., 'De L'Herbe à L'Acacia: l'arbre généalogique de Claude Simon', French Review, vol. 65, no. 5, 1992, pp. 746–53.

Perrin, N., 'Les Rapports d'une lecture et d'une écriture', Sud, nos. 5–6, 1971, pp. 127–35.

Peyroux, M., 'Claude Simon et Proust', Bulletin de la Société des Amis de Marcel Proust et des Amis de Combray, no. 37, 1987, pp. 23–32.

Piégay-Gros, N., 'La Ligne brisée et les cercles concentriques: les parenthèses dans Les Géorgiques de Claude Simon', Textuel, vol. 28, avril 1994, pp. 93–99.

Piégay-Gros, N., 'Des Limites de l'informe aux limites de l'humain: l'objet dans les romans de Claude Simon', in R. Navarri (ed.), Ecritures de l'objet, Bordeaux, Presses Universitaires de Bordeaux, 1997, pp. 179–89.

Piégay-Gros, N., 'Un réalisme de la perception: éléments pour une épigraphie simonienne', *Littérature*, vol. 94, 1994, pp. 16–24.

Piégay-Gros, N., 'La Voix dans les romans de Claude Simon: vocalité, représentation, expression', *Poétique*, no. 116, 1998, pp. 487–94.

Poiana, P., *'L'Acacia* de Claude Simon: la voie du sensible', *Romanic Review*, vol. 86, no. 4, 1995, pp. 721–34.

Predal, R., 'Des mots et des images sur *La Route des Flandres*', in J.-B. Guiran (ed.), *Hommage à Jean Onimus*, Paris, Les Belles-Lettres (*Annales de la Faculté des Lettres et Sciences Humaines de Nice*, 38), 1979, pp. 331–42.

Prevost, C., 'Aragon, Gracq, Simon: l'écriture du désastre', *La Pensée: Revue du Rationalisme Moderne*, vol. 280, 1991, pp. 55–71.

Pugh, A. C., 'Du *Tricheur* à *Triptyque*, et inversement', *Etudes littéraires*, vol. 9, no. 1, 1976, pp. 137–60.

Pugh, A. C., 'Histoire d'une lecture, lecture d'*Histoire* ou comment lire un roman "circulaire"', in A. Montandon (ed.), *Le Lecteur et la lecture dans l'œuvre*, Clermont-Ferrand, Publications de la Faculté des Lettres de Clermont, 1982, pp. 177–88.

Pugh, A. C., 'Defeat, May 1940: Claude Simon, Marc Bloch and the Writing of Disaster', *Forum for Modern Language Studies*, vol. 22, 1985, pp. 59–70.

Pugh, A. C., 'Retours et répétitions dans *L'Acacia* de Claude Simon', in A. Montandon (ed.), *La Répétition*, Clermont-Ferrand, Publications de la Faculté des Lettres de Clermont , 1994, pp. 217–329.

Raillard, G., 'Les Trois Hautes Fenêtres', in R. Debray-Genette and J. Neefs (eds), *Romans d'archives*, Lille, Presses Universitaires de Lille, 1987, pp. 137–74.

Raillon, J.-C., 'Propositions pour une théorie de la fiction: *Triptyque*', *Etudes Littéraires*, vol. 9, no. 1, 1976, pp. 81–123.

Rannoux, C., 'Commencer: comment est-ce? Quelques incipits simoniens', in L. Louvel (ed.), *La Licorne, Hors Série: L'incipit*, Poitiers, Université de Poitiers, 1996.

Rebate, D., 'Ni début ni fin? Claude Simon et la physique du roman contemporain', *Op. Cit.: Revue de littératures française et comparée*, no. 12, 1999, pp. 173–79.

Rebollar, P., 'Sur la pratique adjectivesque de Claude Simon', in *Frantex: autour d'une base de données textuelles*, Paris, Didier Erudition, 1992, pp. 140–48.

Rebollar, P., 'Simonesque, sur quelques adjectifs dans l'oeuvre de Claude Simon', in *Le Texte, un objet d'études interdisciplinaires: mélanges offerts à Véronique Huynh-Armanet*, Paris, Presses de l'Université Paris VIII, 1994.

Reitsma-La Brujeere, C., 'Récit et métarécit, texte et intertexte dans *Les Géorgiques* de Claude Simon', *French Forum*, vol. 9, no. 2, 1984, pp. 225–35.

Ricardou, J., 'Un ordre dans la débâcle', *Critique*, no. 163, décembre 1960, pp. 1011–24 (reprinted in *Problèmes du nouveau roman*, Paris, Editions du Seuil, 1967, pp. 44–55).

Ricardou, J., 'La Bataille de la phrase', *Critique*, no. 274, mars 1970, pp. 226–56 (reprinted in J. Ricardou, *Pour une théorie du nouveau roman*, Paris, Seuil, 1971, pp. 118–58).

Ricardou, J., 'L'Essence et les sens', in J. Ricardou, *Pour une théorie du nouveau roman*, Paris, Seuil, 1971, pp. 200–10.

Ricardou, J., 'Le Dispositif osiriaque', *Etudes Littéraires*, vol. 9, no. 1, avril 1976, pp. 9–79 (reprinted in J. Ricardou, *Nouveaux problèmes du roman*, Paris, Seuil, 1978, pp. 179–243).

Rice, D., and P. Schofer, 'Simon's Lesson', in D. Rice and P. Schofer, *Rhetorical Poetics. Theory and Practice of Figural and Symbolic Reading in Modern French Literature*, Madison, WI, The University of Wisconsin Press, 1983, pp.188–211.

Rogers, M., 'Fonction des quatre photographies publiées dans *Orion aveugle* de Claude Simon', *French Review*, 1985, vol. 59, no.1, pp. 74–83.

Rossum-Guyon, F. van, 'De Claude Simon à Proust: un exemple d'intertextualité', *Marche Romane*, vol. 21, 1971, pp. 71–92.

Rossum-Guyon, F. van, '*Ut pictura poesis*: une lecture de *La Bataille de Pharsale*', *Degrés*, vol. 1, no. 3, 1973, K1–K15.

Roubichou, G., 'Continu et discontinu, ou l'hérétique alinéa (Notes sur la lecture d'*Histoire)*', *Etudes littéraires*, vol. 9, no. 1, 1976, pp. 125–36.

Roubichou, G., 'Langage et roman: la stratégie de l'écriture dans l'œuvre de Claude Simon', *Francographies: Bulletin de la Société des Professeurs français et francophones*, no. 1, 1995, pp. 45–55.

Rousset, J., '*Histoire* de Claude Simon. Le jeu des cartes postales', *Versants*, no. 1, 1981, pp. 121–133 (reprinted in J. Rousset, *Passages, échanges et transpositions*, Paris, Corti, 1992, pp. 155–63).

Rousset, J., 'Trois romanciers de la mémoire: Butor, Simon, Pinget', *Cahiers Internationaux de Symbolisme*, nos. 9–10, 1965–1966, pp. 75–84.

Rousset, J., 'Écrire la peinture: Claude Simon', in J. Rousset, *Passages, échanges et transpositions*, Paris, Corti, 1992, pp. 153–54.

Saad, G., 'Deux romans qui renouvellent l'histoire: *Moi, le suprême* de Augusto Roa Bastos et *Les Géorgiques* de Claude Simon', in J. Bessière, *Récit et Histoire*, Paris, Presses Universitaires de France, 1984, pp. 37–46.

Sarkonak, R., 'Dans l'entrelacs d'*Histoire*: construction d'un réseau textuel chez Claude Simon', *La Revue des lettres modernes*, nos. 605–610, 1981, pp. 115–50.

Sarkonak, R., 'Comment fait-on un cocktail simonien? Ou, *Les Géorgiques* relues et corrigées', *Romanic Review*, vol. 81, no. 2, 1990, pp. 236–47.

Sarkonak, R., 'Un drôle d'arbre: *L'Acacia* de Claude Simon', *Romanic Review*, vol. 82, 1991, pp. 210–32.

Sarkonak, R., 'Du non-dit politique à l'auto-référence: *L'Invitation* de Claude Simon', *Texte*, vol. 11, 1991, pp. 93–116.

Sarkonak, R., 'Towards a Simonian mimetics', in L. Oppenheim (ed.), *Three Decades of the French New Novel*, Urbana, IL, University of Illinois Press, 1986, pp. 87–103.

Scarpetta, G., 'L'Arbre de l'écriture: sur *L'Acacia* de Claude Simon', *L'Atelier du roman*, 3, novembre 1994, pp. 73–112 (reprinted in Guy Scarpetta, *L'Age d'or du roman*, Paris, Grasset, 1996, pp. 113–58).

Schuerewegen, F., 'Orphée au téléphone: appel et interpellation chez Claude Simon', *Poétique*, no. 76, 1988, pp. 451–61.

Schoentjes, P., 'L'Ironie des personnages et celle d'une écriture: *Les Géorgiques* de Claude Simon', in G. Lavergne (ed.), *Le Personnage romanesque*, Nice, Presses Universitaires de Nice, 1995, pp. 411–24.

Serna, A., 'L'Espace simonien: un jeu avec le mur du langage', *Queste*, vol. 4,

1988, pp. 133–63.

Serna Rodriguez, A., 'Pour une analyse grammatextuelle: inscription et figuration dans l'œuvre de Claude Simon', in Felix Menchacatorre (ed.), *Ensayos de literatura europea e hispanoamericana*, San Sebastian, Universidad del Pais Vasco, 1990, pp. 535–42.

Seylaz, J.-L., 'Du *Vent* à *La Route des Flandres:* la conquête d'une forme romanesque', *Revue des lettres modernes*, vols. 94–99, no. 1, 1964, pp. 225–40.

Sherzer, D., 'Ubiquité de la répétition dans *Les Géorgiques* de Claude Simon', *Neophilologus*, vol. 70, no. 3, 1986, pp. 372–80.

Sherzer, D., '*Triptyque*: Paronomasia of things', in D. Sherzer, *Representation in Contemporary French Fiction*, Lincoln, NE, University of Nebraska Press, 1986, pp. 25–31.

Simon, J. K., 'Perception and Metaphor in the New Novel: Notes on Robbe-Grillet, Claude Simon and Butor', *Tri-Quartely*, vol. 4, 1965, pp. 153–82.

Sims, R. L., 'The Myths of Revolution and the City in Claude Simon's *Le Palace*', *Studies in the Twentieth Century*, no. 16, 1975, pp. 53–87.

Sims, R. L., 'Myth and Historico-primordial Memory in Claude Simon's *La Route des Flandres*', *Nottingham French Studies*, 1978, vol. 17, no. 2, pp. 74–86.

Sims, R. L., 'Claude Simon's *Bricolage* Technique in *La Route des Flandres*, *Le Palace* and *Histoire*', *Degré Second*, vol. 7, 1983, pp. 81–108.

Sims, R. L., 'War and Myth in the Twentieth Century: Drieu La Rochelle, Céline and Claude Simon', *Neophilologus*, vol. 68, no. 2, 1984, pp. 179–91.

Sims, R. L., 'L'Influence du cinéma et ses techniques sur quelques romans de Claude Simon', *Les Bonnes Feuilles*, vol. 5, no. 1, 1975, pp. 33–46.

Sims, R. L., 'Memory, Structure and Time in *La Route des Flandres*', *Les Bonnes Feuilles*, vol. 5, no. 2, 1976, pp. 41–58.

Sol, A., '*Les Géorgiques* de Claude Simon: la particularité de la généralisation', *Paroles Gelées: UCLA French Studies*, no. 7, 1989, pp. 63–71.

Solomon, P. H., 'Flights of Time Lost: Bird Imagery in Simon's *Le Palace*', in G. Stambolian (ed.), *Twentieth Century French Fiction: Essays for Germaine Brée*, New Brunswick, NJ, Rutgers University Press, 1975, pp. 166–83.

Sullivan, F. D., 'Recherche pour une textualité dans *Histoire* de Claude Simon', *Romanic Review*, vol. 79, no. 2, 1988, pp. 354–65.

Suter, P., 'Rythme et corporéité chez Claude Simon (*L'Acacia*)', *Poétique*, vol. 97, 1994, pp. 19–39.

Sykes, S., 'Mise en abyme in the Novels of Claude Simon', *Forum for Modern Language Studies*, vol. 9, no. 4, 1973, pp. 333–45.

Sykes, S., 'Claude Simon: Visions of Life in Microcosm', *Modern Language Review*, vol. 71, no. 1, 1976, pp. 42–50.

Sykes, S., 'Ternary Form in Three Novels by Claude Simon', *Symposium*, vol. 32, no. 1, 1978, pp. 25–40.

Sykes, S., 'The Novel as Conjuration: *Absalom, Absalom!* and *La Route des Flandres*', *Revue de littérature comparée*, vol. 53, 1979, pp. 348–57.

Sykes, S., '*Les Géorgiques*: "une reconversion totale"?', *Romance Studies*, no. 2, 1983, pp. 80–89.

Thouillot, M., 'Guerres et écriture chez Claude Simon', *Poétique*, no. 109, 1997, pp. 65–81.

Urbye, R., 'La Texture de l'énoncé littéraire', *Revue Romane*, vol. 18, 1979, pp. 111–27.

Valette-Fondo, M., 'L'Ordre descriptif dans *Les Corps conducteurs*', in J. Bessière (ed.), *L'Ordre du descriptif*, Paris, Presses Universitaires de France,1988, pp. 79–95.

Vareille, J.-C., 'A propos de Claude Simon: langage du cosmos, cosmos du langage', *Etudes Littéraires*, vol. 17, no. 1, 1984, pp. 13–44 (reprinted in J.-C. Vareille, *Fragments d'un imaginaire contemporain* (*Pinget, Robbe-Grillet, Simon*), Paris, José Corti, 1989, pp. 77–108).

Vareille, J.-C., '*L'Acacia* ou Simon à la recherche du temps perdu', in *Le Nouveau Roman en question, tome I: Nouveau Roman et archétypes, Revue des lettres modernes*, 1992, pp. 95–118.

Verheye, W., 'L'Ouverture et l'ensemble dans *Le Vent* de Claude Simon', in C. Grivel (ed.), *Recherches sur le roman II*, Groningen, Institut de Langues Romanes, Rijksuniversiteit, 1984, pp. 70–79.

Viart, D., '"Mais comment appeler cela?": Claude Simon, la mémoire et la guerre', *Nord*, no. 20, 1992, pp. 80–102.

Vidal, J.-P., '*Le Palace*, palais des mirages intestins ou l'auberge espagnole', *Etudes Littéraires*, vol. 9, no. 1, 1976, pp. 189–214.

Vinken, B., 'Claude Simon: The Stained Paper', *Yale French Studies*, 1988, pp. 45–50.

Vinken, B., 'Makulatur oder von der Schwierigkeit zu lesen: Claude Simons *Leçon de choses*', *Poetica: Zeitschrift für Sprache und Literaturwissenschaft*, vol. 21, no. 4, 1989, pp. 403–28.

Vogel, C., 'Le Travail de l'écriture et de la mémoire dans les romans *Histoire* et *L'Acacia* de Claude Simon', *Versants*, no. 36, 1999, pp. 37–52.

Zupancic, M., 'Les Générateurs picturaux dans l'écriture simonienne', *Acta Neophilologica*, vol. 15, 1982, pp. 105–12.

Zupancic, M., 'Eurydice à la recherche d'Orphée: lecture orphique de *L'Acacia* de Claude Simon', in M. Zupancic (ed.), *Mythes dans la littérature contemporaine d'expression française*, Ottawa, Le Nordir, 1994, pp. 200–08.

Zupancic, M., 'Claude Simon: l'écriture face à l'absurde, à la mort, au chaos', in M. Wathee-Delmotte and M. Zupancic (eds), *Le Mal dans l'imaginaire littéraire français (1850–1950)*, Paris, L'Harmattan, 1998, pp. 421–32.

Websites

http://perso.cybercable.fr/naintern/labyrinthe/framesimon.html
http://www.nobel.se/laureates/literature-1985-1-bio.html
http://www.kirjasto.sci.fi/csimon.htm
http://www.twics.com/~berlol/poitiers.htm
http://nobelprizes.com/nobel/literature/1985a.html
http://www.nieuwsbank.nl/inp/1997/06/06050053.htm
http://www.nuitblanche.com/archives/s/simon_entrev.htm
http://www.cavi.univ-paris3.fr/phalese/cspr.htm
http://www.dumag.ch/backlist/inhalt.DU9901.html
http://www.mle.asso.fr/banquet/n38/edito.htm
http://www.chass.utoronto.ca/french/foire2000/colloque/grodek.htm

Notes on Contributors

Mária Minich Brewer, Associate Professor of French, University of Minnesota. She is the author of *Claude Simon: Narrativities Without Narrative* (1995) and, among other articles, of '(Ré)inventions référentielles et culturelles chez Claude Simon', *Revue des Lettres Modernes* (1994), 'Parodies, répliques, écritures', *Revue des Sciences Humaines* (1990), 'Narrative Fission: Event, History, and Writing in *Les Géorgiques*', *Michigan Romance Studies* (1986), 'The Critical Properties of Painting in Claude Simon', *The Review of Contemporary Fiction* (1985). She edited the 'Claude Simon' issue of *L'Esprit Créateur* (1987).

Celia Britton is Carnegie Professor of French and the Director of the Centre for Francophone Studies at the University of Aberdeen. She is the author of *Claude Simon: Writing the Visible* (1987) and *The Nouveau Roman: Fiction, Theory and Politics* (1992), as well as numerous articles on Simon and other *nouveaux romanciers*. More recently she has been working on French Caribbean literature; she published *Edouard Glissant and Postcolonial Theory: Strategies of Language and Resistance* in 1999.

Mireille Calle-Gruber is Professor of French Literature at the Université de Paris-Vincennes and co-director of the Centre d'études féminines. Her publications include studies on the theory of the novel (*L'Effet-fiction. De l'illusion romanesque*, 1989) and on twentieth-century French literature (*Histoire de la littérature française du XXe siècle ou les Repentirs de la littérature*, 2000), an edited volume on Claude Simon (*Chemins de la mémoire*, 1993), a monograph and an edited volume on Michel Butor (*La Ville dans 'L'Emploi du temps'*, 1995; *Les Métamorphoses-Butor*, 1991), a monograph on Claude Ollier (*Les Partitions de Claude Ollier*, 1996) and a collaborative volume with Hélène Cixous (*Photos de racines*, 1994, published by Routledge in 1997 as *Rootprints*). She is also the author of three 'récits de fiction' (*Arabesques*, 1985; *La Division de l'intérieur* and *Midis. Scènes aux bords de l'oubli*, 2000). She is a fellow of the Royal Society of Canada.

David Carroll is Professor of French and Chair of the Department of French and Italian at the University of California Irvine. His books include *French Literary Fascism: Nationalism, Anti-Semitism, and the Ideology of Culture* (1995); *Paraesthetics: Foucault, Lyotard, Derrida* (1987); and a study of the novels of Claude Simon entitled *The Subject in Question: the Languages of Theory and the Strategies of Fiction* (1982). He is currently working on a book on Albert Camus and Algeria.

Alastair Duncan is Senior Lecturer in French at the University of Stirling. He has published on Flaubert and Mauriac, Butor, Robbe-Grillet and Sarraute, as well as on advertising in France. His long-standing interest in Claude Simon has resulted in many publications in French and English, including a contribution to *Claude Simon: Colloque de Cerisy* (1975), the edited volume *Claude Simon: New Directions* (1985) and the monograph *Claude Simon: Adventures in Words* (1994).

Jean H. Duffy is Professor of French at the University of Edinburgh. Her publications include monographs on Colette (1988) and Michel Butor (1990) and articles on the *nouveau roman*, Monique Wittig and Gabriel Josipovici. In recent years, the principal focus of her research has been the relationship between literature and the visual arts. In 1998 she published *Reading between the Lines: Claude Simon and the Visual Arts*. She is currently working on a study of visual culture in Butor's fiction.

David Ellison is Professor of French and Chairman of the Department of Foreign Languages at the University of Miami. He is the author of *The Reading of Proust* (The Johns Hopkins University Press, 1984), *Understanding Albert Camus* (The University of South Carolina Press, 1990), *Of Words and the World: Referential Anxiety in Contemporary French Fiction* (Princeton University Press, 1993) and *Ethics and Aesthetics in European Modernist Literature: From the Sublime to the Uncanny* (Cambridge University Press, 2001). He has published articles on narrative theory and practice, literature and psychoanalysis, literature and philosophy, and the *nouveau roman*.

J. A. E. Loubère graduated from University College, London and spent several years teaching in France at the Collège Morel de Jeunes Filles in Lyon and the Lycée Victor Hugo in Paris. Since then she has divided her time between assisting Leo Loubère in research on the economics of wine in France, overseeing American students abroad, and lecturing at the State University of New York at Buffalo. Her work includes *The Novels of Claude Simon* (1975) and articles on Simon, Valéry, Borges and Balzac. She is currently retired.

Wolfram Nitsch is Professor in Romance Philology at the University of Köln. He is the author of a book on language and violence in Claude Simon (*Sprache und Gewalt bei Claude Simon*, 1992) and of a study on the role of play in the Spanish drama of the Golden Age (*Barocktheater als Spielraum*, 2000). He has also written on various modern French and Latin American novelists as well as on the theory and history of French cinema.

Mary Orr has a Personal Chair in Modern French Studies at the University of Exeter. Among her main research interests are Flaubert, intertextuality, the *nouveau roman* including Claude Simon, autobiography and gender studies. Among her recent publications are two monographs on Flaubert: *Flaubert's 'Madame Bovary': Representations of the Masculine* (1999) and *Flaubert: Writing the Masculine* (2000). She is currently working on a book entitled *Intertextualities: Debates and Contexts*.